Discover Economi GCSE

Graham Teager

Pitman

PITMAN PUBLISHING
128 Long Acre, London, WC2E 9AN
A Division of Longman Group UK Limited

First edition published in Great Britain 1985
Second edition published 1989

British Library Cataloguing in Publication Data
Teager, Graham
  Discover economics. – 2nd ed.
  1. Economics. Questions & answers – For schools
  I. Title
  330'.076

ISBN 0 273 03033 7

Printed and bound in Great Britain

Contents

Preface

In writing this second edition of *Discover Economics* I have had the benefit of both knowing the content of all GCSE syllabuses and seeing the first crop of GCSE examinations as an examiner and Chief Course Work Moderator.

I have still remained true to my original style and indeed much of the book remains the same with the addition of up-to-date figures. I believe that economics is all around us and that it is there to be discovered in real-life case studies. Some people argue that the case study over-complicates – well, real life is complicated and, because of that, far more interesting.

To this basic formula – presenting new concepts through case study – I have added three new chapters covering supply and demand, economic development and government management. Multinationals, economies of scale, market types, etc have also been added to existing chapters with many new and up-to-date case studies such as the Thompson/Horizon take-over, Ford wage dispute of 1988, Balance of Payments crisis of Summer 1988, CAP price cuts in August 1988 and 1992 legislation. I believe that the book now fully covers all GCSE syllabuses.

Each chapter contains tasks and exercises which are intended for class and homework use – for this reason, answers are not provided in the back. Hopefully, the questions stimulate thought not simple factual recall. I have **not** provided a glossary for the same reason. Students ought to be encouraged to work out their own definitions – the GCSE has moved a long way from note learning and this book aims to help students to discover economic principles, not read them at the back of a book.

The last two chapters are also new. In one, I give advice on course work and present some 'study guides' based on my moderating experience. Students often have much to say through course work but lose marks through poor technique. Real economics is about testing theory and involves data collection and analysis: if the 'skills' are not taught in mathematics then we must be prepared to teach them through economics.

Chapter 18 contains questions taken from recent GCSE papers, followed by my *suggested* answers. I would hope the students would use this chapter during revision and examination preparation by writing or planning their own answers and then comparing them with the suggested answers.

Acknowledgments

The author and publishers would like to thank the following for permission to reproduce copyright material:

Andrew Aarons
Anglia Television Ltd
Bairstow Eves
Barclays Bank
British Caledonian Airways Ltd
British Insurance Association
British Petroleum plc
Building Societies Association

Coal Board
Controller of Her Majesty's Stationery Office
Cooperative Development Agency
Cooperative Union Ltd

Daily Express
Daily Mail
Daily Star
Department of Employment
Department of Trade and Industry

Engineering Careers Information Service
Everest Double Glazing
Northums County Council
European Parliament

Ford Motor Company Ltd

Granada Television
Guardian Newspaper

HMSO

Independent Newspaper

Ilford Recorder

LBC Radio
Lloyds Bank
Londis (Holdings) Ltd
London & East Anglian Group
Low Pay Unit

Mauritius Trade Delegation
Midland Examining Group

National Union of Public Employees
National Westminster Bank plc
Northern Examining Association
Northern Ireland Schools Examination Council

Observer

Redbridge Area Health Authority
Royal Mint

Sainsbury plc

Selfridges

Tesco plc
The Bank of England
The CBI
The Mail on Sunday
The Stock Exchange
The Transport and General Workers Union
Town and County Building Society
The TUC
Times Newspapers

Unilever

Welsh Joint Education Committee

1 The Economic Problem

CASE STUDY

There's no such thing as a free school meal!

'Good feedback on fast food'

The van outside the gates of Holloway School in Islington was doing less than brisk business last Tuesday, the first official day of FADS – Fast Ace Dinners at School, an ILEA* pilot scheme. Concerned about the numbers of boys buying food from vans outside, the school put out a questionnaire which found that of the 77 per cent who did so, nearly a quarter said queues were too long in school and over half said the variety was not great enough. 'When asked if they would like a fast food service provided in school,' said headmaster Paul Smith, '91 per cent of the pupils said yes.'

Thus encouraged, the school has done just that. In addition to the normal two-choice school dinners, two fast food trolleys had been set up in the hall and, as the steel band played, were doing a roaring trade in takeaway jacket potatoes and burgers and chips.

Twenty-five minutes after the start the sold out signs were up.

'The boys are responding very enthusiastically,' said Leighton Crooks, school meals supervisor, 'there is less queueing and greater choice.'

'We saw we'd have to make school meals more commercial, promote the product and sell it,' said Janet Bloomfield, ILEA* education catering organiser. 'We already have the healthy eating, the multi-cultural food, the proverbial chips, but we needed something else here too. I see this as the forerunner of things to come, though in other schools the demand may be for soup and sandwiches, or a salad bar.'

Note: *ILEA stands for the Inner London Education Authority which is being disbanded and replaced by individual London Boroughs.

Adapted from The Guardian – *Ad Hoc 14.6.88*

Tasks

1 Why was the headmaster concerned about the number of boys buying food from vans outside the school?
2 Why was the school meals service concerned about the number of boys buying food from vans outside the school?
3 How did the school find out why the boys ate outside school?
4 If you were in charge of meals at Holloway School would you have produced more or less fast food on, Wednesday, the second FADS day? Explain your answer.
5 If a questionnaire conducted by the boys showed that 25 per cent of 14 year olds regularly smoked, and bought their cigarettes on the way to school, do you think that the headmaster would put cigarette dispensing machines into the school? Explain your answer.

Have you ever wondered where a school dinner comes from? Look at the flow chart shown in Fig 1.1.

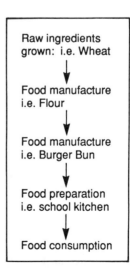

Raw ingredients grown: i.e. Wheat

↓

Food manufacture i.e. Flour

↓

Food manufacture i.e. Burger Bun

↓

Food preparation i.e. school kitchen

↓

Food consumption

Fig 1.1

Chain of production

Food would not be grown unless the farmer knew that people wanted it and were willing to pay for it. This is true right down the line of production.

At the end of the chain, the customer buys what he wants. In the Holloway school the boys wanted variety and no queueing – so they bought from the vans outside. Faced with this, the schools meals service offered a greater choice and more points of sale – and the boys came back into school. Some students and staff are given 'free school meals'. But they are not free; someone has to pay for them.

There are two types of cost. First, there is a **money cost**. As we have seen, a complex chain is involved in providing a meal at school – at each stage people expect to be financially rewarded or they would not undertake their link in the chain. Either the customer must pay or government can collect taxes and pay for you (with school meals it is often a combination of both) – there is no such thing as a free school meal. In addition, there is a second cost: the **resources** used to provide school meals cannot be used for anything else. Instead of paying for kitchen staff, food, etc and devoting large areas of the school for a kitchen and dining area, the school could have more teachers and classrooms. Then we would all buy burgers from the vans outside, or would we?

Opportunity costs

This second cost is known by economists as **opportunity cost**, i.e. what must be given up or sacrificed in order to provide a certain good or service. Looked at for the individual, such costs are well known to us. In a toy shop little children often end up in tears when the reality of oppor-

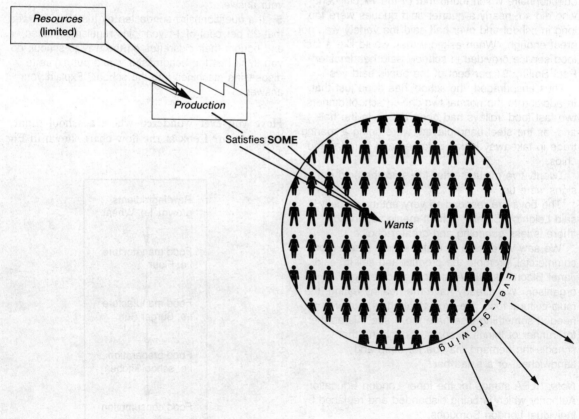

Fig 1.2   The growing wants of the world's population

tunity cost comes home to them. The £5.00 Aunt Jennifer gave them for Christmas just cannot buy both the Lego and Action Man; if they buy one the other must be sacrificed. Such problems often face communities. If the local authority builds that new sports centre then the old people's home must be sacrificed.

Opportunity costs must be faced by the whole world. A few years ago it was calculated that the that the money required to provide adequate food, water, education, health and housing for all the people of the world was £17 billion per year. A huge sum of money – about how much the world then spent on arms every two weeks! The economist might say that the opportunity cost of war and mistrust is malnutrition and homelessness.

The resources of the world are limited. There is a fixed amount of minerals and chemicals, land and sea and they have been here for millions of years. Many resources have yet to be discovered but the total is limited. The population of the world is vast and growing quickly – 6.1 billion by the year 2000. These people all have **wants** – as the population grows so their wants increase (see Fig 1.2).

Economics is about just how we decide which of the ever growing wants of the world to satisfy. Also how best to use the limited resources available to maximise production.

If we satisfy some wants we will not be able to satisfy others. If we use metal and wood to make guns we cannot use the same metal and wood to make a kidney machine. The opportunity cost is the lost alternative use of given resources.

Most of the goods and services that people want do not occur naturally so have to be manufactured or **produced**. Economics investigates how decisions about what to produce – which wants to satisfy – are made. Not all of these wants can be satisfied and for this reason economics has been called the 'gloomy science' or the 'science of scarcity'. Neither is correct. Economics can be fun, interesting and even exciting. The economist looks at the problem of scarcity and suggests how production can be made more efficient so that more wants can be satisfied. He helps businessmen and politicians make good decisions by looking at alternative uses of resources and comparing them in a systematic and logical way.

The study of economics should help you make sensible choices in your life.

Wants and needs

It is important to distinguish between **wants** and **needs**.

In order to survive we **need**:

1 Air
2 Water
3 Food
4 Warmth/shelter

These are listed in the order in which, if they were not supplied, people would cease to exist most quickly. If a person were denied **air** for example they would last for only a few seconds but they could survive for several days without food. Air is very important to a person's survival but it is free which at first appears strange. Air is one of the few basic human needs which is not scarce in most places on earth. It is free for people to use as they need and is called a **free good**.

If all the goods and services which people wanted were listed it would fill the rest of this book. It is certain that for many people most of their wants will never be satisfied and for some even basic needs are barely catered for.

Exercise

1 Where might **air** not be free?
2 Where might the other needs listed above be **free goods?**
3 Give **one** want which would be satisfied, in this country, for a person even if they could not afford to buy it.
4 Give **one** want which might not be satisfied for a person however rich they might be.
5 What is the **opportunity cost** of air?

Classifying resources

The resources used in the production of goods and services are not all of the same type. They can be classified into four main types.

The following assignment highlights these.

ASSIGNMENT

An unemployed school leaver discovers a new board game similar to chess but not quite so complicated. With the aid of her father she makes a prototype in her garden shed. To her surprise everyone likes it which leads her to think of starting her own business.

List all of the things she would need to start a small business to make and sell this game. It is mainly constructed from wood. (Do not put down money – which she would clearly need – only the resources she would need to buy.)

The resources listed in your answer to the assignment (the resources needed for production), ought to fall into four categories:

1 Natural resources

To produce anything you will need some land – to produce it on. This, however, is not the only resource included here. You will also need raw materials and minerals to produce most goods and perhaps geographical features, like the sea or rivers or even climatic conditions.

2 Human resources

Machines can do a great deal but we still need people to help produce goods and services – even if it is only to push buttons! Here we must include all contributions made by humans whether it be with their hands, as with a carpenter, or their minds, as with an accountant.

3 Man-made resources

Some goods called either **producer goods** or **capital goods** are made in order to help make other goods and services to satisfy certain wants. For example, factory buildings, machines and equipment. We do not want these to satisfy wants directly – nobody wants a fork-lift truck in the garage instead of a car – nor would you want to sit and watch a lathe instead of a television. We need to produce these capital goods in order to produce those goods we do want.

4 Enterprise/risk taking

This is a special type of human resource. To make anything you need natural, human and man-made resources. These resources will not come together to satisfy wants on their own. In our example you would have to decide to make the board game and bring together the necessary resources even if these were only the back garden, you, a friend, a rusty saw and a few pieces of wood. The people who bring together the resources necessary for production and start that production; the person who decides to take these resources and make cars, plastic garden gnomes or kidney machines is called an **entrepreneur**. These people start or initiate production and in so doing they take a risk. It is their money and expertise that are put into the project and if the good or service sells well they will be rewarded with large profits.

If you look at Fig 1.3 you will see that it is much the same as Fig 1.2 only more complicated. At the top are the world's resources broken down into different types. To produce anything we need natural, human and man-made resources brought together by enterprise.

As you can see, the actual making of the good is called **production**. Not all goods are the same.

Types of goods

Consumer goods

These are all those products which satisfy wants. We can see them, touch them, buy them and take them home. Some we call **durable consumer goods** because they last a long time, e.g. washing machines, televisions and cars. Others only last a very short while and are called **non-durable consumer goods**, e.g. food, matches or a pint of beer.

Services

Sometimes our wants are satisfied by someone doing something for us. We call these **services**. An example would be a visit to the dentist.

Capital goods

These are pieces of equipment wanted by a producer to help make consumer goods.

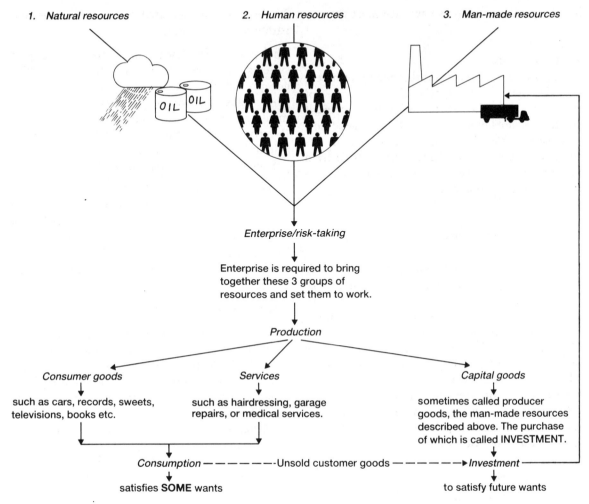

Fig 1.3 Resources for production

Exercise

The following is a list of factors of production, goods and services. For each one see whether you can say which it is:

An accountant	A bank manager
A sales representative's car	A garden shed
	A child's bicycle
A packet of crisps	A postman's bicycle
A haircut	A farmer's cow
A bricklayer	A farmer's wife
A ploughed field	
A tractor	

In our list of goods we missed out two very important types of good.

1 Public goods

Some goods are consumed by all of us at the same time. They are satisfying public wants. An example would be defence. The problem with such goods is that you cannot sell them to people. Imagine a door-to-door salesman selling defence. He knocks on your door. 'Excuse me Sir,' he says, 'Would you like to buy some defence – we have a very special offer today just £10 per head to defend the Falklands against Argentina.'

Do you think he would sell very much? Of course not. What would he do if you did not buy any? The only way such goods can be provided is if the Government provides them. They still have to be paid for – by us – but the Government has the power to make us pay – we must pay our taxes!

2 Merit goods

Some goods are so important that the Government provides them for those who deserve them, not those who can afford them. We call these **merit goods**. You are enjoying one such merit good now – education. We all receive education, and in this country medical attention and basic housing from the Government if we have insufficient money to provide them for ourselves.

Types of economy

The production of goods and services to satisfy wants takes place because the resources necessary for production have been brought together. In some economies all resources are brought together by the State or Government. These are called **planned** economies. In others, resources are brought together by groups of private individuals. These are called **market** economies. In the UK we have a mixture of both. Education is provided for most by local government whereas most food retailers are owned by private shareholders. This is known as a **mixed** economy.

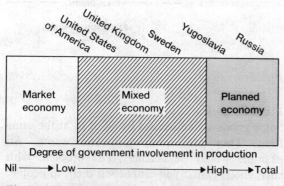

Fig 1.4 Types of economy

Planned economies

A planned economy has two main features:

1 All resources are owned and controlled by the State.

2 Resources are allocated by a centralised administration (bureaucracy).

The government owns all factories, transport systems, schools, hospitals, shops etc. The government also decides what shall be produced. This means that most people work for the government which will also control prices and wages. Poverty can be eliminated and most people enjoy a similar standard of living.

Such a system has many advantages:

• The government can decide upon priorities.
• Resources are not wasted on useless items and can be concentrated upon the provision of important things like education, health care and housing.
• Too much choice is avoided and wasteful advertising unnecessary.

There are disadvantages:

• Since everyone works for the state and receives similar wages there is no incentive to work hard. Production is inefficient.
• As companies do not compete they have no need to improve their products so innovation is slow.
• Planning has proved very difficult and sometimes the state gets its figures wrong and people must queue for goods which are in short supply.

Market economies

A market economy has two main features:

1 All resources are owned and controlled by private individuals.
2 Resources are allocated by the price mechanism.

Individuals on their own or in groups bring together the resources needed to produce goods and services in order to make a profit. If the good or service they produce is popular it will sell well and they will make a good profit. Other individuals will see this and produce similar or better goods and services. Consumers will have their wants satisfied and producers will secure high profits. [Burger vans outside Holloway School!].

Such a system has many advantages:

- Producers are in competition and must therefore be as efficient as possible and constantly improve the product.
- Consumers have much choice. The system responds quickly to changes in taste.
- Individuals who work hard and have good ideas can become very rich.

There are disadvantages:

- There is much wasteful advertising and overproduction.
- Some producers can control a market for a particular product – they become monopolists and can charge what they like.
- Not all our needs are necessarily satisfied – only the wants of people with money.

In a country like Russia, which has a planned economy, people often spend hours queueing for essential goods like bread and meat. In a country like America, which has an economy based upon the market system, a pop star like Michael Jackson can have his nose and lips altered whilst poor people can wait years for essential health care.

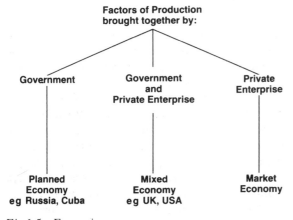

Fig 1.5 Economic systems

Tasks

1 Under which economic system are **public** goods most likely to be produced?
2 Under which system are **merit** goods likely to be produced?

The mixed economy tries to incorporate the advantages of both systems. The state provides the basic public and merit goods and holds out a safety net to catch unfortunate citizens who are unable to fend for themselves while allowing the market to provide all other goods under competition for efficiency. In the UK we have a **private** and **public** sector.

The private sector includes all enterprises owned and run by private individuals. Fig. 1.6 illustrates the different types of private sector enterprises. These are discussed in greater detail in Chapter 2.

The public sector includes all enterprises owned and run by central and local government. This ranges from the provision of merit and public goods like education and defence to large nationalised industries like Coal and Railways. These are discussed in greater detail in Chapter 3.

It is possible for workers to collectively own their own shops and factories and customers their own shops and factories. These are known as cooperative enterprises and are examined in Chapter 4.

Look again at our original case study – 'There's no such thing as a free school meal'.

Recent legislation has compelled local authorities to offer the school meals service out to private tender. This means that private companies can compete to provide school meals. The meals in your school may well be provided in this way.

Exercise

1 Why should private sector provision of school meals differ from state provision?
2 How would private sector provision of school meals differ from state provision? (Remember the Holloway experiment and others referred to in the article are state provision!)
3 Would private sector school meals cost students more?
4 Would private sector school meals cost taxpayers more?
5 Would private sector meals provide specialist meals for vegetarians and ethnic minorities?
6 Would more or less people be employed by private sector meals?

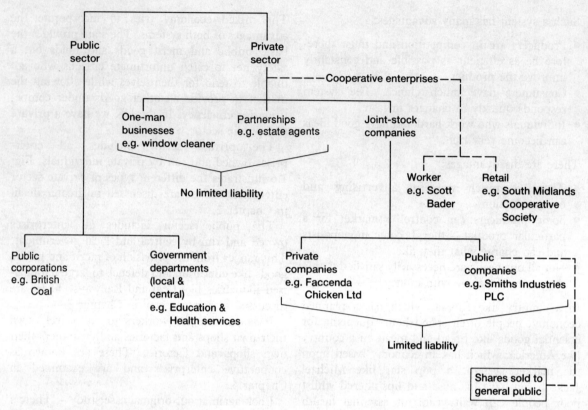

Fig 1.6 Types of private sector enterprise

(If your school has recently changed you ought to be able to check your answers).

Note In economics ordinary words have precise meanings. Before going any further learn these three:

a plant   is one factory or place of production
a firm   is any business unit, e.g. a company
an industry is all the firms producing similar products

Example The Ford plant at Dagenham is part of the Ford Motor Company (firm), which in turn is part of the motorcar industry. List two examples from your area.

In this country the population supply labour, sometimes land and a few people enterprise to firms. This is not done for the fun of it but for the return or income received. We usually call the payment by businesses to their workers wages but this covers all payments to workers whether they be on a weekly wage or salary. People who own land and let others use it receive rent and people who take risks as entrepreneurs do so because they expect to make profits.

Those who work or supply some other resource for production receive an income. What do they do with this income? Much of it will be spent on goods and services. If you look at Fig 1.7 you will see a diagram of how this works. People supply the resources to businesses, all, that is except man-made resources, which, if you remember, are produced by businesses anyway. In return they are rewarded with money payments called factor payments. These are broken down into wages, profits and rent.

The people who now have money spend it on goods and services so that it becomes income for the businesses again. Money is constantly changing hands from people to businesses and back to people; this is known as the circular flow of income.

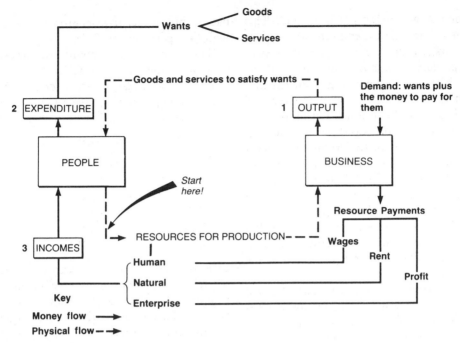

Fig 1.7 The circular flow of income

Measuring output

The value of goods and services produced in the UK for consumption, purchases of new capital and exports, in any given year, is called the **Gross Domestic Product** (GDP). Study the circular flow of income. You will notice that what is produced (1) **output**, is sold – (2) **expenditure**, and the money generated is distributed in (3) factor **income(s)**. The value of output can therefore be determined by measuring any of these three flows over a year. In fact each year all three methods are used by the government to estimate the value of output for that year. Where that value is used in this book it is in general an average of all three.

It is, of course very much more complicated than our diagram because we have foreign trade and a government sector. Looking at one method in detail will highlight these difficulties (*see* Table 1.1).

Using the expenditure method, all forms of spending are added together – consumer spending, government spending and business spending on machinery and other forms of capital. To this is added the value of the increase in stocks of finished and partly finished goods during the year

Table 1.1

Gross Domestic Product (at factor cost) 1986 – Expenditure Method

	£ m.	%
Consumer Expenditure	+234 167	49.2
General government final consumption	+ 79 432	16.2
Gross domestic fixed capital formation	+ 64 227	13.5
Value of physical increase in stocks and work in progress	+ 551	0.1
Total domestic expenditure	= 378 368	79.5
Exports of goods & services	+ 97 835	20.5
Total final expenditure	= 476 203	100
less imports of goods and services	−101 308	—
Gross Domestic Product (at factor cost)	= 374 895	—
less factor costs adjustment (expenditure taxes less subsidies)	− 55 806	
Gross Domestic Product at factor cost	= 319 089	
plus net property income from abroad	+ 4 686	
Gross National Product at factor cost	= 323 775	
less capital consumption	− 46 004	
National Income	= 277 771	

Source: *United Kingdom National Accounts*, 1987 edition.

since it is output which has not been sold. This gives the total **domestic** expenditure to which is added the value of exports, i.e. goods and services made in this country and therefore part of our production. The total is known as **final expenditure**. From this must be deducted the value of foreign-produced goods consumed during the year (after all they were not produced in this country). The result is **Gross Domestic Product** at market prices. When asked how much a pint of beer costs, I do not answer 56p, but include the 30p tax. The beer actually costs 56p to produce and it is this figure we need – thus, expenditure taxes are deducted but, for the same reason, subsidies are added. This leaves Gross Domestic Product at factor cost – the value of output produced in the UK in the given year.

Sometimes economists wish to calculate **National Income** which is the value of goods and services becoming available in a particular country in a given year. This is a subtle difference to Gross Domestic Product. Households and businesses in the UK hold shares in foreign companies and own property abroad: from this they earn an income. Foreigners own shares in UK companies and parts of the UK – from this they earn income. This income is known a property income from, and paid, abroad. In the UK it usually a positive nett figure and if added to GDP it gives Gross National Product (GNP) at factor cost. Each year machines wear out and and become worth less. Firms make an allowance for this known as depreciation. If the total depreciation or capital consumption is deducted from GNP the resulting figure is known as National Income.

Gross Domestic Product and the standard of living

Gross Domestic Product is used as a measure of a country's relative prosperity. In 1986, the UK had the world's sixth largest GDP after the USA, Japan, USSR, West Germany and France. Economic growth is a measure of the percentage increase in GDP in each year. During most of the post war period the UK has experienced much lower growth rates than many of the developed

nations but in recent years growth rates have been high (4.5 per cent in 1987).

Comparison between countries, however, needs to reduce the value of GDP to one currency (normally the US $) and to divide the GDP by the country's population to give a figure for GDP per capita (head). Comparisons can then be made:

GDP US$ per capita 1985:

UK	7 943
France	9 251
West Germany	10 243
Italy	6 278
Japan	10 997
USA	16 494

Even this figure is not necessarily a good measure of relative prosperity or wellbeing within a country. By reducing everything to its monetary value we have no idea **what** is being produced. A country could achieve very high levels of GDP by producing large quantities of weapons. In addition the **distribution** of income in a country could be very uneven with a few very rich and millions' starving. GDP per capita simply divides the value of output by the population and is therefore implying that everyone receives an equal share! To look at a country's welfare it is necessary to look at the percentage of homes with basic necessities and luxuries; to look at the literacy rate; the child mortality rate; the number of doctors per head of population etc. This aspect of growth and GDP is looked at in detail in Chapters 10 and 17.

SUMMARY EXERCISE

1 Explain the difference between a **want** and a **need**.
2 Why is it that all of the World's **wants** cannot be satisfied?
3 Could all of the World's **needs** ever be satisfied?
4 Explain what economists mean by the term **opportunity cost** using as an example the steel used to produce a motorcar.
5 For each of the following list the type of resource:

Teacher   Washing machine (in
Lathe   laundry)

Lorry   Bricks
Machine operator   Washing machine (in
Nurse   private house)
Iron ore   Water

6 Give an example of a **public good**.
7 What is meant by the term **mixed economy?**

8 List any disadvantages that could occur while living in a **planned economy**.
9 List any advantages that could occur while living in a **planned economy**.
10 What is the difference between Gross National Product at factor cost and National Income?

2 Private Sector Enterprise

To produce anything resources, human, man-made and natural, are needed. These are sometimes known as the **factors of production**. These resources are not in a form which will satisfy **wants** until they have been brought together and set to work. This is performed by the **entrepreneur** – in other words the person in control of the enterprise or business. The following case is about Jack Cohen, the founder of the famous Tesco chain of supermarkets and without a doubt an entrepreneur.

CASE STUDY
'Pile it high sell it cheap'

The story of Jack Cohen and his creation, Tesco, is so remarkable that Maurice Corina has written a

Fig 2.1

book called *Pile it high sell it cheap* which gives the full account and facts behind his life.

When Jack Cohen left the flying corps after the First World War he had just £30. Although his family were not in favour he spent this money on tins of surplus war rations and sold them from a hand cart in the London street markets.

He continued to buy cheap goods and sell them in markets. It was hard work, getting up early to secure a good position and working until late.

The name Tesco was first used by Jack to name tea bought from importers by the chest and re-packed. One of the owners of the tea importing firm was called T E Stockwell. By taking his initials TES and adding the first two letters of his own surname Jack Cohen invented the brand name Tesco.

As years went by Jack started selling large quantities of goods to fellow stall holders – he acted as a middleman, or wholesaler, operating from a small warehouse. He used his talent to spot a good bargain, then fill his small warehouse with cheap

goods he could re-sell to the London street traders. For example, in 1930 he bought 87 000 cases of 'Snowflake milk' at 10 shillings per case (50p) – which he sold at 12–14 shillings per case (60–70p). The milk was a condensed variety which had proved difficult to sell for the importers, Amalgamated Dairies. Jack was soon buying 500 cases a week.

As time went by it became obvious Jack was capable of selling far more stock and, therefore, making far more profit if he had a greater number of outlets. In 1930 he opened a shop in a covered arcade in Tooting with a partner, Sam Freeman. The next year he opened a second shop in partnership with a nephew in Chatham and a third was built in partnership with Michael Kaye. (This last venture blossomed into Pricerite Ltd which became a private company in 1934 and a public company in 1963, Jack Cohen having sold his 50 per cent stake in 1956.) More shops followed in Becontree and Edgware.

In 1932–33 he formed two private companies,

Fig 2.2

Tesco and J E Cohen & Co Ltd (the first for retailing, the second wholesaling). Both businesses grew and by 1938 had a turnover (value of goods sold) of £2 million and 100 shops.

Jack Cohen now moved into production buying farm land to grow his own vegetables and fruit. Many Tesco brands already existed including the now famous original tea.

Visits to America convinced Jack that self-service supermarkets were the future for retailing and soon after the Second World War he experimented in one shop. However, it failed.

In 1947 all his different companies were brought together in one holding company – Tesco Stores (Holding) Ltd. In December 1947 the company became a public company with 250 000 shares sold at 75p each. (A public company sells shares to the public who then own a tiny part of the company. They receive their share of the profits and have the right to vote at annual meetings to elect the directors to run the company.)

In the first full year of trading this new public company made enough profit to pay each shareholder a 20 per cent return on the price of their shares. This influx of money resulted in larger stores and the introduction of American style self-service stores which proved successful. Further sales of shares allowed the company to expand during the 50s and 60s. Less profitable smaller groceries were bought and unlikely sites such as churches and cinemas were converted into supermarkets. By 1988 Tesco ran 379 stores (130 of them superstores) and employed 50 192 people – quite a jump from a barrow and £30!

Not only did Jack Cohen pioneer self-service supermarkets, he also took part in the campaign to remove **resale price maintenance** (RPM). Under this practice a manufacturer could tell a retailer the price at which he wanted his products sold. Tesco could buy in bulk and sell at lower prices. Jack Cohen's whole philosophy was to pile his goods high and sell them cheap. In this way he might not make much profit upon each item but he sold so many this did not matter. RPM prevented him from operating like this. In 1964 after a long campaign RPM was banned and Tesco were able to drop the prices on many lines, for example a 20 per cent reduction in the price of Gillette razor blades.

The story of Tesco is of particular interest for, as the student's summary table shows (see opposite), it has passed through most of the forms of business which have been developed in the UK private sector.

Types of business

One-man businesses

A one-man business is very easy to form. When Jack Cohen bought his first £30 of stock and hand-cart he had formed a business. In such a case there is one entrepreneur who takes all of the risk, makes all the decisions and takes all the profits.

Constraints

Money The one-man business has very limited sources of finance – his own savings and any loans he might be able to negotiate from banks or even friends.

Skill Although a talented man, Jack Cohen needed the selling skills of his partners when he expanded his business. A brilliant craftsman may be a poor salesman and this could hold back the business.

Benefits

Independence Some people like to work for themselves, to make their own decisions and, therefore, like to run a one-man business. Some plumbers or shopkeepers who are their own bosses could earn far more money working for someone else but prefer to work for themselves. They also have an incentive or reason to work hard since all the profits are their own!

Partnership

To overcome some of the constraints of a one-man business people can join together to take an equal share in the running and ownership of a business. They are called partners and the business a **partnership**. Jack Cohen took on partners who had experience as salesmen to run shops. Other people take on partners to share the costs of the business. Many professional people, such as opticians, solicitors and estate agents, are partners. Two or more professionals can share accommodation and secretarial help, split the costs of telephones, premises, heating bills etc. They can also specialise in one aspect of their profession. The **Partnership Act (1890)** limits the number of partners

Exercise

Complete this summary chart of the growth of
Tesco by filling in the gaps, using the case study.

The Growth of Tesco

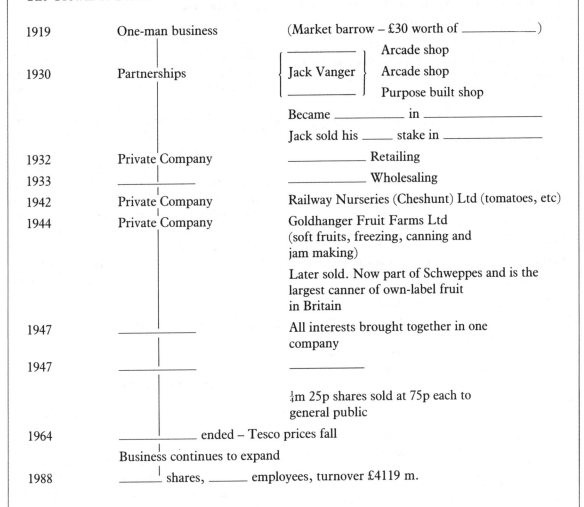

1919	One-man business	(Market barrow – £30 worth of _____)
		_____ ⎫ Arcade shop
1930	Partnerships	Jack Vanger ⎬ Arcade shop
		_____ ⎭ Purpose built shop
		Became _____ in _____
		Jack sold his _____ stake in _____
1932	Private Company	_____ Retailing
1933	_____	_____ Wholesaling
1942	Private Company	Railway Nurseries (Cheshunt) Ltd (tomatoes, etc)
1944	Private Company	Goldhanger Fruit Farms Ltd (soft fruits, freezing, canning and jam making)
		Later sold. Now part of Schweppes and is the largest canner of own-label fruit in Britain
1947	_____	All interests brought together in one company
1947	_____	_____
		$\frac{1}{4}$m 25p shares sold at 75p each to general public
1964	_____ ended – Tesco prices fall	
	Business continues to expand	
1988	_____ shares, _____ employees, turnover £4119 m.	

1 Jack Cohen was an entrepreneur. Using the case study explain fully the term **entrepreneur**.
2 Using the case study give one example of each of the following resources or factors of production used by Jack in his early street trading days:

(*a*) Capital
(*b*) Labour
(*c*) Land

3 How did Jack compete against other entrepreneurs and what made him so successfull?
4 When Jack took on partners in 1930 and again when the company became public in 1947 he gained more money to expand his operations – but what did he lose?
5 Some one-man businesses do not expand as Jack Cohen's market stall did but prefer to remain small. Why do you think this is so?

to 20 (although the Department of Trade and Industry can now permit more).

Constraints

Money   Although additional funds are available from partners money for expansion is still limited and borrowing from a bank the only other source.

Liability   The business and the partners are in law seen as being the same. This means that if the business makes a loss and owes money the property and the wealth of the partners would be used to settle these debts. The partners are said to have **unlimited liability**. They are collectively liable for any debts the business might have. This is also true for a one-man business.

Benefits

Additional money   Extra partners mean money for expansion.

Additional skill   New partners might bring fresh ideas or skills to the business.

Control   Although a one-man business has total control a partner has a great deal of say in the running of the business. On some issues, such as the introduction of a new partner, there must be a unanimous decision by all existing partners.

Costs

Loss of control   Every partner has the right to take decisions and enter into agreements on behalf of the other partners. The one-man business who forms a partnership therefore will face this cost. It is an opportunity cost – the cost of increasing the money available for expansion or expertise is a loss of personal control and independence.

The **Limited Partnership Act 1907** made it possible for some partners to be known as **limited partners** who would only contribute money to the business and not play any part in the running of it. The advantage to the limited partner is that they gain **limited liability** and, unlike the ordinary partner, if the business fell into debt would only be liable to lose the money they had originally put into the business. Their own personal wealth

could not be touched. This would encourage people with savings to put them into a partnership. They are sometimes known as **sleeping partners**.

The company

The constraint shared by the two forms of business discussed previously is the lack of funds for investment. Over time a company evolved into a business owned by a number of people who might or might not take an active role in the running of the business. Each would own only part or a share of the business and would receive part or a share of its profits which would be paid in the form of a dividend. To encourage people to purchase shares in a business Acts of Parliament during the mid-nineteenth century gave such shareholders limited liability (they could not be asked to sell their own property to pay the debts of the company). A company is seen in law to be separate from its owners. There are two main types of company controlled by the Companies Act 1948 as amended in 1967 and 1976. All companies must register certain facts with the Registrar of Companies and follow certain rules. (*See* Table 2.1.)

Private limited company

Such a company is often a small family affair although very popular. Before the Companies Act 1980 changed the law the private limited company was restricted to 50 shareholders. The Act abolished this constraint, and private limited companies are no longer restricted in terms of growth. They cannot, however, advertise shares to the general public.

Benefits

Limited liability   Every shareholder has limited liability which certainly makes buying such shares an attractive proposition.

Continuity   A company can exist for ever. It does not die with the shareholders, the ownership simply passes from one person to another.

Costs

Loss of control When an entrepreneur sells shares it is no longer his company. He may keep the majority of shares himself and since voting is on the basis of the number of shares each shareholder owns he could retain control. He would lose independence but gain limited liability and funds for expansion.

Public limited company

These are the forms of business which have produced the massive international companies, as shown in Fig 2.3.

Benefits

Unlimited source of funds A public company can have as many shareholders as needed. This can often be several thousand and means that vast sums of money for expansion can be raised. Shares can be advertised to the general public and anyone can buy them. If a shareholder wishes to sell his part ownership of the firm he firm he can do so in the special market place which has developed for this purpose called **The Stock Exchange**.

Limited liability As with a private company all shareholders have limited liability.

Costs

Gulf between owners and managers Public companies are owned by so many shareholders it is impossible for them all to have a say in the decision making of the firm. They elect Directors therefore to control the firm. A small shareholder is at a disadvantage since votes are allocated on the basis of one vote per share. Institutions such as pension funds and insurance companies often own vast quantities of shares and can out-vote the small shareholder. The cost of unlimited funds is that control becomes remote from the ownership.

Shares

Raising capital in a public company

A public company will need additional funds if it wishes to expand. Indeed, as we saw from our case study, this is often the reason for changing from a private company to a public company.

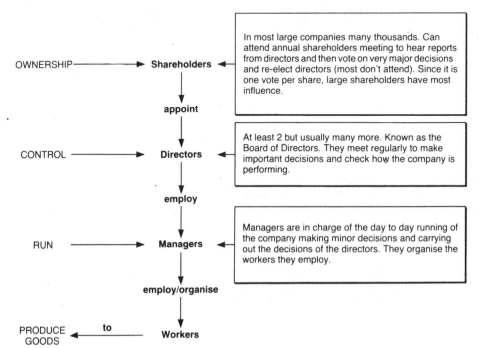

Fig 2.3 Public joint stock company

If it is performing well a public company may well keep back some of last year's profits and use this money for expansion – **retained profits**. It can always borrow money either from a bank or from the public. Such loans are often called **stock** or **debentures**. A firm will borrow a certain amount from a person at a fixed rate of interest for a fixed length of time. They are given a certificate and twice a year receive interest. At the end of the set period of time the loan is repaid. If the person who lent the money wants it back before the time is up they can sell it to somebody else.

The public company has no limit upon the number of shares or shareholders it can have, so another way of raising money for expansion is to sell more shares. This can be done in several ways. The most usual way is to advertise in quality newspapers that there are shares on offer – **an offer for sale**. People who are interested answer the advertisement and send a cheque for all or part of the cost and later will receive their share certificate.

An alternative method is called a **rights issue**. Here existing shareholders are given the chance to buy more shares. If they do not wish to buy them the remainder will be offered to the general public.

Illustrated on page 22 is the front cover of the Offer for Sale of shares in J Sainsbury in 1973. Look at it carefully and answer the questions.

Selling shares for the first time is called **issuing** and it is a very complicated business. It is important to get the price of the shares just right. If the price is too high people will not buy them, too low and you will not make as much money as you could. For this reason companies often pay for the help of a special bank to do it for them. Such banks are called **merchant banks**.

Before shares in public companies can be bought and sold on the Stock Exchange permission must be obtained from the Stock Exchange Council which will need to look at the books of the company over the last five years. In this way potential investors are protected from bogus companies selling shares and then disappearing with the money.

Table 2.1 Summary of forms of Private Sector Enterprise

Type	Features	Advantages
Sole trader i.e. builders plumbers hairdressers printers 'corner shop'	• most common type of business • easy to establish • owners capital • owners labour • many bankruptcies	• owner makes decisions • personal contact with employees and customers
Partnership Two types: 1 Unlimited partnership: typical of professions: i.e. doctors, accountants, solicitors (Partnership Act 1890) 2 Limited Partnership Act 1901	• 2–20 partners • no upper limit in a professional partnership like solicitors • profits and losses equally divided • no salary for partners • agreement by one partner is binding on all • all partners entitled to a role in management • same as above • very few of these, some often better to form a private limited company	• more capital available • use of specialist partners who make capital contribution • accounts only have to be submitted to Inland Revenue • expansion is its own affair • Limited Liability providing

The Stock Exchange

The role of the Stock Exchange

When a private company turns into a public company it is fully investigated by the Stock Exchange Council. Most people have heard of the Stock Exchange, but what does it do? When a public company wishes to sell shares it will advertise them in a newspaper or offer them to existing shareholders. Why do we need a Stock Exchange?

It is unlikely that people would be so happy to buy shares if they were not sure they could sell them again without too much difficulty. The Stock Exchange makes this possible. It is a market place for second-hand stocks and shares. When people sell shares they sell them to someone else who wants to own part of that public company for a while. Public companies can last for ever so that people who buy shares in them need some way of getting back their money.

Note When shares are sold at any time other than the **first** time the company receives no money,

only the ownership of the firm changes. For this reason the company must be told of the transfer so that they know where to send the dividends. This is done on a **stock transfer form** (*see* Fig 2.5). On 27 October 1986 The Stock Exchange implemented a large number of changes in the way in which shares are bought and sold. These changes, introduced on one day, were known as 'Big Bang'. At the heart of the change is new technology. All 'deals' to buy or sell shares are now recorded on a computerised dealing system called **SEAQ (Stock Exchange Automated Quotations)**. Members of The Stock Exchange are now known as **Broker/Dealers**. They can be individuals or represent large financial institutions (corporate members). Some of the Broker/Dealers are also **Market Makers** – that is they will undertake to buy or sell certain types of shares on a continuous basis. Market Makers 'advertise' the prices at which they are willing to buy or sell certain shares via TOPIC, The Stock Exchange videotext information system. All Broker/Dealers have this information as do financial institutions and

Drawbacks	Sources of capital	Additional information
• Unlimited Liability. Liable for all the debts of a company, and can mean loss of personal wealth • no continuity on owner's death • interest on loans often higher than larger firms • lots of competition • on one's own • technological shortages and hence efficiency difficulties	• savings • plough-back profits • bank loan • overdraft • trade credit	• personal stock of savings • primary source of cash for growth or expansion • 'high street' banks such as National Westminster, Barclays, Lloyds and Midland. • loans can cover periods of up to 20 years or more, usually for specific projects (e.g. new equipment) • overdrafts are usually short-term to support day-day operations.

• unlimited Liability
• if one partner dies, partnership ends, and a new one has to be formed
• since agreements made by one partner are binding on all of them, each 'active' partner should have good business sense.
• delays and arguments may occur since all partners have a management role
• limited number of partners may restrict expansion
• partners take no part in running business
• at least one general partner has unlimited liability
• register with Registrar of Companies.
	• same as above plus Loans from Partners – can only carry 5% interest p.a.
	• savings from partners
		• from suppliers by delaying payment
		• terms of business contracts like time for payments is a key part of business operation, especially for export orders
		• large companies need credit control departments
		• loans could also come from:
		  (a) Merchant Banks and organisations which provide venture capital such as Investors in Industry Ltd (3i)
		  (b) insurance companies, building societies and other institutions such as pension funds
		• other funding is available through the Loan Guarantee Scheme and Business Expansion Scheme

Table 2.1 (cont'd)

Type Limited companies	Features	Advantages
1 Private Limited Company. An expanded small business, often the remains of a family business.	• company has own legal identity, separate from shareholders • familiar where large scale operations necessary • under 1980 Companies Act all companies are private unless they meet the necessary requirements for public companies • name must end with 'Limited' • not permitted to issue shares or debentures to the general public • no limit to the number of shareholders • no secrecy since accounts must be filed annually with Registrar of Companies	• Limited Liability Act of 1856 • own legal identity • continuity is not threatened by death of shareholder(s) • capital attracted from people who might not have invested • founders of the business can maintain control by holding a majority of shares • no limit to the number of shareholders
2 Public Limited Company. Tend to be large companies and are quoted on the Stock Exchange.	• Memorandum of Association must state company is public. • name must end with 'public limited company'. (plc) • issued capital must be at least £50 000 • two owners as minimum	• allowed to appeal to the public for funds • no restriction on the transfer of shares

Drawbacks

- many formalities required under Companies Acts 1948–1981
- must produce:
  (a) Memorandum of Association, i.e. relationship with outside world – name, address, objectives, capital amount and share types.
  (b) Articles of Association, i.e. internal running of business covering election and rights of directors, borrowing powers of company
  (c) Statutory Declaration, i.e. statement that company has complied with Companies acts.
- must register with Registrar of Companies.
- transfer of shares can only occur with consent of the company
- company not allowed to make a public appeal for extra capital
- tend to rely on friends and relatives for capital
- no secrecy, so competitors can see your 'situation'
- complicated and expensive process in forming a plc

- size of operation may create problems for management like:
  communication with shareholders and employees. Co-ordination of varied parts control of the organisation and the power of management.
Many legal requirements so that shareholders and general public can be protected.
No secrecy about affairs since accounts must be published.

Sources of capital

- same as above
- shareholders' capital unlimited number

- private placing

- Stock Exchange placing

- Offer for Sale

- Public Issue

- Rights Issue

Additional information

- loans and grants can be obtained through government departments (e.g. Department of Trade and Industry) and development agencies

- often done through a financial advisor whereby the shares are 'placed' privately with individuals
- often by Merchant Banks – shares are 'placed' with institutions like insurance companies
- shares are offered to an Issuing House (part of a Merchant Bank) who will gradually sell them to the public
- simply shares are sold directly to the public through advertisements in national newspapers and through the company's prospectus
- existing shareholders are given the chance to buy more shares, those shares left over will be sold to the public

Types

- ordinary shares – risk capital: dividend depends on size of profit: voting rights
- preference shares basic – fixed dividends: paid before ordinary shareholders: often no say in control of company, since privileged position given with divident payment.
  cumulative – dividend missed one year is carried forward to next year.
  participating – entitles holder to further share of profits once they reach a certain level.
- debentures – loans to company: fixed rate of interest: paid before anything else: failure to pay debenture holders can cause bankruptcy. Debentures are **not** shares and debenture holders do not share in ownership of company.

A copy of this Offer for Sale, having attached thereto the documents specified below, has been delivered to the Registrar of Companies for registration. Application has been made to the Council of The Stock Exchange for the ordinary share capital of the Company to be admitted to the Official List. This Offer for Sale contains particulars given in compliance with the Regulations of the Council of The Stock Exchange for the purpose of giving information to the public with regard to the Company. The Directors collectively and individually accept full responsibility for the accuracy of the information given and confirm, having made all reasonable enquiries, that to the best of their knowledge and belief there are no other facts the omission of which would make any statement herein misleading.

The Application List for the Ordinary Shares now offered for sale will open at 10 a.m. on Thursday 12th July, 1973 and will close at any time thereafter.

J Sainsbury Limited

(Incorporated under the Companies Acts 1908 to 1917: registered in England No. 185,647)

Offer for Sale

by

S. G. Warburg & Co. Ltd.

of

10,000,000 Ordinary Shares of 25p each
at
145p per share

payable in full on application

The Ordinary Shares now offered for sale rank in full for all dividends hereafter declared or paid on the ordinary share capital of the Company.

Share Capital

Authorised

Issued and fully paid
or to be fully paid

£25,000,000 in 100,000,000, Ordinary Shares of 25p each £20,174,751

The Company has outstanding £1 499 995 7 per cent. Irredeemable Unsecured Loan Stock. A subsidiary has outstanding £2 749 942 6½ per cent. First Mortgage Debenture Stock 1988/93, £2 887 547 7¼ per cent. First Mortgage Debenture Stock 1987/92 (of which £2 000 000 is held by the Company) and £1 500 000 8 per cent. Guaranteed Unsecured Loan Stock, guaranteed by the Company. The Company has guaranteed the bank indebtedness of associated companies to a maximum principal amount of £6 651 200 (of which £2 617 172 was outstanding at the close of business on 22nd June, 1973). At the same date, there were also outstanding other guarantees by the Company to an aggregate principal amount not exceeding £295 000. Save as aforesaid and except for inter-company liabilities between the Company and its subsidiaries ("the Group"), no company in the Group had outstanding at that date any loan capital, mortgages or charges, borrowings or indebtedness in the nature of borrowing, including bank overdrafts, liabilities under acceptances (other than normal trade bills) or acceptance credits, hire purchase commitments or (other than in the ordinary course of business) guarantees or other material contingent liabilities.

Fig 2.4   Offer for Sale

Fig 2.5 Stock Transfer Form

1 Who are the merchant bankers employed by Sainsbury to sell these shares?

2 What is the **face** or **nominal value** of the shares on offer?

3 What price are people asked to pay for each share?

4 Why is the price of each share so much higher than its face value?

5 When do the shareholders have to pay for their shares?

6 If J Sainsbury sold all of the shares on offer how much capital would be raised?

7 What would they do with this money do you think?

8 Why would people wish to buy shares in such a firm?

wealthy investors. The SEAQ system sorts the Market Maker's prices so that the cheapest is at the top of each page. For most leading shares there are about 16 Market Makers in competition. If a Broker/Dealer wishes to buy from or sell to a Market Maker he will either telephone him or visit him in person, as they can operate from the floor of The Stock Exchange or their own dealing rooms. Deals are fed into the SEAQ system within five minutes so that the information is up-to-data. Investors can deal with any Broker/Dealer whether or not they are a Market Maker. The constantly up-dated data, available to all, gives investors total information and since all deals are recorded on the computer it is hoped that there now is greater protection for the investor.

Fig 2.6 The Stock Exchange
(Courtesy: The Stock Photobank – London)

How The Stock Exchange works

A retired couple sold their house and moved to a smaller cottage near the sea. They were left with £10 000 to spend or save. Since the man had worked for BP for many years he decided to buy shares in his old company with his spare £10 000.

They had never purchased shares before so they went to their Building Society who offered a share service. The Building Society contacted a Broker/Dealer who consulted a SEAQ screen. With such a well-known company many Market Makers dealt in these shares but the lowest selling price is at the top of the screen. (If selling the highest

purchase price is shown.) The Broker/Dealer contacted the Market Maker selected by telephone. (It can be done in person on the floor of The Stock Exchange as it once had to be.) The deal was agreed by word of mouth but then entered into SEAQ, displayed and recorded. The investors knew they had paid the lowest possible price. Within a couple of days they received a contract note which gave full details of the amount owed and when it had to be paid. This invoice included not only the price of the shares but also 'Commission' (the amount charged by the Broker/Dealer) and various Government taxes. BP was sent a stock transfer form to tell them of the change in ownership and in due course, after they had paid the balance due,

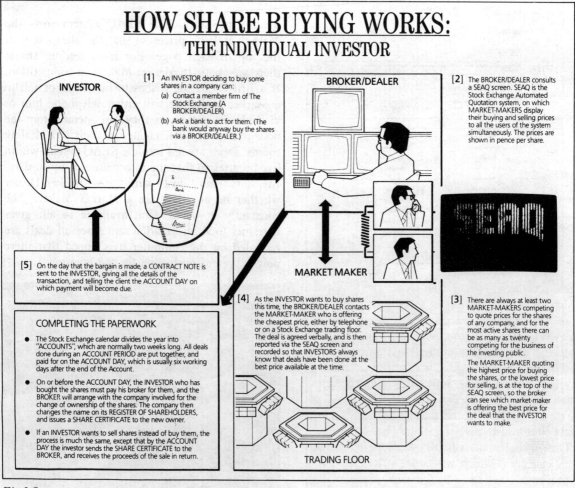

HOW SHARE BUYING WORKS:
THE INDIVIDUAL INVESTOR

INVESTOR

[1] An INVESTOR deciding to buy some shares in a company can:
(a) Contact a member firm of The Stock Exchange (A BROKER/DEALER)
(b) Ask a bank to act for them. (The bank would anyway buy the shares via a BROKER/DEALER.)

BROKER/DEALER

[2] The BROKER/DEALER consults a SEAQ screen. SEAQ is the Stock Exchange Automated Quotation system, on which MARKET-MAKERS display their buying and selling prices to all the users of the system simultaneously. The prices are shown in pence per share.

[5] On the day that the bargain is made, a CONTRACT NOTE is sent to the INVESTOR, giving all the details of the transaction, and telling the client the ACCOUNT DAY on which payment will become due.

MARKET MAKER

COMPLETING THE PAPERWORK

- The Stock Exchange calendar divides the year into "ACCOUNTS", which are normally two weeks long. All deals done during an ACCOUNT PERIOD are put together, and paid for on the ACCOUNT DAY, which is usually six working days after the end of the Account.

- On or before the ACCOUNT DAY, the INVESTOR who has bought the shares must pay his broker for them, and the BROKER will arrange with the company involved for the change of ownership of the shares. The company then changes the name on its REGISTER OF SHAREHOLDERS, and issues a SHARE CERTIFICATE to the new owner.

- If an INVESTOR wants to sell shares instead of buy them, the process is much the same, except that by the ACCOUNT DAY the investor sends the SHARE CERTIFICATE to the BROKER, and receives the proceeds of the sale in return.

[4] As the INVESTOR wants to buy shares this time, the BROKER/DEALER contacts the MARKET-MAKER who is offering the cheapest price, either by telephone or on a Stock Exchange trading floor. The deal is agreed verbally, and is then reported via the SEAQ screen and recorded so that INVESTORS always know that deals have been done at the best price available at the time.

[3] There are always at least two MARKET-MAKERS competing to quote prices for the shares of any company, and for the most active shares there can be as many as twenty competing for the business of the investing public.
The MARKET-MAKER quoting the highest price for buying the shares, or the lowest price for selling, is at the top of the SEAQ screen, so the broker can see which market-maker is offering the best price for the deal that the INVESTOR wants to make.

TRADING FLOOR

Fig 2.7

1571998

ORDINARY SHARE CERTIFICATE

THE BRITISH PETROLEUM COMPANY p.l.c.

INCORPORATED UNDER THE COMPANIES (CONSOLIDATION) ACT 1908

BP

THIS IS TO CERTIFY THAT

IS/ARE THE REGISTERED HOLDER(S) OF

CERTIFICATE NUMBER	NUMBER OF SHARES OF 25p EACH (IN WORDS)	(IN FIGURES)

ORDINARY SHARES OF TWENTY FIVE PENCE EACH, FULLY PAID, IN THE COMPANY, SUBJECT TO THE MEMORANDUM AND ARTICLES OF ASSOCIATION.

THE COMMON SEAL OF THE COMPANY WAS AFFIXED PURSUANT TO ARTICLE 113 OF THE COMPANY'S ARTICLES OF ASSOCIATION.

EXAMINED

THE COMPANY WILL NOT REGISTER THE TRANSFER OF ANY SHARE WITHOUT THE PRODUCTION OF THE RELATIVE CERTIFICATE.
REGISTRAR'S OFFICE: BP HOUSE, THIRD AVENUE, HARLOW, ESSEX, CM19 5AG.

PRINTED IN ENGLAND BY METCALFE CALDWELL.

Fig 2.8 A share certificate

our retired couple received their share certificate (*see* Fig 2.8).

Stock Exchange Account Days 1981

First Day of Dealings	Option Declaration Day	Last Day of Dealings	Account Day
Dec 8 1980	Dec 22 *a*	Dec 23 *b*	Jan 5*
Dec 24 *c*	Jan 8	Jan 9	Jan 19
Jan 12	Jan 22	Jan 23	Feb 2
Jan 26	Feb 5	Feb 6	Feb 16
Feb 9	Feb 26	Feb 27	Mar 9*
Mar 2	Mar 12	Mar 13	Mar 23
Mar 16	Mar 26	Mar 27	Apr 6
Mar 30	Apr 8 *c*	Apr 9 *d*	Apr 21 *b*
Apr 10 *e*	Apr 29 *c*	Apr 30 *d*	May 11*
May 1 *e*	May 14	May 15	May 26 *b*
May 18	May 28	May 29	Jun 8
Jun 1	Jun 11	Jun 12	Jun 22*
Jun 15	Jun 25	Jun 26	Jul 6
Jun 29	Jul 9	Jul 10	Jul 20
Jul 13	Jul 23	Jul 24	Aug 3
Jul 27	Aug 6	Aug 7	Aug 17
Aug 10	Aug 26 *c*	Aug 27 *d*	Sep 7*
Aug 28 *e*	Sep 10	Sep 11	Sep 21
Sep 14	Sep 24	Sep 25	Oct 5
Sep 28	Oct 8	Oct 9	Oct 19
Oct 12	Oct 22	Oct 23	Nov 2
Oct 26	Nov 5	Nov 6	Nov 16
Nov 9	Nov 19	Nov 20	Nov 30
Nov 23	Dec 3	Dec 4	Dec 14

* = 3-Week Account
a Monday *b* Tuesday *c* Wednesday
d Thursday *e* Friday

Fig 2.9

Speculation

Figure 2.9 shows that the Stock Exchange year is divided into 20 two-week accounts and four three-week accounts. This means that any transaction which takes place during an account does not have to be settled until the account day which is always one week after the close of the account. So if we take the account underlined and you were to purchase shares on 1 June you would not have to pay for them until 22 June. It would also mean that if you sold shares on 1 June you would not have to give them to the purchaser until 22 June nor would you receive the money until then.

This arrangement allows people to **speculate**. They can guess which way share prices are going to move and buy and sell the same shares within the one account. If they guess correctly they can make a lot of money. To help illustrate this Fig 2.9 shows some of the share prices for the first and last days of the account underlined. Remember, if you were a speculator you would only know the first days prices! Figure 2.10 shows the prices for oil and gas shares for the two dates. Three shares are underlined. The first is the Century Oil Group Ltd.

On 1 June 10p shares in this company were sold for 76p. Even if there were no shares to sell some could still be sold on 1 June allowing enough to be bought to cover the sale later in the account. This is called **selling short**. It works because the share certificates do not have to be produced until 22 June. So if 100 000 Century Oil shares were

1 June, 1981

OIL AND GAS

Dividends Paid	Stock	Price	Last xd	Div Net	C'yr	Y'ld Gr's	P/E
Jan. July	Do. 8% Pf. £1	64	24.12	5.6%	1435	12.5	—
Jan. July	Burmah £1	147	1.5	6.5	q2.2	6.3	(8.3)
Jan. July	Carless Capel 10p	136	8.12	12.5	4.1	2.6	12.9
Jan. Aug.	Century 10p	76	8.12	h2.25	5.5	4.2	4.6
—	Ceres Res. C$5.00	150	—	—	—	—	—
—	Charterhall 5p	67	3.67	—	—	—	—
—	Charterhouse Pet.	81	10.4	1.0	3.8	1.8	21.3
July	Cie Fr. Petroles B.	£12¼	7.77	Q54%	φ	19.0	φ
—	Jessel Trust 5p	20½	—	—	—	—	—
Oct. June	KCA	182xd	18.5	5.25	1.2	4.1	(26.1)
—	LASMO	580	—	—	—	—	19.5
Feb. Aug.	LASMO 14% 1981–83	£99½	26.1	Q14%	—	14.1	—
Apr. Oct.	LASMO "Ops" 10p	962	30.3	71.19	—	10.6	—
—	Magellan Pet.	470	—	—	—	—	—
—	Magnet Metals 10c	20	10.12	—	—	—	—
—	‡‡Marinex Pet. 10p	132	—	—	—	φ	—
—	††Penine Res.	48	—	—	—	—	—
—	•Pict. Petroleum	280	—	—	—	—	—
June	Premier Cons. 5p	68	—	—	—	—	—
—	Ranger Oil	580	—	—	—	—	—
May Oct.	Royal Dutch Fl.10	£16½xd	18.5	Q68½%	3.9	7.8	3.3

12 June, 1981

OIL AND GAS

Dividends Paid	Stock	Price	Last xd	Div Net	C'yr	Y'ld Gr's	P/E
Nov. May	Brit. Petroleum	352	16.3	20.25	3.4	8.2	4.0
Jan. July	Do. 8% Pf. £1	61	24.12	5.6%	1435	13.1	—
—	Brunswick Oil NL	13	—	—	—	—	—
Jan. July	Burmah £1	141	1.5	6.5	q2.2	6.6	(8.0)
Jan. July	Carless Capel 10p	120	8.12	2.75	φ	3.3	φ
Jan. Aug.	Century 10p	70	8.12	2.8	φ	5.9	φ
—	Ceres Res. C$5.00	155	—	—	—	—	—
—	Charterhall 5p	60	3.67	—	—	—	—
—	Charterhouse Pet.	75	10.4	1.0	3.8	1.9	19.7
July	Cie Fr. Petroles B.	£12	1.7	Q54%	φ	19.6	φ
—	Jessel Trust 5p	23½	—	—	—	—	—
Oct. June	KCA	160	18.5	5.25	1.2	4.7	(23.0)
—	LASMO	525	—	—	—	—	17.6
Feb. Aug.	LASMO 14% 1981–83	£99½	26.1	Q14%	—	14.1	—
Apr. Oct.	LASMO "Ops" 10p	900	30.3	71.19	—	11.3	—
—	Magellan Pet.	510	—	—	—	—	—
—	Magnet Metals 10c	17	10.12	—	—	—	—
—	‡‡Marinex Pet. 10p	120	—	—	—	φ	—
—	††Penine Res.	42	—	—	—	—	—
—	•Pict. Pet. £1	235	—	—	—	—	—
—	Premiers Cons 5p	65	—	—	φ	—	φ
—	Ranger Oil	630	—	—	—	—	—
May Oct.	Royal Dutch Fl.10	£16½	18.5	Q68½%	3.9	7.9	3.3

Fig 2.10 Share prices

sold on 1 June you would receive £76 000 on 22 June but would have to present the purchaser with the shares on that day as well – and you have not got any. By 12 June the price of Century Oil shares has fallen to 70p each so 100 000 shares will only cost you £70 000 and you will not have to pay until 22 June which is when you are paid £76 000. You will also now have 100 000 Century Oil shares to hand over to the original purchaser. This will leave you with a capital gain of £6000. Some of this goes to the stockbroker who charges a fee or commission which in this case reduces your gain to £5767.50 upon which you would be taxed at a special rate.

This commission is how the broker makes his living and is charged at different rates depending upon how large the deal is and how important the customer is.

If you look at the third share underlined, Ranger Oil, you will see that unlike Century Oil share price its price rose during our account. To make money here the speculator would have to buy at the beginning of the account and sell at the end. If say, he were to buy 10 000 at the beginning of the account he would owe the broker on the 22 June £58 000. If he then sells at the end of the account he would be paid £63 000, a gain

of £5000 from which would be deducted commission and tax.

When prices are rising as in this second case it is sometimes called a **bull** market and such speculators are known as **bulls**. When prices are falling as in the first example it is said to be a **bear** market and such speculators are said to be **bears**.

Exercise

1 Using the second share underlined, LASMO, show in detail how you could make £2750 gain (before tax and commission).
2 Look at the mining shares. Give the names of shares where bulls and bears could have made a gain. (One of each.)
3 Using the table of Stock Exchange Account days on page 25 write down when the four three week account days are. Why do you think these are so timed?
4 Speculators who buy new issues of shares in order to sell them quickly for a gain are called **stags**.
   Put this into everyday language: ' . . . stags (who are really a form of bull) profited handsomely from an issue of Penguins.'
(Taken from page 33 Guide to the British Economy, *Donaldson Peter, Penguin, 1965.)*

The size and growth of companies

There are about 600 000 companies in the UK, most of these are private (99 per cent) and most of them are small.

The bar chart shows just how many small firms existed in the manufacturing sector in this country in 1982. Nearly three quarters (73 per cent) of all manufacturing establishments employed less than 20 people whereas just 386 establishments (0.5 per cent) employed over 1500 people. The number of small firms has grown as a percentage of total manufacturing establishments over the last few years, with Government help to the unemployed to start their own businesses. It is a sad fact, however, that between 1979 and 1982 the total number of manufacturing establishments fell by some 5000. Small firms only account for 10 per cent of total employment in the manufacturing sector.

Task

The figures used in Fig. 2.11 refer to manufacturing establishments only. If tertiary sector businesses were to be included how would you expect the bar chart to alter?

A second way is to look at the value of a company's assets. Figure 2.12 shows that of the new companies formed in 1981 well over half had a recorded capital value of less than £100.

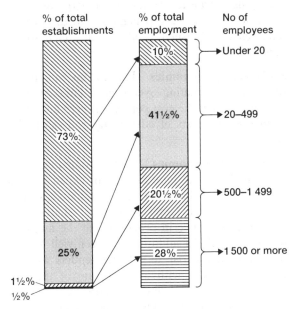

Fig 2.11   The size of distribution of manufacturing establishments in the UK 1982 (Source: Report on the Census of Production 1982)

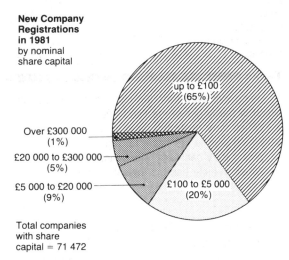

Fig 2.12   New Company registrations 1981 (Source: Barclays Bank Review February 1983) (Taken from The Independent 19.06.88)

Table 2.2: Manufacturing: Size Distribution of Establishments

Number of employees	Number of establishments	% of total establishments	% of total employment
Under 20	75 001	73.3	10.0
20 to 499	25 633	25.0	41.6
500 to 1499	1 367	1.3	20.5
1500 or more	386	0.4	27.9

Economies of scale

> ### CASE STUDY EXERCISE:

Table 2.3: Selected monthly vehicle running costs (£)

Fixed costs	Vehicle 1	Vehicle 2
Road tax	235	99
Insurance	46	36
Depreciation	1 885	823
Total	2 166	958
Variable costs		
Fuel	853	554
Service/repairs	1 140	536
Labour	1 054	1 054
Total	3 047	2 144
Fixed + variable	5 213	3 012
Miles	5 125	5 993
Fuel (litres)	3 091	2 009
MPG	7.5	13.5
Cost/mile	101.6	51.7
Cases delivered	27 995	10 613
Cost/case	18.6p	29.2p

Tasks

1 Using evidence from the table try to distinguish which is the larger of the two lorries.
2 Which lorry costs the most to run?
3 Which cost is the same for both vehicle?
4 Which lorry can carry most cases?
5 Which vehicle has the lowest cost for delivering cases?

If you completed the task above you will soon discover that the larger of the two lorries is much more expensive to run. It has higher fuel consumption, higher road tax and insurance. In fact, it costs nearly twice as much per mile to run *but*, since it can carry nearly **three** times as many cases it can deliver them at a much lower unit cost.

This is an example of the savings enjoyed by larger firms. These savings are collectively known as **economies of scale**. There are several types of savings economies.

1 Technical economies Large firms use bigger machines. As in the case above. It has been estimated that the unit costs (the cost of transporting each item) are 175 per cent higher using a 7.5 tonne lorry rather than a 32.5 tonne lorry. Such savings do not only apply to transporting the finished goods or raw materials. Larger machinery is often more efficient, and it is also possible to use labour in a more efficient way. Workers can specialise. (*See* Chapter 7 Mass Production and Automation).

2 Purchasing economies Do your parents sometimes buy in bulk? Many families find that they can make huge savings by buying food in bulk – but they must have the space to store it and of course, the money to pay for such a large order. Many poor families are forced to buy small quantities of food which works out more expensive. The same is true for businesses. A large firm can buy raw materials, components or, in the case of retail chains, finished products, at much lower unit costs.

3 Marketing economies Large firms can spread the cost of marketing over such a large number of products that the cost per item is very low. This applies to the costs of advertising and sales staff etc.

4 Financial economies Larger companies find it much cheaper to raise finance for expansion. As with marketing above, the cost of a share issue can be spread over a larger number of shares, and indeed, fees do rise in proportion to the numbers of shares sold. In addition, a larger well known firm presents less risk to potential lenders who are therefore content with a lower rate of interest. (Ask your local bank for the interest rate charge on business loans. They will quote several different rates but the actual rate charged will depend upon the size of the firm).

5 Managerial economies Large firms will employ specialist managers who have greater expertise and are therefore more efficient; for example, accountants, marketing and personnel experts, buyers, production managers etc. The number of such experts required will not increase in proportion to the size of the firm. The company would not have to double the number of accountants if output were to double for example.

The above are all types of internal economies of scale – the savings are internal to the firm.

Collectively, they mean that as a firm grows the **average** cost of producing one item (total costs of production/total output) will fall: this will not necessarily continue for all levels of production. A firm may grow so large that delays in communication begin to increase costs. This would be an example of an internal diseconomy of scale.

In general, firms are able to reduce average costs if they become larger. This will enable them to compete with rivals by offering lower prices and increase profits.

The growth of firms

As was shown in the case study, Tesco grew in several ways.

Task

Look back at the Case Study: 'Pile it high sell it cheap.' List down as many ways as you can that Tesco grew giving actual examples for each way. You ought to be able to find:
(a) New shops were opened using retained profits or borrowed funds
(b) Existing businesses were bought or taken over.

Integration

Firms can grow by building/opening new plants or by joining together with existing firms. This latter form of growth is known as **integration** and can either occur when a company buys all of the shares in another company (takeover) or when two or more companies decide it is in there mutual interest to join together (merger).

There are four main types of integration:

1 Horizontal – where firms engaged in the same industry at the same level of production join together: for example, the 1988 takeover of Rowntree-Mackintosh by Nestle or British Caledonian by British Airways.

2 Vertical – where firms engaged in the same industry at different levels of production join together: for example, when a tea producer like Brooke Bond buys a tea plantation.

Task

Using the case study 'Pile it high sell it cheap' give an example of:
(a) Horizontal integration
(b) Vertical integration

3 Lateral integration – where firms engaged in same industry but not directly competitive join together: for example, Grand Metropolitan's take over of Smirnoff in 1987.

4 Conglomerate integration – where firms in completely different industries join together: for example the takeover of The Rover Group in 1988 by British Aerospace, or Brooke Bond by Unilever in 1984.

Clearly, integration takes place for many reasons:

1 To be able to enjoy the economies of scale.
2 Rationalisation: a strong company may take-over a weak competitor and then close down the unprofitable/loss making parts of the weaker company leaving a rationalised industry. (*See* Case Study 2 – British Airways/British Caledonian).
3 To increase market power: if a firm can take-over competitors it might be able to increase price due to the absence of competition and thus profits.
4 To secure supplies and sales: Unilever companies operate 65 000 hectares of oil palm plantations originally bought to ensure supplies for their margarine and soap factories.
5 Diversification: by producing many different products in different industries, a firm can spread the risks of production and is more likely to survive. If, due to a change in demand, or change in commodity prices one particular product becomes unprofitable the large company has other products to produce profits. For example, BP has diversified into chemicals, nutrition, minerals, coal, shipping, detergents and information technology.

Tasks

1 How might the consumer benefit from integration?

2 How might the shareholder benefit from integration?
3 How might the consumer suffer from integration?

Competition/monopolies

A growing firm may be able to enjoy increased economies of scale and therefore pass on lower costs to the consumer. However, if integration means fewer firms in a particular industry and less competition it could lead to higher prices and less choice. Economists identify several different market structures:

Perfect competition – a very large number of small firms in a particular market each unable to affect the price producing identical products. This is an unrealistic situation – perhaps only true in some types of agriculture.

Imperfect competition – a few large firms with several smaller firms in a particular market. The larger firms having 'brand loyalty' are able to increase prices within reason. Very realistic – much of the Western world's output is produced in this way.

Duopoly – only two large firms in a particular market. Tate & Lyle and the British Sugar Corporation control 94 per cent of the UK sugar market.

Monopoly – only one firm in a market. Able to charge what it likes.

Task

Why do monopolies occur?
List as many reasons you can think for the development of a monopoly. (*Hint* – think about how entry into a particular industry is restricted either naturally or deliberately).

Under all these market forms except perfect competition a large firm may have a certain amount of monopoly power: that is an ability to control output and price. As we have seen entrepreneurs aim to maximise profits – in the absence of legal controls firms will aim to grow and exploit their monopoly power or join together and fix prices (restrictive practices).

Monopoly legislation

In the UK we have a Monopolies and Mergers Commission (MMC) which is an independent body of representatives from employers, higher education and trade unions (a full-time chairman and up to 31 part-time commissioners backed by a staff of 110 civil servants).

Any proposed takeover or merger can be referred to the MMC by the Secretary of State for Trade and Industry acting on the recommendation of the Office of Fair Trading if a monopoly would result (25 per cent plus share of market), or be intensified or where the total assets would exceed £30m. Once referred, any such proposal will be examined in detail by a small group of about six commissioners who will invite written evidence from interested parties and take oral evidence from those they believe to be most relevant. The MMC must report within six months. If they find that the proposed integration is not in the public interest then the Secretary of State has the power to prevent such a merger from taking place.

CASE STUDY 1

Concentration in the package holiday business

Read the article opposite carefully and then attempt these questions.
1 Before Horizon was sold to Thomson for £75m, it was briefly part of the Bass Brewing and Leisure Group. When Bass bought Horizon in May 1987 it was an example of what sort of integration?
2 What reasons are given by Bass for the sale of Horizon after just 15 months?
3 Which part of Horizon is Bass **not** selling to Thomson and why?
4 What share of the UK package tour market will the expanded Thomson group now have?
5 What share of UK foreign holidays will the expanded Thomson group now provide?
6 Explain the difference between your answers to questions 4 and 5 above.
7 On what grounds do some people think that the take-over ought to be referred to the Monopolies Commission?
8 What is a 'price war'. Why might Intasun think that the take-over might lead to lower prices and what are they prepared to do about it?

Thomson gets 40% of market with £75m Horizon purchase

THE SHAPE of the UK packaged holiday market changed dramatically yesterday, when market leader Thomson Travel Group boosted its position through the £75m acquisition of Horizon Travel from Bass, the brewing and leisure group.

The deal could face the hurdle of a reference to the Monopolies and Mergers Commission. The acquisition of Horizon, the third largest tour operator, will give Thomson close to 40 per cent of the packaged tour market.

A spokesman for the Office of Fair Trading said the OFT was aware of the deal and looking at it.

Thomson has calculated its combined share of all foreign holidays, including those made by independent holidaymakers, at 22.9 per cent. The combination of its Britannia Airways and Horizon's Orion airline will give it 22.2 per cent of the charter market behind British Airways at 25.8 per cent.

Paul Brett, managing director of Thomson Travel, said he did not believe there was a monopoly case to answer, because of the competitive nature of the travel industry. "There are no barriers

By Alison Eadie

to entry and there are price wars."

He pointed out that Thomson had been forced to reduce its prices last October, because it had pitched them too high compared with other operators. He also said that of 600 tour operators licensed by the Civil Aviation Authority, 300 had started up in the last six years.

Harry Goodman, chairman of International Leisure Group

whose Intasun subsidiary is the second largest tour operator with 21 per cent of the market, said if Thomson's increased dominance led to more predatory pricing, Intasun would respond in kind.

"We may have to cut £50 off prices and add one million holidays", he said, adding that ILG could afford to invest £25m and sit out the battle for three years.

He said ILG had considered

buying Horizon, but had been deterred by the likelihood of a monopolies reference.

Other tour operators thought the greater power of Thomson could lead to higher prices, which would not necessarily hurt the consumer.

Keith Webber, sales and marketing director of Redwing Holidays, the fourth largest tour firm with a 6.5 per cent market share, said he viewed the deal in a positive light. "For a modest increase in price, we could produce a better product and better value at the end of the day. We cannot continue with delays and surcharges for ever".

Horizon is making a loss having fallen between the two stools of the larger operators with their economies of scale and the smaller, niche operators.

Ben Hanbury, director of corporate affairs for Bass, said the industry background had not improved in the way Bass had hoped. Economies of scale were not as great as expected, the fiercely competitive climate had continued and the air traffic problems had not been resolved.

Bass, which last year bought the Holiday Inns business, believes

that hotels have better potential. Mr Hanbury said Bass had broken even on its involvement in Horizon.

It bought a 25 per cent stake in 1985 and the rest in May last year. The business was then valued at £93.5m, but included the Pontinental Hotels, which Bass is keeping.

Thomson Travel's chairman and chief executive Roger Davies said that despite the trading loss, Thomson was delighted to have bought a group of businesses with such an excellent reputation. Horizon's tour operations will continue to be run as a separate business.

Mr Goodman suggested that the £75m price was "a bit heavy for a lossmaking operation", but Thomson said it was buying 10 aircraft and a good brand name.

Source: NOP

	0	10	20	30 % of total
THOMSON	15.5%	18.1%		
ILG	7.8%	10.4%		
HORIZON	4.0%	4.8%		
REDWING	2.8%			
AIRTOURS	1.5%			
COSMOS	1.4%			
OTHER TOUR OPERATORS				30.8%
INDEPENDENT				30.4%

UK FOREIGN HOLIDAYS- COMPANY SHARES 1987

100% = 20.9m foreign holidays of 1+ nights

■ inclusive holidays   □ seat only passengers

Thomson, Horizon and ILG figures include seat only passengers, other operators figures are only inclusive tours

(Courtesy The Independent)

9 Other people think that this take-over might lead to higher prices. Explain why this might happen.

10 Before the take-over Horizon was making a loss. Why was this?

Using the evidence in this article do you think consumers gain or lose from unchecked competition in the short term and long term?

CASE STUDY 2

British Airways/British Caledonian

On 16th July 1987, the Boards of British Airways (BA) and British Caledonian (B-Cal) announced that they had agreed terms of an offer to be made by Lazard Brothers on behalf of BA for the whole of the issued capital of B-Cal. BA is the largest airline in Western Europe, operating then a fleet of 159 aircraft carrying 20 million passengers a year and employing about 41 000 people. BA flew to 145 different cities in 70 countries and was making a large and healthy profit. B-Cal was much smaller airline, operating a mere 25 aircraft to 37 cities. At the time B-Cal had announced a pre-tax loss of £19.3m., BA wished to buy B-Cal in order to grow –

to be able to compete against the much larger American Airlines. This is not as easy as it sounds, since to fly a route, an airline must have international route licences and airport take-off and landing slots. By purchasing B-Cal, BA hoped to acquire B-Cal's licences and slots (mainly at Gatwick), and BA also hoped to reduce competition on internal and some European routes. (9 out of 17 routes in the UK and 7 out of 11 in Europe would become monopolies for BA). This would lead to rationalisation – instead of two half full planes flying from London to Edinburgh they could fly just one.

The Secretary of State ordered a MMC report on August 6th 1987. The MMC took evidence from the airlines and the National Consumer Council which made a case against integration saying that it was not in the public interest since it would strengthen BA's monopoly power and reduce consumer choice. They made the point that large aeroplanes were efficient, **not** necessarily large airlines. The MMC reported on November 5th 1987. The Secretary of State announced that the Government would allow the proposed integration to go ahead, but with the condition that 8 of B-Cal's domestic and international route licences and a minimum of 5000 take-off and landing slots at Gatwick be given up.

BA reduced the offer price and eventually took over the ailing B-Cal. BA now controls 93 per cent of UK scheduled airline capacity.

Tasks

1 Why did BA wish to take over B-Cal?
2 Given that there are considerable economies of scale, on a per seat basis, related to aircraft size, does the integration of BA and B-Cal increase the efficiency of BA?
3 How might a businessman travelling between London and Edinburgh suffer as a result of the integration? How might they gain?
4 How did the MMC try to reduce the increase in BA's monopoly power?
5 After the take-over the new company saw more than 2000 job losses. What is this evidence of?

Restrictive practices

As we have seen, monopoly might be prevented by law. Firms in the same industry could, however, agree to fix prices and all enjoy higher profits. This is illegal. Under the 1976 Restrictive Practices Act any such agreement between firms must first be registered and is then considered by the Restrictive Practices Court. This Court assumes that the agreement is **not** in the public interest unless the firms can prove otherwise.

Multinational companies

Look at the list below of branded consumer products. What do they all have in common?:

Bachelors Soups, Birds Eye, Surf, Mattessons, Timotei, Brooke Bond, Blue Band, Impulse, Denim, Fray Bentos, OMO, Lifebuoy, Lux, Signal, Flora, Liptons, Vim, Persil, Sunlight, Comfort, Jif, Pears, Wisk, Shield, Pepsodent, Sunsilk.

Did you know that they were all manufactured by one company – Unilever?

If you have had holidays in other European countries you may have seen products which look very similar to those sold in the UK but which have different brand names. Cornetto icecream is

Fig 2.13

sold in 20 countries under different names. The fabric softener, 'Huggie', is sold in the same distinctive blue plastic bottle, with the same cuddly teddy bear on the label throughout the world – only the brand name varies from country to country. This same product is known as Snuggle, Kuschewelch, Mimosin, Cajoline.

Unilever is an Anglo-Dutch business formed in 1930 by the merger of the British soap manufacturers, Lever Brothers, and the Dutch margerine manufacturers, Margarine Unie. It is now one of the world's largest producers of consumer goods employing 300 000 people in more than 75 different countries.

The company makes 60 per cent of its sales in Europe, 20 per cent in North America and 20 per cent to the rest of the world.

Unilever is the world's largest manufacturer of detergents – it sells four million tonnes per year and owns 65 000 hectares of oil palm plantations and 16 000 hectares of tea and coffee estates. The company has diversified into many different areas such as fish farming, animal feeds, medical products and even paperboard and packaging materials.

Unilever is an international company: it has two Head Offices, one in London and one in Rotterdam and operates in most countries in the Western world.

A company which **produces** goods or services in more than one politically separate state is known as a **multinational**. Ford, for example, produces cars in the UK, and many other countries around the world.

Multinationals fall into three major categories:

1 Raw material seeking companies: For example BP – the UK's largest business – operates in 70 countries. Although diversified, BP is an oil producing company and must continue to look for this important raw material. The company produces oil in more than a dozen geographically diverse areas from Alaska to Egypt and is currently exploring in 25 countries.

2 Economy seeking manufacturing companies: this may be to avoid high tariffs – which was the original motive behind the formation of Unilever – or the desire to reduce transport costs. Nissan have recently built their own production plant in the UK. This enables them to export components and assemble cars closer to the market, thus reducing transport costs. Locally available components eventually replace the export content and the profits of the parent company increase.

3 Market seeking companies: In order to expand into new markets, a company may take over a smaller company in the new market. This also enables the company to 'get closer to the new market' to understand consumer tastes.

Multinationals are perhaps a logical extension of the desire of a company to grow and enjoy the economies of large scale production. A company such as Ford is thought of by many as a British company. It has produced wealth in Dagenham and other areas around the UK for many years. It adds to our export earnings and reduces the need to import cars, recruits and trains local workers, spreads new ideas and technologies and produces cars for the UK and European market. Most people would argue that as a country we have benefited from Ford operating in the UK.

Others feel that multinationals become too large and powerful: they are able to exploit cheap labour in the underdeveloped/third world; they can switch profits from one country to another to avoid company taxes. They are so large that they can stifle the development of home-grown industries and influence weak governments.

It must be remembered that any multinational is answerable to the laws of the country in which it operates and can only operate successfully in cooperation with local government and opinion.

Survival of the small firm

Task

Look back at Fig 2.11
  (a) What percentage of manufacturing establishments employ 20 or less people?
  (b) What percentage of manufacturing establishments employ 500 or less people?

It is at first surprising to find so many of our businesses are small. Why do small businesses survive given the economies of large scale production?

Here are some suggestions:

1 Lack of finance. Small businesses find it difficult to expand because they cannot raise finance. Large companies have huge retained profits and are able to approach the general public through share/debenture issues. The small firm by definition does not have these large profits and cannot approach the general public.

2 Limited market. Your town may well have a number of efficient, profitable fast food shops. It is not worth expanding because the demand for pizza or burgers is limited in any particular area. It would be rather silly for a ballet shoe manufacturing company to expand given the extremely limited demand for ballet shoes. There are thousands of small companies which supply a specialised good or service to a limited market, sometimes to the general public and sometimes to other producers.

3 Desire to remain in control. Small businesses often wish to remain small: the owner enjoys being in charge. Often, the owner will work for longer hours and less financial reward than if he or she worked for someone else. This keeps the business going. Small shop keepers often link together in voluntary chains to gain purchasing and marketing economies. In this way, they can survive as independent retailers but gain economies of scale. (*See* page 177.)

4 Lack of knowledge. Perhaps a small firm could expand but lacks the managerial skills necessary for such expansion.

5 Growth stage. Firms do not start large. Think back to our original case study: Jack Cohen

started with one barrow and £30 of groceries. He would have been considered small – but look how his business grew! Many of today's small businesses will be the multinationals of the future.

6 Government aid. The government has placed much emphasis upon helping small businesses in an aim to reduce unemployment. (*See* page 73.)

SUMMARY EXERCISE

1 Give one example of each of the following types of business from your local area: (*a*) a one-man business (*b*) a partnership (*c*) a company
2 A one-man business can increase the funds available for expansion by taking on one or more partners. List two further advantages taking on partners would give.

3 Give one reason for the legal requirement on companies to register with the Registrar of Companies.
4 State two differences between private and public companies.
5 What is a rights issue of shares? Why do companies make use of such issues?
6 In spite of the economies of scale enjoyed by large companies the vast majority of UK firms employ less than 500 people. Explain why this is.
7 Give one advantage to the UK from the existence of so many small firms.
8 List three examples of horizontal integration. Give one reason for such expansion.
9 What is a multinational company. Name three multinationals based in the UK.
10 What is a diseconomy of scale?

ASSIGNMENT

A distant relative, Mr Elwin Griffiths, has been made redundant. He was a coal miner for many years and has received £10 000 redundancy pay. Together with his life savings and the sale of this cottage he can raise £20 000 towards buying and opening a small shop. He is well thought of by his bank manager.

Taking into account what you have learnt in this chapter would you advise Elwin to open a shop or not? Remember to consider:

(*a*) What competition might he face?
(*b*) What problems might he run into?
(*c*) What would the advantages be?
(*d*) What are the **alternative** uses for his savings?

3 | Public Sector Organisations

The **public sector** can be described as that part of the economy which is directly controlled by the Government. This includes:

- **Public corporations**, e.g. British Rail
- **Central Government departments**, e.g. the National Health Service
- **Local Government departments**, e.g. schools

Many of the industries which are now controlled by the Government as public corporations were originally a large number of privately owned companies.

The public corporation

CASE STUDY

British coal

On 1 January 1947 coal became the first British Industry to be **nationalised**. The Coal Industry Nationalisation Act gave the government the power to take over the whole coal mining industry. All 958 collieries became part of the National Coal Board: organised and controlled by a Board appointed and overseen by the Government.

The private sector owners were compensated; £164 million was paid to the private shareholders. Today, 40 years after nationalisation, the name has changed to the 'British Coal Corporation' but the 1947 Act still holds and in its general provisions set out the 'rules' under which the industry is run.

The original act gave the National Coal Board total control over all coal production in this country and the duty to make supplies of coal available in quantities and prices thought to be in the public interest. In the early days, just after the war, there was a considerable shortage of coal – then the major source of primary energy in the UK:

Table 3.1   UK Primary energy provision

	% (approx)		
	1947	1973*	1986
Coal	90	38	35
Oil	9	46	32
Natural gas	—	12	25
Nuclear/hydro	1	4	8

* 1973 was the year of highest demand for energy in the UK – since then conservation and the recession has reduced demand

Adapted from *British Coal Supplement*

The coal industry is now in competition with many alternative sources of energy. This trend is known as primary fuel diversity; Britain is a 'four fuel economy'. Fewer homes and firms buy coal directly and most coal is sold to power stations. Today coal provides a fairly stable one-third share.

Table 3.2   Coal markets

	%	
	1947	1985/6
Power stations	14	73
Industry	20	7
Domestic	19	8
Coke ovens	11	11
Railways	8	—
Gasworks (town)	12	—
Misc. and colleries	16	1

Adapted from *British Coal Supplement*

In 1947 the major objective was to increase and maintain supplies of this vital source of energy. For years the coal industry had suffered from too many small mines owned by different groups of private individuals. Since they were in competition they would not share inventions and new ideas. Each mine owner was too small to be able to afford the expensive new machinery; British mines lagged behind the rest of the world.

Fig 3.1 (Courtesy: National Coal Board)

For example:

- In the early 1880s output per worker in coal stood at over 300 tons per year. By 1913 this had fallen to 250 tons, and output per worker continued to fall in the early 1920's!
- In the 1930's Britain mines still used over 70 000 pit ponies to haul coal underground. This was slow and labour intensive – in Britain one haulage worker was required for every five tons of coal mined; in Holland one haulage worker was required for every 25 tons mined!
- In 1938 in British mines 60% of coal was cut by machine – in Germany 97%!

After nationalisation it was possible, for the first time, to co-ordinate the activities of the mining industry as a whole. The first National Plan for Coal was drawn up. Small uneconomic pits were gradually closed down (130 within ten years) with younger miners being moved to expanding areas. Much more investment in new machinery was undertaken with government money (£60 million a year). Injuries dropped and output increased. By the

Fig 3.2   Coal mining in Scotland
(Courtesy: National Coal Board)

late 1950s a new problem arose. Oil began to replace coal and the discovery of natural gas and the introduction of nuclear power left the coal industry with stockpiles of unsold coal. (*See* Table 3.1.) Many more pits were closed and the new slimmer industry concentrated upon those areas where coal could be mined most economically.

Table 3.3   Summary of statistics

	1947	1985/6
Output (m tonnes)	200	104.5
Output per man year (tonnes)	267	571
No. of colleries	958	133
No. of miners ('000)	704	155

Source: National Coal Board Report & Annual Accounts

The original act did not require the Coal Board to make a profit but to 'break-even' on day-to-day production costs and sales, not including capital costs (new machinery etc.) taking an average of good and bad years. Most of the expensive capital investment in British Coal has come directly from the government, with the Secretary of State for Energy being consulted about major policy such as the opening of new mines. In 1986 the Board made a £50 million loss which was covered by a government grant. Today, a far more commercial view is taken with break-even planned for 1988/9 and increasing profitability after that and the hope that British Coal will be able to finance capital expenditure from surpluses:

'British Coal consider that in the longer term (i.e. after 1989), it is essential to improve on break-even and to achieve a progressive ability to finance capital expenditure from their own internal resources.'

(Michael Butler, Finance Director, British Coal)

Many more pits are being closed so that only the most profitable are left in operation.

Recently the organisational structure has been streamlined to achieve: 'appropriate and clear allocation of responsibilities; to facilitate policy responses to business threats and opportunities; and to ensure speedy, consistent and effective implementation of policy.'

(David Brandick, Secretary, British Coal)

The Board, appointed by the Secretary of State for Energy, is responsible for policy decisions. Not only does the Board report to the Secretary of State but an all party committee of MPs – the 'Select Committee on Energy' acts as a parliamentary watch-dog constantly reviewing the work of the Board.

Fig 3.3   Modern coal cutting 'Shearer in Bentink Colliery'
(Courtesy: National Coal Board)

Nationalisation

Not all of the reasons given in favour of national-isation apply to coal. During the period between 1945 and 1951 many private sector industries were taken into public ownership by the elected Labour Government. Railways and electricity distribution in 1947, gas 1948 and iron and steel 1949, for example.

All the reasons given in the preceding assign-ment were used during this period of nationalis-ation. The gas industry, for example, is a **natural monopoly**. Once *one* private sector company has put gas pipes into a housing estate it is not worth a second and third company repeating the exer-cise. Further, there are tremendous economies of scale allowing one large monopoly to supply gas at a lower price than two or more companies in competition. Unlike sweet manufacturers, gas companies had little or no competition. They were monopolies (the only producers) and able to charge whatever price they liked.

Public accountability

Nationalised industries were organised as **public corporations**. A Board was appointed by the government to control the industry much like a public company. These Boards were given finan-cial and other targets and were answerable to the government minister responsible for that industry.

ASSIGNMENT

Listed below are reasons that are given in **favour** of nationalisation. Take each one and, using the case study above, try to find evidence to support each reason.

Arguments used in favour of nationalisation:

1 Possible to co-ordinate and plan for the whole industry.
2 Greater efficiency.
3 Better labour relations.
4 No wasted competition and advertising.
5 It is a very important industry and should be under government control.
6 Profits should go to the government.
7 Needs much capital to modernise – only possible source being the government.
8 It is a 'natural monopoly' and ought to be controlled by the government.

Parliament could ask questions about the public corporation and Select Committees would watch over their conduct and report to parliament.

Some public corporations with private customers have **consumer consultative councils** to represent the public and take-up minor complaints with the Board. Major complaints can be made to the Government Minister in charge of that industry via an MP who can ask questions in Parliament. In this way nationalised industries are accountable to Parliament and to the public; they are not necessarily expected to operate for profit but in the public interest. (*See* Fig 3.4.)

The public sector includes those goods and services produced and supplied directly to us from local and national government.

In the introduction to this book both **merit** goods and **public** goods were explained. The government supplies both types of good or service in the UK directly or through local government councils. Defence, a public good, is supplied by the

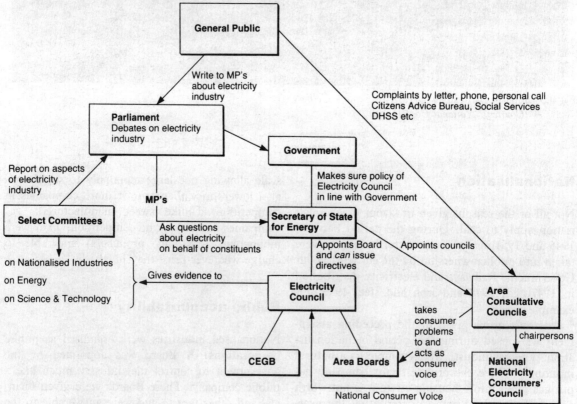

Fig 3.4 Public accountability in the electricity industry before privatisation in 1989

ASSIGNMENT

For each of the goods and services listed below state which comes from a public corporation, which a central government department and which your local government:

- a train journey
- education
- an operation in a hospital
- an interview with a careers officer
- coal
- defence

Ministry of Defence; street lighting, another public good, by local councils; education, a merit good, is supplied by local councils and hospitals, also a merit good, by the Ministry of Health.

The government can buy shares in a public limited company either to help them out and prevent collapse or to take a control in an important area of production. This form of joint ownership exists in British Leyland. It is not the same as nationalisation as it is not the whole industry which is taken over but only one firm. No act has been passed and the company operates as a normal public limited company.

Privatisation

Not everyone believes that nationalised industries are a good idea. Some reasons for this are:

1 **Inefficiency** – relying on government finance rather than having to make a profit.

2 **Bureaucracy** – too much 'red tape' because they are too big.

3 People should have **freedom of choice** and not just one public corporation to deal with.

4 **Over-staffing** – too many workers for each job.

5 **Poor industrial relations** – too many strikes.

6 **Unresponsive** – they do not respond quickly to changes in public demand.

7 **Unprofitable** – they may make a loss and need to be subsidised.

For these and other reasons the government during the 1980s has been **privatising** nationalised industries, in other words, the public corporation is turned into a Public Limited Company (plc), shares being sold to the general public through an 'offer for sale'. Advertisements are placed in newspapers and appear on television. By filling in a form and sending a cheque members of the general public have been able to buy very small numbers of shares in these privatised companies. This has greatly increased the number of private shareholders. (In 1986, after the sale of British Telecom which attracted two million shareholders, it was estimated that 14% of the adult population in the UK owned shares). The government has sold British Telecom and British Gas very successfully in this way. By the end of 1987 public sector industrial ownership had fallen by 40%. When a public corporation is privatised in this way the government keeps a special 'golden' share which gives it the power to prevent any major changes in the way the company is run.

Privatisation has one further important benefit to the Government – **income**. The vast sums of money raised by the sale of public corporations has increased the Governments income over the period of privatisation and has allowed the Government to both reduce taxation and borrowing to the lowest levels since the war. (*See* page 204.)

(*See* page 204.)

CASE STUDY

Rolls-Royce shares fly

Rolls-Royce is probably one of the most famous British company names; mainly due to the illustrious luxury motorcar rather than the aero-engines which bear the name. It must not be forgotten that the Rolls-Royce 'Merlin' engine powered the Lancaster bombers and Spitfires of the Second World War and that today the equally well known Concord and Harrier jump-jet and a hanger full of other civil and military planes are powered by Rolls-Royce.

The company shocked the world when it announced financial problems in 1971, caused by the development and sale of the RB211 engine to Lockheed. The company was taken into public ownership by the conservative government led by Edward Heath. By 1973 the motorcar division was back in the private sector leaving the government in control of the loss-making aero-engine division, which remained one of the three large aircraft engine manufacturers, supplying engines to British civil and military aircraft and an important employer. Since then over £520 million of tax-payers' money has been spent returning the company to a profit-making concern.

In 1987, 16 years after the spectacular collapse, Rolls-Royce was returned to the private sector, making it the fifteenth company to be privatised since 1979. On 28 April 1987 the price for the 800 million ordinary shares was set at £1.70 each giving the company a stock exchange value of £1.36 bn. The share issue was similar to other flotations of public sector concerns. Private individuals wishing to purchase shares applied using the widely available application forms. In this case these stipulated a minimum purchase of 400 shares with half of the total cost paid on application by no later than 7 May 1987 (individuals being limited in the number they could purchase and to just one application each). Successful applicants paid the remaining 85 p per share by 23 September 1987 at which point the company became a Public Limited Company again.

Only 40 per cent of the total shares were initially offered to the general public; the remainder were 'placed' with institutional investors (pension funds, banks, insurance companies etc). The government itself purchasing £283 m. The proportion of foreign-owned shares was limited to 15 per cent thus preventing the company from passing into foreign control. Instant profits of up to 70 p in the £ were made when the shares were first sold, 284 million shares changing hands in the first 90 minutes of trading.

The opposition estimated that at current values the £520 m. spent rescuing Rolls-Royce and the £283 m. spent on the issue by the government totalled £1.34 bn. leaving a mere £20 m. gain to the taxpayer. In addition they pointed out that Rolls-Royce collapsed when privately owned and last year made a healthy profit while publically owned. The government claimed that the company would thrive unfettered by government control.

Tasks

1 For what reason was Rolls-Royce taken into public ownership in 1971?
2 What had changed to make it possible to sell Rolls-Royce back to the private sector 16 years later?
3 Why was 'foreign' ownership of the shares limited?
4 Why did the opposition believe the sale was bad for the taxpayer?
5 Why did the government believe privatisation was good for the company?

Competitive tendering for local authority services

The policy of privatisation is also being used for local and central government **services**.

The Government has made it compulsory for all local government services such as street cleaning, office and school cleaning, refuse collection and school meals to be put out to 'competitive tendering'. This means that private sectors firms can 'tender,' i.e. offer a price for providing the service. It is also possible for the existing local government department to tender for the service. In general, the lowest price will secure the contract. This has led to a great deal of private enterprise in local government services.

Some local governments have had services provided by the private sector for many years –

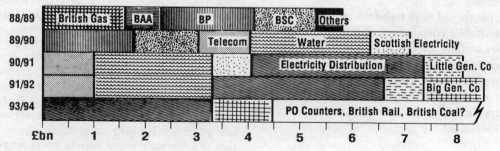

Fig 3.5   Income from 'privatisation'
(Taken from The Observer 10.07.88)

for example Southend and refuse collection. (This is not the same as privatisation since the general public do not have any choice and cannot shop around for, say, refuse collection.)

Many believe that this reduces the costs of local government, and therefore local taxation, but others claim that local services suffer and are not so well provided.

Tasks

1 List as many services provided by your local government as you can.

2 From your list above, find one service you think could be privatised and one you think could not. For each state why.

3 Either by visiting your local council offices or from your parents' rate demand, discover how many goods and services are provided by the council.

4 Visit your local Electricity Board shop and discover whether there is a Area Consumer Council. (Perhaps one person in the group could write to the Council to discover how many customer complaints were dealth with last year and what sort of problems they were.)

5 British Gas is one public corporation that has been privatised. Write down one difference you think this has made to the organisation of British Gas and one difference it might make to the workers. Has privatisation increased competition in the gas industry? Give reasons for your answer.

Course work

Follow the privatisation of a public sector concern, local or national. Use newspaper articles, the company prospectus and any other information to write your own case study/diary. Try to examine why the business was taken into public ownership and why it is now being privatised.

SUMMARY EXERCISE

1 What is meant by (a) the private sector and (b) the public sector?

2 Name two public corporations.

3 Name two public companies.

4 Name two central government departments which provide services.

5 How are public corporations 'accountable' in a way in which public companies are not?

6 For what reasons are public companies said to be more efficient than public corporations?

7 What is 'privatisation'? State and explain three reasons given in favour of privatisation.

8 Give three reasons against further privatisation.

9 Give one advantage for the 'contracting out' of local authority services. Which group of workers might object to this?

10 Name two government services **not** suitable for competitive tendering.

4 Cooperative Enterprise

Cooperative enterprise can take very many forms.

Worker   Business owned and controlled by its workers

Housing   Homes run and owned by tenants collectively

Community   Groups from a community joining together to run recreational facilities etc

Retail   Shops owned and run by their customers

We shall be looking at two in detail – the worker and retail cooperative.

Worker cooperatives

This is a business where all the workers are part owners. This means that they not only undertake to work for the firm, but also share in the important decisions which have to be made and of course share in the profits.

CASE STUDY

Richard Baxendale & Sons Ltd (Baxi Heating)

Richard Baxendale & Sons Ltd was founded over 100 years ago in Preston and until 1983 was a private company owned mainly by the Baxendale family. The company manufactures domestic heating equipment – you may well have one of their products in your fireplace at home. Richard Baxendale, who founded the firm in 1866, did not then know that his name would be given to a type of grate. In those days it was a small iron foundry supplying other firms with metal parts to order. The turning point came in 1935 when Richard's son, John invented a new type of grate – the Baxi Burnall. These grates are still very popular and the

Baxi Burnall, today often fitted with a back boiler and pump to heat radiators, sells about 15 000 a year or 80 per cent of the market. During the 1960s people started to change over to gas central heating which they found cheaper and more convenient. The Baxendale company was the first to realise that most houses have very small kitchens allowing little room for a gas boiler.

Using the experience they had built up over the years they were able to develop a gas boiler that fitted into the old fireplace, heated the water and radiators and also looked good in the room with a normal gas fire at the front. The idea caught on and is still very popular – the Baxi Bermuda.

By 1973, four out of every 10 gas heating systems were powered by this system. Since then the company has developed wall boilers, very useful in flats and smaller houses and more recently floor standing boilers and wall mounted gas space heaters. This small family company grew by producing new products the customer wanted until in 1982 it employed 900 people and made an annual profit of nearly £6 m.

The firm remained a **private company** – owned by the family. There were detectable differences however. In 1963 a system of 'worker participation' was introduced. This meant that the workers elected representatives who, along with members of the management and a trade union representative, formed a 'works council' where problems, ideas, production targets etc could be discussed.

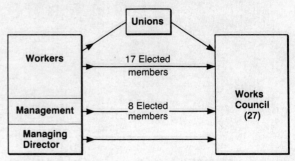

Fig 4.1   Baxi heating works council 1963–83

This system was introduced for several reasons:

- To make jobs more interesting.
- To give workers a say in important decisions.
- To help spread important information.

In 1965 a next step was to introduce a limited profit sharing scheme. Under this scheme any workers who had worked for more 12 months would receive a cash bonus if profits were higher than a specified amount. The final change came in 1983 when the firm converted from a private company into a worker cooperative.

The shares were bought from the family by the company at a cost of £5¼ m. and placed in a trust – the **employee trust**. These shares are owned by the workers who work at the company and their interests are looked after by a number of **trustees** who themselves do not own shares. Up to 49 per cent of the shares can be sold to individual workers at the factory who will then watch the value of these shares grow if the company makes a profit. The major decisions are made by the 'partnership council' which comprises part trustees and part elected representatives of the workforce. The **trustees** appoint a managing director who in turn appoints his executive board to run the company. The trustees will always have the majority vote of 51 per cent of the shares but they cannot use this to out-vote the partnership council without a full meeting of all the workers where all sides of the arguments will be heard. This is a very complicated system since this is a large company with many workers but in principle it is like many others. The shares are owned by the workers, who have a say in the running of the firm. Profits are still shared as before, with cash bonuses.

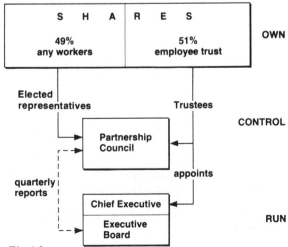

Fig 4.2

Baxi Heating was and is an efficient, profitable company. We can probably see that this form of enterprise has advantages for the workers but why did the family owners decide upon this form of enterprise? Why not 'go public'?

In their official publications about this conversion to a worker cooperative they give two main reasons for their actions:

- **Job security**
  If the firm became a large public company it might well be taken over by a giant company who could well decide to close down the plant or sack workers.
- **Efficiency**
  Since the workers own the firm they are likely to work harder, because they are working for themselves. It is interesting to note that there has never been a strike at this firm.

Exercise

The Baxi Heating example highlighted two major advantages of worker cooperatives. These were job security and efficiency. Assume you have just secured a job at Baxi Heating. A list of possible advantages of a worker cooperative follows. For each advantage award a mark from 1 to 5, where 5 indicates that you think this advantage would definitely exist in your job, 4 it is likely to exist and so on until 1 it is very unlikely to exist in your new job.

Possible Advantages of a Worker Cooperative

	Mark: 1	2	3	4	5
Less boring work					
Better labour relations					
Job security					
Workers work harder					
More responsible workers					
Workers produce better products					
Workers earn more					

Your teacher will compare the results of the class and discuss your answers with you.

Types of worker cooperative

Baxi Heating is just one of the 1050 worker cooperatives in the UK. Most are much smaller and employ on average approximately 18 people. In other countries like France and Spain there are many more cooperatives employing a more significant number of workers. All worker cooperatives are different, but the Cooperative Development Agency identifies five main types:

Conversions   An old established firm is given or sold to its workers.

New Starts   A group of workers set up in business as a cooperative.

Rescue   An attempt to save a factory which has been closed by its owners, by the workers.

Phoenix   An attempt to save part of a business which has been closed down.

Job Creation Schemes   In areas of high unemployment local authorities often help unemployed people form cooperatives.

Table 4.1

Growth in Cooperatives by Trade Sector 1980–1986

Trade Sector	Aug 1980	Number of Cooperatives Aug 1982	June 1984	June 1986	Growth % 1984–1986
Manufacturing					
Crafts, arts, carpentry, furniture-making and joinery	19	40	20	39	
Engineering, electronics, chemicals, general manufacturing	26	41	57	85	
Footwear, clothing and textile manufacture	19	32	51	81	
TOTAL	**64**	**113**	**128**	**205**	**60.16%**
Services					
Advisory, consultative, educational & office services	21	33	60	93	
Building, house renovation and decoration, cleaning, waste recycling, architecture, gardening services	33	69	230	194	
Printing and publishing	61	75	91	127	
Provision and hire of transport, bicycle & motor vehicle repairs	11	13	25	68	
Record, film & music making theatre, theatrical agencies, leisure	28	46	111	301	
Umbrella co-operatives, workspaces, Community services		15	45	147	
TOTAL	**154**	**251**	**562**	**930**	**65.48%**
Wholesale/retail					
Retail, distributive, catering and food processing	112	151	221	341	54.30%
Total number of co-ops	**305**	**498**	**911**	**1476**	**62.02%**

A Cautionary Note:

The tabulation of this data was altered quite substantially in 1984.

Consequently the changes within a particular sector between 1980–1986 must not be too strictly interpreted.

1. In 1980 and 1982 cooperatives engaged substantially in more than one trade are included within each appropriate sector. In 1984 each co-op is listed only once.
2. In 1986 the trade sectors have been expanded to provide a greater degree of accuracy. For purposes of comparison the sectors have been put together to approximate the previous breakdown.

Finance of worker cooperatives

The methods of raising finance for a worker cooperative are limited, not so much in the number of
different methods available, but in the amount of
money that can be raised. Public companies can
raise millions of pounds by selling shares, however
a worker cooperative is unable to do this. The
main sources are:

- Savings of workers
- Borrowing from friends, relatives, community
  groups, churches, trade unions and other
  sympathisers

- Borrowing from a bank
- Trade credit, that is pay for supplies **after** using
  them and selling service or product
- Official sources – loans/grants from local
  authority
- Leasing equipment, that is renting expensive
  items

Finance is a problem. The worker cooperative will
find if difficult to raise the necessary cash for
expansion unless it is already a profitable
company, for then it can use some of the profits
it is making. It will come as no surprise to note
that the majority of worker cooperatives in this
country are small and to be found in the service
areas. Such production as house decorating, motor
car repairs, computer software need very little
capital. They can be undertaken from home and
need little specialised equipment. Figure 4.3 illustrates the types of worker cooperatives listed by

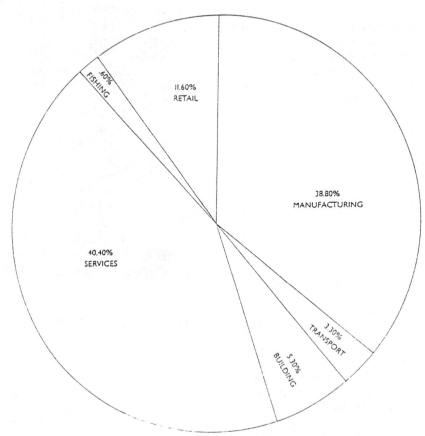

Fig 4.3   Proportion of full-time workers within cooperatives each trade sector

the CDA in their 1986 Directory. Where they exist in industries which require large amounts of capital they are more often conversions or very old and have grown slowly over the years.

Retail cooperative movement

CASE STUDY

The retail cooperative society

Most high streets in the country have a Cooperative shop and at some time in your life you must have been into such a shop. They are not very different to any other supermarket or department store – the difference is in the ownership. Retail cooperatives are owned by their members. Anyone over 16 who shops in a Cooperative can become a member if they buy part of a share in the society which costs as little as 5 p. The full shares cost £1 and one can own up to £2000 worth.

The Cooperative principle for running shops dates back to the 1840s when a group of workers in Rochdale saved up enough money to start their own shop (below right). They hoped to grow into what we now call a commune owning their own land and houses and producing their own food. From these early beginnings the cooperative movement was formed and the societies of today are still based upon the same principles:

- Open membership – anyone over 16 can belong.
- Democratic control – the people who control the Cooperative, the Board, are elected by the members all of whom have **one vote** no matter how many shares they own.
- Fixed return on shares. Although interest is paid to those who own shares the amount is low and fixed.
- Profits are distributed in proportion to the amount **bought** from the society.
- Promotion of education.
- International cooperative with other cooperatives.

The shop in Rochdale was a great success and led the original members to buy a corn mill as a joint venture with others. As other retail societies were formed in different areas they began to act together in buying goods in bulk (wholesaling) and set up the Cooperative Wholesale Society and from there it was a logical step to become involved in producing their own goods.

Fig 4.4

Fig 4.5

In 1872 the CWS started a loan and deposit department for member societies. This has since developed into a proper bank just like any other high street bank with branches and customers all over the country.

Coursework

Some Co-operative facts

Co-operative Retail Societies

Turnover	£4440 Million (approx)
Staff	90 500
Number of Societies	107
Annual repayment of dividend	£20 Million (1983)
Number of shops	6400 (60 Superstores)
Number of members	8 687 000

The Co-operative Wholesale Society

Turnover	£2232 Million
Staff	19 700
Productive units	90
Farms	34 600 acres
Distribution centres	19
Co-op Brand Lines	1200

The Co-operative Bank Group

Assets	Over £1.1 Billion
Staff	3728
Branches	79
Handybanks	705
ChequePost (with cash-a-cheque support)	540
Cash-a-cheque points	3021
Customer accounts	1 500 000

The Co-operative Insurance Society

Premium Income	£466 Million
Assets	£3160 Million
Number of policies in force	14 Million
Number of families insured	$3\frac{1}{2}$ Million
Staff	10 600
District Offices	220

Co-operative Travel	150 Branches
Co-operative Travel	89 Practices
Opticians Worker Co-operatives (UK)	1 050

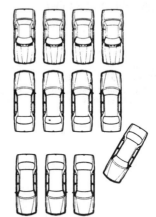

If you look at Fig 4.6 it shows just how the cooperative movement works in the UK today.

In the early days and until quite recently any profit or surpluses would be distributed in the form of a dividend. Every time a member purchased something they would give the cashier their membership number which would be recorded along with the amount spent. Then, at the end of the year, their account would be credited with so much back in the pound. The member could either draw this out or leave it as part of their share capital. Later the system of stamps was introduced. Any shopper

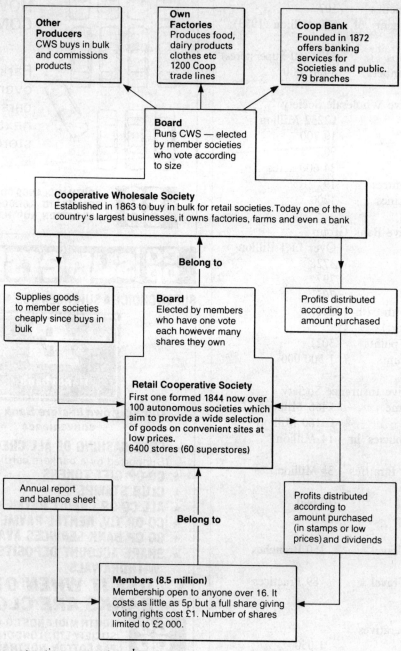

Fig 4.6   *How the cooperative movement works*

was given stamps which were stuck into a book and exchanged for goods or added to share capital or changed for cash. A member wrote their number into the book and received a bonus. In some areas this system has been replaced by lower prices.

In order to promote education of their members and workers the Cooperative movement have their own college which runs courses along with local training.

The Co-operative is more than just a shop owned by its customers. It has been referred to already as a movement, which it is.

The CWS and the different retail societies belong to the Cooperative Union which looks after all the activities of the cooperative movement in Great Britain. These include not only those we have already discussed but also its own political party formed in 1917. This endeavours to return MPs to parliament so that the voice of the Cooperative movement is heard there. (In 1984 there were seven such MPs.)

Lastly, the Cooperative Union is affiliated to the International Cooperative Alliance which has 161 members from 64 countries and represents a total of 336 667 519 individual members. The aim of this organisation, which was formed as long ago as 1895, is to gather information about cooperatives from all over the world and then pass this information on to people who wish to form a cooperative.

Exercise

The following is a chart which aims to compare public joint stock companies, about which you learnt in Chapter 2, and Cooperative enterprises about which you learnt in this chapter. As you will see it is incomplete. Using the information that you have been given in these two chapters try and complete it.

	Retail Cooperative	*Worker Cooperative*	*Public Joint–Stock Company*
Ownership			Large number of shareholders. Often pension funds and other institutions. There is no limit on the number of shares owned.
Control	Shareholders have only one vote however many shares. They elect a board which managess the society.		
Capital Source			Many different types of shares are sold. Also loans from the public – debentures and banks. Value of shares varies from day-to-day but can be sold.
Distribution of Profits		Profits distributed to workers in a bonus which is either a percentage of income or a fixed amount each.	

Exercise

Here is a sketch of an imaginary shopping centre:

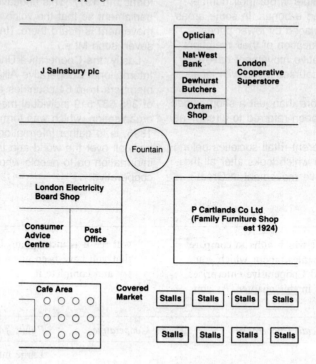

Either

From the imaginary shopping centre above find an example of:

(*a*) a likely one-man business
(*b*) a service which is likely to be provided by a partnership
(*c*) a service provided by the local authority
(*d*) a shop run by a public corporation
(*e*) a shop which sells durable consumer goods
(*f*) a shop run by volunteers
(*g*) a shop which shares its profits with its customers

(*h*) a shop which is part of a public company
(*i*) a business which has obviously been involved in some form of horizontal integration
(*j*) a shop which is likely to be a private company
(*k*) a branch of a public corporation which was not formed as a result of nationalisation.

or

Draw a plan of your local shopping centre or high street and mark on it as many of the features listed in (*a-k*) above as you can.

SUMMARY EXERCISE

1 List the four main forms of cooperative enterprise in this country.
2 What are the differences between the following types of **worker cooperatives** in this country:

(*a*) Phoenix
(*b*) Conversion
(*c*) Rescue

3 Give two advantages to the worker of belonging to a worker cooperative.
4 Give two disadvantages to a worker of belonging to a worker cooperative.
5 What source of finance open to public companies is not open to a cooperative enterprise?
6 In what main industrial area are most British cooperatives to be found?
Why is this so?

7 How are the profits of a retail cooperative distributed?

8 List as many differences as you can between a share in a retail cooperative and one in a public company.

9 How are the members of the Board of a retail cooperative selected?

10 List two other interests of the retail cooperative movement other than providing cheap goods for members.

ASSIGNMENT

Imagine that after working for a small engineering firm for a year it is announced the owners are making a loss and have decided to close the factory. Many of the workers are proposing to take over the firm and run it as a worker cooperative. Using the evidence given in this chapter decide whether you would be in favour of such a change. Write a brief summary of your reasons.

5 | People at Work

Specialisation

People work in order to earn money to buy things they need and want. In the past families provided for themselves, each household being able to satisfy all of its members' needs. This is called **self-sufficiency**. It has great limitations and in general results in a poorer way of life. As people came together in groups and lived in settlements they gradually realised it was better for people only to work at one job – **to specialise**. There are many advantages:

- a person can fully utilise a natural ability
- a person can develop a skill and become very good at a job
- each person would only require one set of tools or piece of equipment
- no time is lost changing from task to task

All of these advantages combine to give the main gain from specialisation – greater output.

A doctor and an assembly line worker are both specialised workers. There is however, a difference. The doctor is a specialist, studying the subject of medicine in great depth for many years. An assembly line worker is quickly trained and performs one or two simple repetitive tasks day after day. The doctor probably finds the work interesting and rewarding, however, the assembly line worker may well become bored.

The working population

In a developed economy such as ours not everyone works. Those people who offer themselves for work are collectively known as the **working popu-**

WHO WORKS IN THE UK (1984)

Total population 56½ million people

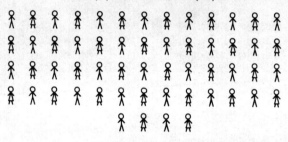

Not all of the population are the right age to work

less

Those under 16 22% and over 60/65 18%

Total in working age group

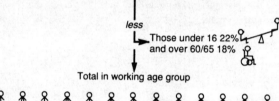

Not all those people of the right age do work

less

Those of retirement age who still work

Housewives
Students

plus

Total working population (27 000 000 people)

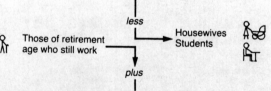

Not all those who want to work can find work. Of this 27 million, potential work force 8½% are currently unemployed.

Fig 5.1 (*Source: Britain: An Official Handbook, 1987 HMSO*)

lation. This includes those people unemployed since it is the potential work force (those who could work, not those who are working). The size of the working population is very important. A country with a large working population has the ability to produce a great number of goods and services. Those people who are unable to work –

sharply. Many people think this is part of a long-term trend. As people become better educated they realise that a smaller family can lead to a higher standard of living. More reliable forms of contraception have become generally available and many more women wish to pursue a career. Other people believe that the difficult economic

Exercise

1 Give one reason for working other than the financial reward.
2 List three jobs which are not paid. Suggest a reason why these jobs are not paid.
3 Give three examples of specialisation in depth, like a doctor.
4 Give three examples of specialisation by process, like an assembly line worker.
5 Give one disadvantage to the worker of specialisation.
6 Give one advantage to the community of specialisation.
7 Explain this statement: 'In the UK there is no shortage of work simply a shortage of paid employment.'

the very young, the old and parents bringing up children – are known as the **dependent population**. The working population must support the dependent population. In 1984 the working population of the UK was just 27.0 million which is 60 per cent of the population over 16 years old or 47 per cent of the total population.

ASSIGNMENTS

Conduct a class experiment.

1 Divide the class into two groups of equal size.
2 Give each group the same simple task which requires several stages. For example, the cutting out and manufacture of paper aeroplanes or the sorting and stapling of a booklet.
3 Let one team specialise – that is each member undertakes one stage only in the task. The other group is not allowed to specialise, each member must complete the entire task on their own.
4 Each group must be given the same equipment.
5 Count the final output of each group. Write up the results of your experiment to include a conclusion. Comment upon the quality from each group and the feelings of group members.

Factors which affect the size of the working population

1 The size of the total population

A larger population will in general contain more workers. The size of a country's population will depend upon the number of people entering (being born or immigrating) and the number of people who leave (die or emigrate. *See* Fig 5.2). The effects of births and deaths are called **natural changes** and are the major influence upon total population. Figure 5.3 shows that since 1962 the number of births in the UK have been falling

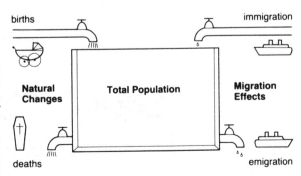

Fig 5.2 Factors affecting total population

conditions over the last few years have caused couples to postpone having children.

Migration effects, immigration and emigration, are relatively small and have little effect upon the total population. It is a great expense and upheaval to move to another country and most, including our own, have strict laws which restrict immigration. Since 1962 more people have emigrated from this country than have immigrated *to* this country. Only on a few occasions has there been a net migration into the UK. For example, during the Second World War when Europeans fled from Hitler (*see* Figs 5.3 and 5.4).

2 The age distribution of the population

Only people of a certain age work. In the UK full-time employment starts when children reach the age of 16 and usually ends at 60 for women and 65 for men, the age at which a state pension can be drawn. A population could be growing not because more children are being born but because people are living longer. Over the last 100 years life expectancy for both men and women has increased dramatically in the developed economies. In the UK the percentage of people who are above the retirement age has increased from five per cent in 1901 to 15 per cent now. This has, however, been matched by a fall in the birth rate leaving a dependent population roughly the same size. If this trend continues the dependent population will increase in size in proportion to the working population. With fewer children being born fewer will be available to work but more and more old people will need to be supported.

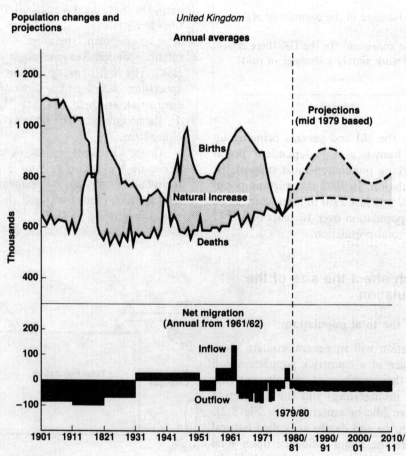

Fig 5.3   Population changes

3 Social changes

Women now form a high percentage of the total working population and this is increasing. It is not considered unusual for a woman to return to work after having children nor for the man in a partnership to look after those children. Laws passed during the last 15 years have ensured that women are paid the same as men, cannot be discriminated against and are allowed maternity leave to have a baby and return to their old job. Changes in the law and attitudes have, therefore, increased the number of economically active women (either working or looking for employment) and therefore the size of the working population.

4 Government influences

The Government will influence the size of the working population in several ways. It is the Government which decides the official retirement age, school leaving age, number of further education places and level of grants. The Government has rarely changed the school leaving age; 1947 to 15 and 1972 to 16, but between 1960-61 and 1975-76 the percentage of young people

Table 5.1

Population changes and projections
United Kingdom   Thousands

	Population at start of period	Average annual change				
		Live births	Deaths	Net natural change	Net civilian migration and other adjustments	Overall annual change
Census enumerated						
1901–11	38 237	1 091	624	467	−82	385
1911–21	42 082	975	689	286	−92	194
1921–31	44 027	824	555	268	−67	201
1931–51	46 038	785	598	188	+25	213
Mid-year estimates						
1951–61	50 290	839	593	246	+ 6	252
1961–66	52 807	988	633	355	+12	367
1966–71	54 643	937	644	293	−40	253
1971–76	55 907	766	670	96	−37	60
1976–81	56 206	705	662	43	− 8	35
1981–82	56 352	722	669	53	−99	−46
1982–83	56 306	722	660	62	−21	41
1983–84	56 347	718	652	66	+47	112
1984–85	56 460	745	659	86	+72	158
Projections[2]						
1987–91	56 891	804	647	157	−17	140
1991–96	57 452	834	645	190	−17	172
1996–2001	58 312	795	648	146	−17	129
2001–06	58 957	732	654	78	−17	61
2006–11	59 259	713	663	50	−17	33
2011–16	59 422	736	677	59	−17	41
2016–21	59 629	763	694	69	−17	52

1 See Appendix, Part 1: Population and population projections.
2 1985-based projections.

Source: Office of Population Censuses and Surveys; Government Actuary's Department

leaving school and *not* seeking employment rose from 14.1 per cent to 22 per cent. This was probably not due to increase in grants but the increased availability of places in higher education.

Exercise

1 Give two reasons why very few people **migrate**.
2 From the graph (Fig. 5.3) in which year did the UK experience a **natural decline** in population?
3 The UK has a growing number of old dependent people. List **two** problems this might cause.

CASE STUDY

Mothercare and the falling birthrate

We have seen that the age distribution of a country's population will help to determine the size of its working population. It will also effect what that population wants. A change in the age distribution will cause changes in the pattern of consumption. If there is a fall in the birth rate it will affect certain businesses more than others. Mothercare, for example, specialise in providing clothes and other products for expectant mothers and their babies. The Chairman of Habitat/ Mothercare, Sir Terrance Conran, was quoted in June 1983 as saying: 'It's only unsuccessful retailers who get worked up about it. These statistics about the ageing population are true but the changes in the market are not going to take place suddenly . . .'
Even so, many people feel that the fall in the birthrate will restrict Mothercare's natural growth. They are also facing increased competition from other stores like Boots, Marks & Spencer and C & A. Mothercare, however, aim to go on expanding and opening new shops.

Exercise

You are a member of the management team of Mothercare who has been asked by Sir Terrance Conran to suggest ways of overcoming the problems of increased competition and a falling birth rate. Remember you wish to keep expanding and to make greater profits for your shareholders.

How many ways did you think of? Here is what Mothercare actually did during 1983-84:

- Revamped shops with attractive new interiors.
- Produced higher priced, more fashionable maternity dresses (£29.95 as well as £19.95). In the words of Sir Terrance, 'the signs are that Mothercare is retrieving the middle classes.'
- Produced clothes for older children 10-13.

Population pyramids

One convenient way to display the composition and characteristics of a particular population is by the use of a 'population pyramid'. It is, in fact, two histograms, with age measured vertically and numbers in each group shown horizontally. Male and female are separated and placed back-to-back. It is known as a 'pyramid' since the numbers fall towards the top.

It is possible to see that the pyramid is slightly unbalanced towards the top because women on average live longer than men. Currently, the life expectation at birth is 71.4 for men but 77.2 for women in the UK. Although almost impossible to detect, slightly more males (boys) are born than females (girls). This results in a sex imbalance of more males than females in the lower ages and more females than males in the higher. It has little or no economic significance.

TASK

1 In which five year period was the birth rate highest?
2 In which five year period was the birth rate lowest?
3 Which of the population pyramids in Fig. 5.5 would best represent the population of:
(a) Bornmouth
(b) Milton Keynes
4 Between 1961 and 1979 the percentage of economically active women (either working or looking for work) between the ages of 25 and 44 rose from 40.3 per cent to 61.9 per cent. Give **one** reason for this change and **one** consequence.
5 In the year 1975-76 19 per cent of boys leaving school entered some form of full-time education but 25.6 per cent of girls leaving school entered some form of full-time education. Explain the difference.

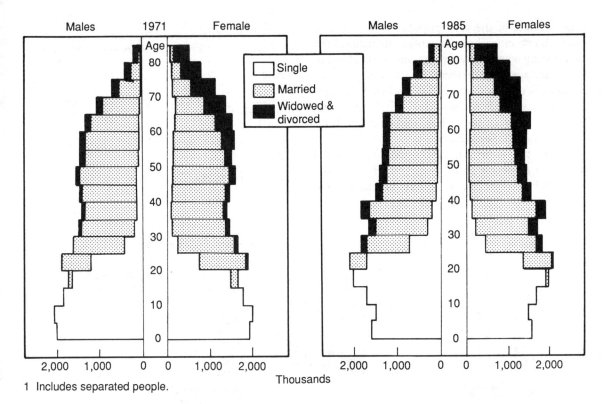

1 Includes separated people.

Source: Office of Population Censuses and Surveys
Fig 5.4

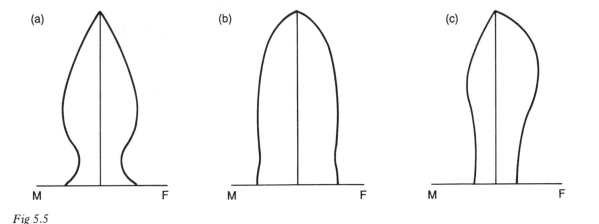

Fig 5.5

Geographical distribution of the population

The population of the UK is unevenly spread throughout the land. There is an uneven distri-
bution between the four countries of the UK. England not only contains the majority of the population (83 per cent) but is more densely packed. The majority of people live in towns or urban areas as opposed to the open country; about

three quarters of the total population now live in towns. Some cities have expanded to include the surrounding towns leaving one vast **conurbation**. There are seven such areas in the UK: Greater London, West Midlands, West Yorkshire, South-East Lancashire, Merseyside, Clydeside, and Tyneside. Between them they hold over one third of the country's population.

During the industrial revolution there was a movement of people towards the major coal fields since coal was the major source of energy and

	Surface area (sq km)	Population (millions)	Population density per sq km
England	130 439	47.0	361
Wales	20 768	2.8	135
Scotland	78 772	5.1	65
Northern Ireland	14 121	1.6	112
United Kingdom	244 100	56.6	232

Source: Social Trends, 1981 HMSO

Exercise

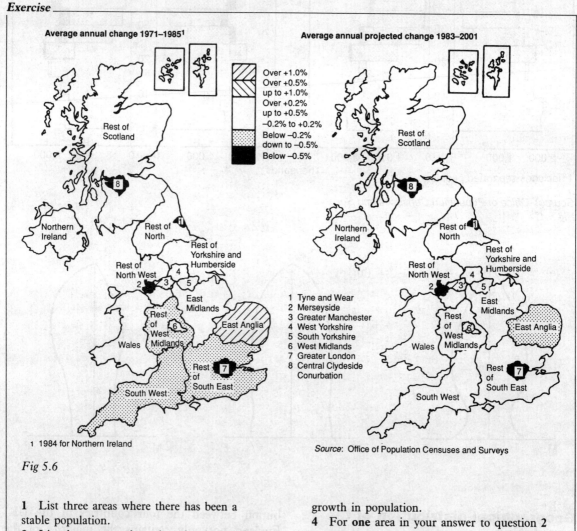

Average annual change 1971–1985[1]

Average annual projected change 1983–2001

Over +1.0%
Over +0.5% up to +1.0%
Over +0.2% up to +0.5%
−0.2% to +0.2%
Below −0.2% down to −0.5%
Below −0.5%

1 Tyne and Wear
2 Merseyside
3 Greater Manchester
4 West Yorkshire
5 South Yorkshire
6 West Midlands
7 Greater London
8 Central Clydeside Conurbation

1 1984 for Northern Ireland

Source: Office of Population Censuses and Surveys

Fig 5.6

1 List three areas where there has been a stable population.
2 List three areas where there has been a fall in population.
3 List three areas where there has been a growth in population.
4 For **one** area in your answer to question **2** suggest one reason for the fall in population.
5 For **one** area in your answer to question **3** suggest one reason for the growth in population.

difficult to transport. Since the beginning of this century there has been a gradual southward shift of the population with Outer London and the South East growing rapidly since the Second World War. The fastest growing regions are now East Anglia and the South West.

The large conurbations do cause problems though. Transport is difficult due to bad congestion. At their centres the conurbations often have poor housing. To help the situation the **New Towns Act (1946)** gave the Secretary of State for the Environment the power to designate areas of the country for development into new towns. By attracting industry to new areas and building new homes for rent or purchase close at hand people would be encouraged to move away from the conurbations. New towns can be planned with modern needs and problems in mind. Cars can be kept away from shopping centres and adequate parking can be provided. The urban sprawl was further halted by the establishment of **green belts** – areas of countryside upon which building has been prohibited – around London, Birmingham and Liverpool.

Types of employment

There are well over 35 000 different occupations in this country, and these occupations can be split into three different classifications. One convenient and quick way is to distinguish between three levels of production.

To produce anything one must start with raw materials, manufacture them into some good or service (often through many different stages) and then distribute and sell the product. The manufacture of a desk, for example, illustrates this process. The desk started life as a tree which had to be cut down. This is the first stage of production or **primary production**. Then it was turned into planks of wood and finally the desk. This we call **secondary production**. The last stage was to sell and deliver it to the school. This is the third or **tertiary stage**. The following diagram illustrates this process more clearly.

Primary Production
Industries concerned with obtaining raw materials

or food eg agriculture, mining, fishing, forestry etc.

Secondary Production
Industries concerned with manufacturing building and construction, or in other words the stage at which things are made.

Tertiary Production
Industries concerned with distribution and services, including civil servants.

Consider the percentage of the working population engaged at each level. An interesting and perhaps surprising picture emerges:

Distribution of Employment by Sector

Category	% of working population 1971	1984
Primary	4.8	4.6
Secondary	42.2	30.7
Tertiary	53.1	64.7

(*These figures exclude unemployed and armed forces and take public utilities as secondary.*)

Source: Department of Employment, HMSO

The percentage of the working population employed in the primary sector is small and falling. This is not perhaps surprising since the UK has very few raw materials and a small land area. What is perhaps surprising is that well over half the working population are employed in the tertiary sector. Increased mechanisation has replaced workers in the primary and secondary sectors but the move towards tertiary employment is part of a long-run trend.

In the days before industrialisation most people worked on the land. However, industrialisation brought the growth of the manufacturing sector. Increased wealth and the fall in price of manufactured goods brought about by mass production meant that everybody wanted goods. As incomes continued to grow so the desire for services grew. The UK has specialised, in fact, in financial and professional services such as insurance and banking which results in more employment in the tertiary sector (*see* Fig 5.7).

Exercise:

1   Between 1982 and 1986 which two Standard Industrial Classifications saw the greatest percentage increase in employment?

2   What, if anything, have the two Industrial Classifications in your answer to question 1 have in common?

3   Between 1982–1986 which two Standard Industrial Classifications saw the greatest percentage decrease in employment?

4   What, if anything, have the two Industrial Classifications in your answer to question 3 have in common?

5   Using an appropriate method, display the information countries in Fig 5.7 in graphic form.

A second way of looking at employment is to break jobs down into **job families**. This is how we approach the classification in careers lessons. You will find that somewhere in your school you have what is called a 'signposts' box file issued by Careers Research and Advisory Centre (CRAC), in which some 800 or so jobs are classified under 10 headings. Some jobs will fit into more than one section. It is often fun to try and think of a job which could fit all 10 – perhaps a first division football manager? This is a very useful way of looking at employment for those who are chossing a career. If, for example, you wanted to work outdoors you would look at section J, or with numbers, section G. Here is the complete list with a few examples. Try to think of further examples

TABLE ONE
Numbers Employed in Different Sectors as a Percentage of Total Working Population

SIC Division		Numbers Employed 000s	% of Total
0	Agriculture, Forestry & Fishing	300.2	1.4%
1	Energy and Water Supply	491.0	2.3%
2	Mineral and ore extraction; metal manufacture	761.8	3.6%
3	Metal goods, engineering and vehicles	2,245	10.5%
4	Other manufacturing industries	2,064	9.7%
5	Construction	988	4.6%
6	Distribution, hotels, catering, repairs	4,387	20.5%
7	Transport and Communication	1,335	6.2%
8	Banking, finance, insurance	2,306	10.8%
9	Other services	6,498	30.4%
TOTAL: 0–9		21,377	100

(Source: *Employment Gazette*, 1988)

TABLE TWO
Changes in Employment: 1982–1986

SIC 1980	Numbers Employed September 1982 000s	Numbers Employed September 1986 000s	% Change
0	363	338	− 6.9%
1	666	519	−22%
2	857	773	− 9.8%
3	2,661	2,306	−13.3%
4	2,172	2,087	− 3.9%
5	1,045	984	− 5.8%
6	4,034	4,322	+ 7.1%
7	1,351	1,332	− 2.1%
8	1,782	2,231	+25.2%
9	5,905	6,268	+ 6.1%
TOTAL	20,838	21,160	+ 1.5%

(Source: *Employment Gazette*, 1987)

Fig 5.7 (SIC = 1980 Standard Industrial Classification)

as you go through. You can always check with the signposts box.

A **Scientific** – Air traffic controller, chiropodist, physicist
B **Social Service** – Nurse, dietition, social worker, youth leader
C **General Service** – Accountant, telephonist, sales assistant
D **Persuading/Influencing** – Estate agent, insurance salesman, journalist
E **Literary** – Archivist, barrister, interpreter
F **Artistic** – Fashion designer, dancer, photographer
G **Computational** – Accountant, actuary, surveyor
H **Practical** – Boatbuilder, cook, dental technician

Levels of entry. For every type of job, there are different levels of entry depending upon the qualifications of the person concerned. For example a person could work in the catering industry as: washing-up/general help; chef; catering manager; or hotel manager.

These different levels of entry may differ in name from job to job but they conform roughly to the pattern shown in Fig 5.8.

Table 5.2

Level of entry	Qualification	Training
Operative	nil	'on the job' few weeks
Craft	four GCSE grades D/E	3–4 years incl. part time at college first two years as part of YTS scheme
Technician	four GCSE grades A/C	as craft but higher level courses
Student	four GCSE grades A/C with two at A' level	4–5 years professional training
Graduate	university degree	further professional training

Task

For each of the levels of entry give an example of an actual job for:
(a) A car factory
(b) A general hospital
(c) Any firm you have visited.

There are several types of training mentioned in the table above. Many people are critical of the amount of training in this country as compared with our competitors. In 1980 for example 44 per

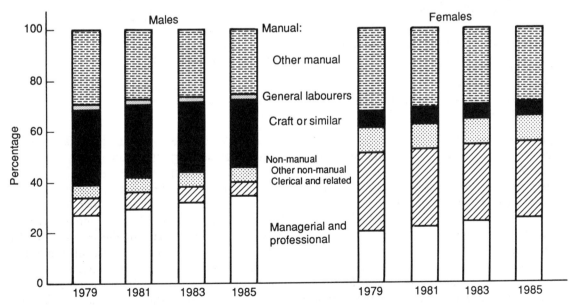

1 Excludes occupation inadequately described or not stated.

Source: Labour Force Surveys, Department of Employment

Fig 5.8 People in employment by sex and occupation

cent of British school leavers went straight into a job with no more than a few weeks on-the-job training.

A very small proportion, 14 per cent gained apprenticeships while 10 per cent went into full-time vocational training (physiotherapy for example) and 32 per cent into full-time higher education. The government YTS scheme in many cases serves as the first two years of an apprenticeship scheme or at least two years with some off-the-job college based vocational training.

Mobility of labour

In a modern economy the demand for goods and services is constantly changing as new products are invented. This means that the jobs people are required to do also change. Ten years ago most schools did not have a computer, most now do. New products are now being invented more quickly than ever before which means that society does not expect workers to remain in the same occupation all of their working lives.

Labour needs to be **mobile**; that is the ability to change quickly from occupation to occupation and area to area, so that industry can adapt to the new technology and take advantage of the benefits it will bring.

Changing jobs can mean one of two things:

(a) A completely new occupation – **occupational mobility**
(b) A similar occupation in a different industry – **industrial mobility**

Either can be associated with a change in the area in which a worker lives – **geographical mobility** (see Fig 5.9).

There are many obstacles or barriers to mobility which prevent a smooth movement of workers from unnecessary jobs to new jobs. Lack of knowledge of the opportunities in different areas or industries for example. One of the major barriers is the **cost** of changing a job. Most people train for an occupation when they first leave school. They are young and have few responsibilities. They are able to survive on the low wage or grant they receive whilst they train. However,

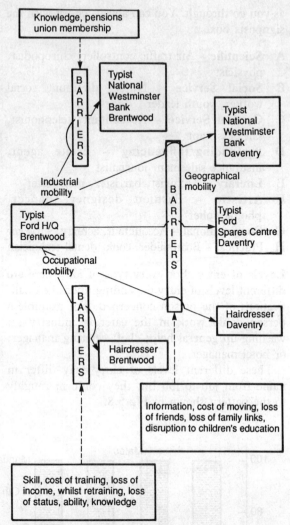

Fig 5.9   Types of labour mobility

an older person, perhaps with financial responsibilities such as a family or home to support might not be able to survive on these low incomes. Moving house is a further problem. Not only does it cost thousands of pounds to move but it might be impossible because of the different prices of houses in different parts of the country (see Fig 5.10). In 1983 the average price of a house in Greater London was 42 per cent higher than in the North of England. It would be almost impossible for an unemployed shipbuilder in Newcastle to move to London even if he could find employment since he would not be able to afford a house.

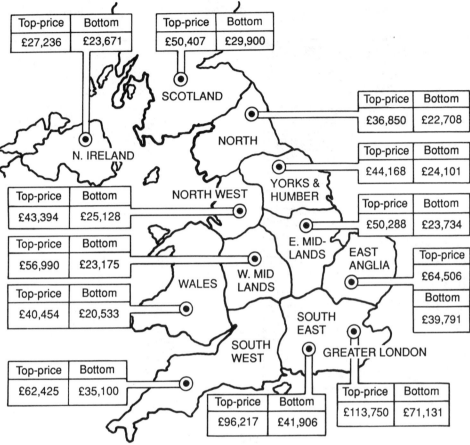

House prices: three bedroom semi-detached

Top-price	Bottom
£27,236	£23,671

Top-price	Bottom
£50,407	£29,900

SCOTLAND

N. IRELAND

NORTH

Top-price	Bottom
£36,850	£22,708

YORKS & HUMBER

Top-price	Bottom
£44,168	£24,101

NORTH WEST

Top-price	Bottom
£43,394	£25,128

Top-price	Bottom
£50,288	£23,734

E. MID-LANDS

EAST ANGLIA

Top-price	Bottom
£56,990	£23,175

W. MID LANDS

WALES

Top-price	Bottom
£40,454	£20,533

Top-price
£64,506

Bottom
£39,791

SOUTH EAST

GREATER LONDON

SOUTH WEST

Top-price	Bottom
£62,425	£35,100

Top-price	Bottom
£96,217	£41,906

Top-price	Bottom
£113,750	£71,131

Fig 5.10

Table 5.3

Average House Prices 1988

Region	£
Greater London	92 440
South East	69 061
East Anglia	52 148
South West	48 762
West Midlands	40 082
Scotland	38 696
East Midlands	37 011
North West	34 261
Yorks & Humber	34 134
Wales	30 493
North	29 779
Northern Ireland	25 453
United Kingdom	44 360

Exercise

1 List **three** occupations/jobs which were common 50 years ago but are no longer required today.

2 List **three** occupations/jobs which are common today but were not required 50 years ago.

3 Give an example of something that you could do to ensure that you remain mobile as a worker.

4 Give one effect on the country if workers remain immobile.

5 Look at the following figures. Give **three** reasons why young people are more mobile than older people.

Job mobility: full-time employees* who had changed employers in the previous 12 months, 1973, 1976, and 1979

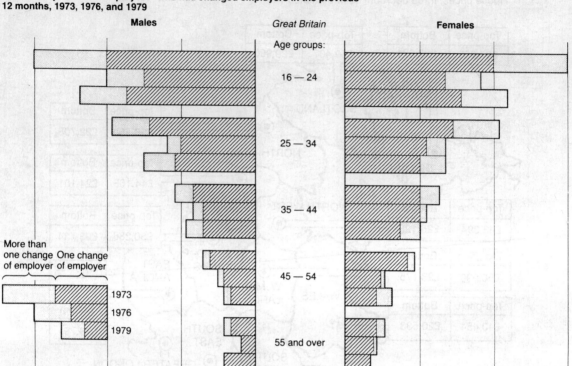

Fig 5.11 (Source: Social Trends 1981 HMSO)

*Includes some self-employed persons who had been an employee during the previous 12 months. Excludes fulltime students who were working in the reference week.

In 1979 11 per cent of male workers and 13 per cent of female workers changed their jobs at least once. The Government tries to increase mobility through the Department of Employment with such schemes as ET and the jobcentres (discussed later in the book).

ASSIGNMENT

Draw Fig 5.9 *Types of labour mobility*, but use examples from your own area.

Finding work

Can you think of the ways people find work? One can:

- write to or approach the employer directly and ask

- go to the employment office (job centre) or careers office
- go to a private agency
- visit the school's careers teacher
- hear of the job through relatives or friends

One other important way to find work is through advertisements. These can be found in most newspapers – local and national. These often appear in categories, e.g. Hotel and Catering, etc. Some professions and trades have their own journals in which you would find advertisements for jobs in that specific field. An example of this is *The Times Educational Supplement* where teaching jobs are advertised. Also trade unions often have their own newspapers where specialist jobs are advertised. The National Union of Teachers has a weekly paper called *The Teacher* in which some teaching jobs are advertised. The following variety of jobs appeared in a local paper. Read through them carefully and then answer the questions.

Exercise

1 *Read the job advertisements.*
(a) Why do they ask for attractive bar staff and not a bar maid?
(b) Can you see any problems with the *Everest* job?
(c) Would you like the first cook's job? If not why not?
(d) Why do the Estate Agents want a car driver?
(e) Can you see two advantages in the Technician job?

Government help in finding employment

The Government provides various facilities for helping people find a job. The following paragraphs explain these services.

1 For the school leaver

At school Schools do not have to employ a careers teacher, but most do. It is not the job of a careers teacher to find employment for school leavers, this is the responsibility of the Careers Advisory Service. The role of a careers teacher in the school is to help students select the correct courses, decide upon a future career and apply for jobs. They arrange interviews with the Careers Advisory Service and organise careers displays and conventions. Often special careers lessons are given in the senior school where students learn how to write a letter of application, present their best image at interviews, etc. Most schools have a careers library where information about different occupations is kept.

The Careers Advisory Service (CAS) This was established in 1909 and was called the 'Youth Employment Service'. It is run and financed by the education department of your council. Each area has a careers office from which careers and employment officers work. It is their responsibility to help young people find their first employment. A list of suitable jobs and training schemes is kept and visits are made to firms and colleges so that each officer has up-to-date information. Careers officers visit schools, take group discussions, interview school leavers and give advice. Often computers are used to help sort out appropriate jobs for students. Special careers officers help find employment for disabled students and older pupils.

2 For adults changing employment

Help is given to adults changing jobs by the Training Agency which is part of the Department of Employment. The Department of Employment runs well over a thousand **jobcentres** which provide information for the unemployed and those seeking a change in job or employment opportunities in the local area.

Most jobcentres have display boards like an estate agency but instead of houses they advertise jobs. Often these are arranged in types like the ones shown on this page. There are sections for local employment, part-time employment, jobs covering a wider area and jobs for the self-employed. People can just walk in and look around in their lunch hour or when they are out shopping. In this way all sorts of people are encouraged to use them, not just people who are redundant. Part-time work may suit someone with young children for example.

This is a completely free service. Employers do not pay to advertise nor do clients who find a job. If one of the cards seems suitable the person simply asks at the counter for further details and an interview is arranged. For the more serious job hunter an interview will be arranged with one of the experts who work at the jobcentre during which they will fill in a form (an *SR1/LNE*) containing the relevant details, eg experience and qualifications. It is then the centre's task to try and match the unemployed person to a suitable vacant job. Computer terminals in the centre enable centres to keep in touch so that all the jobs in a whole area are known to each centre. The client is given help and advice on such things as training and even how to go for an interview if it is needed. There are also a small number of professional executive recruitment offices where unemployed or even employed people of professional or executive status are given advice

```
┌─────────────────────────────────────────────┐
│  SELF EMPLOYMENT                              │
│                                               │
│     JOB: LIFE UNDERWRITERS (SELF EMP)  MAN OR │
│  DISTRICT: 15 MILE AREA OF LOCAL DISTRICT WOMAN│
│    WAGE: £80-£100 (3 NIGHT                     │
│          THEN COMMISSION 0                     │
│   HOURS: TO SUIT APPLICANT                     │
│                                               │
│  DETAILS: AGE 25-40 EXPERIENCE NOT NECESSARY TO COLD│
│           CANVAS BUSINESSESS/HOUSEHOLDERS TO OBTAIN │
│           LIFE ASSURANCE & PENSION CONTRACTS, CAR OWNER│
│           & OWN PHONE PREFERRED, SMART APPEARANCE  │
│                                               │
│           *** SELF EMPLOYED ***                │
│  ASK THE RECEPTIONIST FOR JOB NO               │
└─────────────────────────────────────────────┘
```

```
┌─────────────────────────────────────────────┐
│  LOCAL JOBS                                   │
│                                               │
│     JOB: MOTOR PARTSMAN.                MAN OR │
│  DISTRICT  LOCAL DISTRICT               WOMAN  │
│    WAGE: £1.25. P.H. DEPEND-                   │
│          ING ON EXPERIENCE                     │
│   HOURS: 8.30.AM TO 6.30.PM.MONDAY             │
│          TO SATURDAY.                          │
│  DETAILS: MOTOR PARTSMAN AGE 30 - 40 REQUIRED. │
│           ESSENTIAL TO HAVE KNOWLEDGE OF THE MOTOR│
│           TRADE AND PARTS TO WORK IN STORES. MUST ALSO│
│           HAVE EXPERIENCE OF HANDLING CASH. REFERENCES│
│           WILL BE TAKEN.                       │
│                                               │
│  ASK THE RECEPTIONIST FOR JOB NO               │
└─────────────────────────────────────────────┘
```

on availability of jobs which are kept on a special register.

When a firm moves into an area or if it needs to recruit labour for some reason, such as winning a new contract, it can set up a recruitment stall inside the jobcentre and undertake some initial interviewing and selection. This is clearly an efficient and cheap way of recruiting.

By offering this service the Government is clearly increasing the mobility of labour by giving people better **knowledge** of the jobs available and by helping them apply for them.

ASSIGNMENT

Study the article on page 70 published in the *Sunday Times* in 1980 and construct a bar chart or pie chart to show the education or training of school leavers in the UK in 1980. The chart should have four sections:

- No training
- Full-time higher education
- Time-served apprenticeships
- Full-time vocational education

Exercise

Find out the following:

1 Where is the careers library in your school?
2 What jobs need a knowledge of economics or commerce?
3 What is the COIC library classification for banking?
4 Where is your local careers office?
5 Where is your nearest jobcentre?

Now answer these questions:

1 What is a **time-served apprenticeship scheme**?
2 Give an example of **full-time vocational education**.
3 What evidence is there to suggest that training of school leavers was poor in the UK?
4 Suggest one economic result of poor training for the UK.
5 What evidence is there to suggest that training has improved since 1980?

Training

The article from the newspaper shows that most young people leaving school have no formal training. This does not mean that they will have no training at all before they start work – they will, after all, be 'shown the ropes' at least! There are, however, different types of training available. The following paragraphs show the main types.

'On-the-job' training

Here youngsters are shown what to do, while they are actually doing it. A firm might run a short course to teach new employees about the firm and what it produces, and to show them where things are and where to go for help. This is called an **induction course** and might last a few days. If this is all a young person receives it is very cheap for the firm but the worker might find it difficult to get another job since they have gained no recognised qualifications, only experience.

Apprenticeships

The apprenticeship is one of the oldest forms of training. Here a craftsman will take on a young helper who will perform many of the easy tasks like making the tea, fetching and carrying tools etc whilst learning the trade at the side of the craftsman.

Although this is a fine way to learn, it very much depends on the professionalism of the craftsman. Now, although the principle is much the same, some industries have an **Industrial Training Board** supervised by the Department of Employment, which monitors training in the industry and sets standards (e.g. the Engineering ITB).

The apprentice has to undertake training at a college where they learn the fundamental theory behind the craft. Sometimes this is full-time for a number of weeks (**block release**) or all day for one day per week (**day release**). When at work the apprentice has to complete a number of progressively more difficult tasks which are written up in a log book. The college courses often lead to City and Guilds certificates or the Business and Technical Education Council's (BTEC) general,

UK training is 'West's worst' Report by Robert Taylor

BRITAIN'S system of industrial training for workers is the worst of any major country. Sir Richard O'Brien, chairman of the Manpower Services Commission, warned last week that unless Britain transforms the way it trains its workers, it will cease to be an industrial trading power of any importance by the end of the Eighties.

Apart from Ireland, Britain has the highest proportion among Western countries of school-leavers receiving neither an apprenticeship nor any full-time vocational education as a preparation for a job, and it has the lowest proportion of apprentices in the working population.

As many as 44 per cent of young people go into the labour market in this country straight from school with no training at all, while 14 per cent win a time-served apprenticeship, 10 per cent go into full-time vocational education and 32 per cent into full-time higher education.

In Britain training is mainly left for individual employers to decide with government acting on the margin and in support of what employers see as their own needs. By contrast, in West Germany training is based on the collective employer needs viewed in national terms through powerful industry-based organisations.

With three times as many apprentices as in Britain (1 500 000) the West German economy benefits from having two out of every three men and one out of every two women in the labour market with vocational qualifications through practical and theoretical testing.

The most impressive feature of the West German system is the commitment to a basic vocational training year provided free for 15- or 16-year-old pupils in 13 broad occupational fields. By 1982 as many as 100 000 youngsters will be covered by this scheme. The State plays a vital part in the provision of suitable training through grants and subsidies.

In the United States there is a substantially better system than in Britain.

Americans enjoy a uniquely high rate of enrolment in tertiary education, with about 66 per cent of school-leavers proceeding to some form of post-secondary education and about 50 per cent going to college.

As the needs of industry are for more technical expertise from workers, greater flexibility and mobility between jobs, the archaic *laissez-faire* system which Britain developed in the first industrial revolution looks increasingly moribund and irrelevant.

national and higher national awards. After four or five years (depending upon the industry) if apprentices reach a satisfactory standard, they will be recognised as a qualified craftsman and would be able to find employment all over the world. It is tempting to think of apprenticeships operating only in the manual, male dominated areas such as engineering and construction industries; and it is true these are important areas of apprenticeships but do not forget hairdressing and floristry for example.

Full-time vocational education

Vocation in this sense simply means employment, trade or profession. It is possible to leave school and go to a college or institute and learn one specific job. This is called **full-time vocational education** and accounts for about 10 per cent of all school leavers. There are numerous examples such as physiotherapy, medical schools, secretarial colleges etc. The advantage is that a student becomes very highly skilled but the disadvantage is they only possess one skill which might limit mobility. However, competition is often high to enter such colleges and places are limited which means that, in most cases, a job is almost guaranteed.

There are also some private training colleges, many of which are excellent. Students have to pay for these but most people believe it to be a worthwhile investment for the future.

Higher education

After school some 32 per cent of students continue to study in an academic sense. This may mean attending University or a Polytechnic to study for a degree or a College of Higher Education to study for BTEC national or higher national awards, or perhaps even a College of Further Education to re-take GCSE and A levels or study for general and national awards.

Government training schemes

The government has many training schemes. The Employment Training, for example, where unemployed workers can be trained with a new skill while receiving benefits (*see* Table 5.4). Figure 5.1 shows 8.5 per cent people who wish to work are unable to find paid employment. One reason for this high level of unemployment has been the replacement of people by machines. Increased mobility is one attempt to reduce unemployment.

All school leavers at 16 and 17 are guaranteed a place on the YTS programme if they cannot find a job or a place for further education. The YTS programme is an integrated two year course of work experience and vocational training. The details of this and other schemes are set out in the following table.

Task

Study the table below. For each of the government schemes decide how they aim to tackle the problem of unemployment and which barries to mobility they are trying to remove.

Special needs

The Government provides a number of programmes for those with special needs, e.g. for people with disabilities:

- Special aids to employment (equipment lent)
- Assistance with fares to work (up to £69.25 per week)
- Personal Reader Service (for the visually handicapped)

- Employment rehabilitation
- Sheltered employment
- The Disabled Persons' Register and Quota Scheme – any employer with 20 of more workers must try to employ at least three per cent of workforce from registered disabled
- Employer can receive grants of up to £6000 to adapt their premises or equipment in order to employ a particular disabled person and
- £45 per week to take on a disabled person for a trial period.

In addition, Employment Training will provide work-related English language training for members of ethnic minorities.

ASSIGNMENTS

1 Explain how the size of a country's working population might change even though the toal population of the country stays the same. For what reasons might a Government engineer such a situation?
2 You are a fully qualified, unemployed chef. Explain in detail all the ways in which you would attempt to find employment.
3 Having just left school you are looking for your first job. List all of the ways you and other school leavers might seek employment. Mention the people who could be of help and say who would be most helpful and why.
4 Outline the different sorts of training you could receive after leaving school either as a young employee or as part of the Government's YTS programme.
5 It is important that the workers of a country can change their jobs easily. We call this the **mobility of labour**.

(*a*) State why it is important for workers to be mobile in a modern society.
(*b*) State clearly the three types of mobility, giving an example of each.
(*c*) Describe four barriers to mobility which might affect your mother or father.

Table 5.4

Summary of employment, training and enterprise programmes of the Department of Employment Autumn 1980

Programme name	Eligibility	Main points
1 EMPLOYMENT MEASURES		
Restart Programme	People unemployed for 6 months or more	Counselling interviews every 6 months to explain opportunities to long-term unemployed.
Restart Course	People unemployed for 6 months or more	5-day informal course to improve employment skills.
Jobstart allowance	People unemployed for 12 months over 18 and more than 6 months from retirement	6th month, £20 per week top-up to low wages (£70 per week or less gross for 35 hours)
Jobclubs	People unemployed for 6 months or more	Coaching in job-hunting techniques. Free facilities including telephone and postage.
Community Industry	Unemployed people between 16 and 17	7000 places for disadvantaged young people who are given work experience on community projects or in sheltered workshops for up to 1 year.
Travel to interview scheme	People unemployed for 4 weeks or more	Helps people travel to interviews beyond normal daily travelling distance by meeting the cost of travel and over-night stays.
Jobshare	Employed/unemployed prepared to take part-time employment (16–29 hours per week)	Employers who split full-time job or vacancy to 2 part-time jobs, create new part-time post from overtime or employ 2 new part-time employees from a Government training scheme are given £1000 towards administration costs and training.
2 TRAINING		
Youth Training Scheme (YTS)	All 16 and 17 year olds	2 year training scheme with 20 weeks off-the-job training in addition to on-the-job training and work experience. Opportunity to take recognised vocational qualifications. £29.50 per week at 16 and £35 per week at 17.
Employment Training	All unemployed people aged 18 to 59 who have been unemployed for at least 6 months.	12 months planned training suitable for trainee often in areas of skill shortages. Trainees receive £10 per week more than benefits and travel costs over £5 per week. £50 per week towards childcare costs for loan parents plus training bonuses for people who complete action plan drawn up by independent training agent.
Small Business Development Programme	Suitable employed or self-employed people	Business skills courses for owner/managers of new and existing small businesses.
Business Enterprise Programme	Any suitable people	7 days of free start-up training for small businesses. (Can form part of Employment Training).
Training Grants for Employers	Employers, with priority in some cases for small businesses	Grants for retraining existing employees or new recruits, consultancy grants and grants through the National Priority Skills scheme.
Training Access Points	Everyone	Help to identify training opportunities. TAPs available in 30 areas but will increase.
Open Learning	Everyone	Over 1000 flexible multi-media courses.

Table 5.4 *(cont'd)*

Summary of employment, training and enterprise programmes of the Department of Employment Autumn 1980

Programme name	Eligibility	Main points
Career Development Loans	Anyone over 18 who lives or intends to train in Great Britain	Loans to help cover cost of vocational training (lasting at least one week and less than one year). Loans, from participating Banks only, are interest free during the training and for up to 3 months afterwards.
3 ENTERPRISE Small firms Service	Anyone who is already running or thinking of starting up a small business.	Free information and counselling from experienced people on business problems and Government schemes (below)
Enterprise Allowance Scheme	People 18 and over, under 65 who have been unemployed for at least 8 weeks and who have £1000 to invest in a business.	£40 per week for up to 52 weeks to supplement the receipts of the new business while it is being established.
Loan Guarantee Scheme	Most new or existing small businesses	Government guarantees for 70% of loans to small businesses (up to £75 000). A premium of 2.5% on the guaranteed portion is paid by the borrower.
Business Expansion Scheme	UK residents paying income tax Unquoted new or existing companies incoporated in the UK. (Providing they are not in certain excluded catagories).	Top rate tax relief on equity investments in unquoted companies if investment maintained for at least 5 years. Capital gains tax also not paid. (In 3 years raised £410 m)

SUMMARY EXERCISE

1 We live in a society in which we have specialisation amongst our workers. Give **three** advantages to society of this specialisation and **three** disadvantages to the individual worker.

2 Name **two** categories of people of working age who do not work and one category who are not of working age but do work.

3 Since 1901 there have been 'peaks' or 'booms' in the number of babies born. Give **three** problems this may cause on both the supply of goods and services and the demand for labour?

4 Give examples of primary, secondary and tertiary production found close to your school.

5 Explain how the Government's Employment training attempts to increase the occupational mobility of labour.

6 On a radio phone-in programme a caller asks why it is that the unemployed ship-building workers in Newcastle do not come down to Dagenham as there are always jobs in the local paper. Write down some of the points you would make if able to answer his question.

7 What is the enterprise allowance scheme? How will it help unemployed people?

8 Give an example of a **private employment agency**. Which group of workers often find employment this way?

9 Give an example of a full-time vocational training course other than teaching.

10 Draw a population pyramid for a third world country.

6

Trade Unions Employer Organisations

Trade unions

About 11 million working people belong to trade unions in the UK. A trade union is an organisation of working people who join together because they have something in common such as a skill or craft and by so doing are able to increase their power and influence in discussions with an employer.

Exercise

You and a few friends decide that one of the school rules is silly and ought to be changed. After considerable discussion you arrive at three plans of campaign:

1 You go and see the head teacher as soon as possible and ask that the rule be changed.
2 Ask that it be discussed in form/tutor group and if there is general agreement send a group of students (picking the best speakers!) to see the head teacher.
3 Write the request for a rule change on sheets of paper and ask as many people in the school who agree with it to sign and take all of these signatures to the head teacher.

Which of these alternative plans would you choose and why?

In the example above it is likely that you would choose option **2** or **3** because joining together with other students who feel the same would strengthen your argument. This illustrates the principle of trade unions. By joining together workers have increased power and influence when discussing such matters as wage rates, holidays and working conditions with employers.

CASE STUDY

The Transport and General Workers Union

The Transport and General Workers Union (TGWU) was formed in 1922 through the amalgamation of 14 different unions. A further 80 merged with the TGWU over time to produce by far the largest and arguably most influential union in the UK today. The TGWU had nearly $1\frac{1}{2}$ million members and represents many different types of worker from all over the country and several industries. It is known as a **multi-industrial union**.

It costs under £1 per week to belong to the TGWU. What are the members buying?

Collective bargaining All unions will negotiate with employers about wages (this is what we hear about most in the news). The TGWU also negotiates such things as overtime, hours of work and holidays, redundancy, health and safety, working conditions and pensions.

Individual help Members of the TGWU are given help in such matters as securing compensation from employers if they are injured at work. If they are ill or on strike the union will pay out cash benefits (the Union has its own recuperation centre in Eastbourne). It also runs education courses for members and gives free legal aid and advice to members.

Organisation of trade unions

No two trade unions are exactly the same but most are organised in a similar way to the TGWU outlined above. This organisation or structure is outlined in Fig 6.1.

The members of a trade union will elect a work place representative or shop steward. This worker will continue with his/her normal work but will be given some time and facilities by the employer

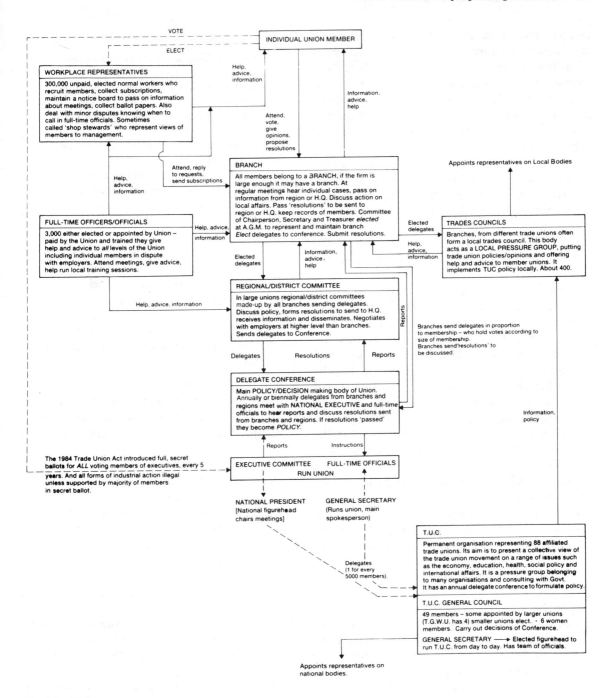

Fig 6.1 Union structure

to carry out union work. They will keep their members in touch with union policy and tell them when branch meetings are to be held. It is their responsibility to negotiate with the employer on issues which affect members like new working conditions, holidays, discipline of members etc. They also recruit new members and collect subscriptions.

Each member belongs to a branch which meets regularly to make decisions about both local and national issues which affect members. This is done by members putting forward motions or statements which are then formally debated and voted upon. The branch will elect a committee and officers (President, Secretary etc) to run the branch each year.

Large unions will group branches geographically into regions or divisions to look after all members in an area. Most employ the services of full-time officials who are paid to look after the interests of members, in particular any legal and technical matters where their expertise can be invaluable. Branches send delegates to regional meetings where a committee is elected to look after regional matters.

The most important body in any union is the Annual Conference. Each branch will send delegates to this large meeting which normally lasts a week. The delegates will discuss motions sent by branches and if passed they will form the policy for that union. Since the Conference only meets for one week the union elects a group of members to put into effect the policies it decides upon. This group is known as the National Executive Committee. It is now elected by a secret ballot of all members.

The National Executive is aided by full-time national officials who are paid to carry out union policy. The membership will elect by secret ballot a General Secretary, a full-time figure-head who will represent the union in negotiations with employers and Government nationally. They often become household names as they are seen on television so often.

It can be seen therefore that unions are organised on democratic lines. Any member has the right to attend branch meetings and vote for or against motions and stand for election to office in that union.

Exercise

1 Name the General Secretary of two unions stating which union they represent.
2 Give two benefits an individual member might expect from joining a trade union.
3 How is national policy decided in a trade union?
4 Give one task a regional official of a trade union might undertake.
5 Describe how a worker might become a regional or divisional president of the union and name one task they might perform in this office.

Summary of the functions and objectives of trade unions

The TUC describe the general objectives of trade unions, those goals they are working to achieve, as follows:

- Improved conditions of employment – better wages, shorter hours and longer holidays
- Improved physical environment at work – heating, lighting, ventilation, health and safety
- Job security
- Job satisfaction and prospects – personal fulfilment, elimination of boring repetitive work, training and retraining
- Income security – protection of income when work is interrupted by illness, accident, old age, redundancy or unemployment
- Full employment
- Redistribution of national income and wealth between those who provide labour and those who provide capital
- A share in the planning and control of industry
- Improvements in the standard of living such as standards of education, health service and the provision of housing
- The defence of trade unions' right to operate freely

Such overall aims should not be confused with their day-to-day functions which can be summarised as:

- Collective negotiation on wages, pensions, health and safety and conditions of service

- Individual representation and help if a member faces redundancy, discipline, etc or has been injured at work
- Free legal aid and advice
- Financial payments if on strike, ill or retired and in need of help
- Collective purchasing schemes – often cheap insurance, travel etc
- Education and training of officers and members
- Research into problems of industry and representation on national and international bodies

Classification of trade unions

A trade union was defined as a group of workers who have something in common. The type of trade union will depend upon what its members have in common (*see* below).

Type of union	Common link of members	Examples
Craft	Skill or trade	Card Setting Machine Tenders' Society National Union of Scalemakers
Industrial	Same industry	National Union of Railwaymen (NUR) National Union of Mineworkers (NUM)
General	None – other than all work	Transport and General Workers Union (TGWU) General and Municipal Workers Union (GMWU)
Non-manual	Nature of work	Association of Scientific, Technical and Managerial Staffs (ASTMS) Association of Professional, Executive, Clerical and Computer Staff (APECCS)

Craft unions represent workers who have a skill, usually acquired after a long apprenticeship. They are known as **closed unions** and aim to protect their skill and maintain standards. They are very small and can result in one firm having several

different unions. In some cases it can lead to disputes between unions about who should do what. In our modern technological world machines have replaced many skills and so the number of craft unions has fallen. An industrial union will recruit from a whole industry. This can mean a company negotiates with only one union – which is obviously of benefit to both sides. General unions, like the TGWU are **open**. Anyone in any industry can join. They are very large and can offer a wide range of services to members and have a great deal of power. Over the last 20 years non-manual or white collar unions have grown rapidly. In 1965 they represented only 18 per cent of total union membership. Now it is closer to 40 per cent. This reflects perhaps the change in the nature of employment. The success of manual unions in increasing pay levels also encourages non-manual workers like teachers and local government workers to form unions.

ASSIGNMENTS

1 Take two trade unions. One that someone you know belongs to and one a person working in your **school** belongs to (a teacher, cleaner, secretary, cook, laboratory assistant). For each list:

(a) The name of the union and type
(b) The cost to join
(c) How it is organised
(d) Services offered to members
(e) Last time union called a strike

2 Add the results in answer 1 to the results of four of your friends.

(a) Is there a pattern in the organisation of unions?
(b) Are certain types of unions more expensive than others?
(c) Do expensive unions offer a greater range of services than smaller?

Collective bargaining

Keith once owned an old Triumph 2000 motorcar. He wanted to sell it and thought that it was worth about £650. He advertised it in a local paper for £700 ono (that stands for 'or near offer' and means that he was prepared to negotiate – haggle the price). The man who bought it told Keith that he would not give more than £750 for the car! He obviously did not understand the game. If he had offered *less* than £700, say £650, Keith would have said that he would take £675 and they could have settled. Instead the buyer offered more than Keith wanted so he took it with both hands.

The above example is not what happens exactly in collective bargaining but similar. If Keith and the buyer had followed the rules Keith would have known that he had sold his Triumph for as much as he could and the buyer would have known that he had spent as little as he could and still bought the motorcar.

When a trade union negotiates a wage claim for its membership it is called **collective bargaining**. Often a union will claim a pay rise which is a maximum, or in other words, the most they would like. The employer will often offer the least amount that they would like to pay. Both sides will then negotiate. Perhaps the employer will

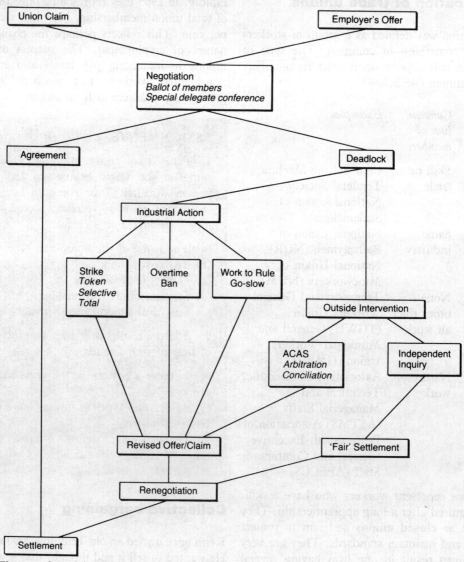

Fig 6.2 The wage bargaining process

offer more but with certain conditions, such as harder work from the employees. This is known as a **productivity deal**. Clearly the employer can pay more if the same number of workers are producing more goods.

Exercise

> Which of the following occupations could not negotiate a productivity deal? State your reasons in each case.
>
> - car workers
> - coal miners
> - nurses
> - school teachers
> - bricklayers
> - bus drivers

A union might accept a lower offer than the claim plus longer holidays or tea breaks. In most cases a compromise is reached which is called a settlement and work will continue as normal. In a few cases agreement cannot be reached. This is called **deadlock**. To indicate their strength of feeling and to try to force the employer to make a better offer the members of a union can take **industrial action**. All members of a union are asked to vote for or against such action and it has to be agreed by the union's Executive. (If individual members of a union take action without permission of their executive it is unofficial action and the workers taking action are not protected by the union nor do they receive any strike pay.) Figure 6.2 shows the course taken by the wage bargaining process.

Industrial action

Strike Union members stop work. Strikes can be '*all out*' – all members involved until employer makes a better offer. '*Selective*' – some workers are called to strike and others stay at work (often those who stay at work pay into a fund to help support those on strike). '*Token*' – workers leave work for a day or even an hour (often used by caring professions, such as nursing to prevent suffering).

Note Although unions often have strike funds to help striking members who obviously receive no pay while on strike very few unions have enough to support an all out strike for more than a few days.

Overtime ban Union members only work normal hours accepting no overtime. (Clearly only effective in industries where overtime is common place.

Work to rule/contract Union members adhere very closely to the letter of the rules or contract which govern their work. They withdraw 'good will' in effect undertaking no work they do not *have* to do.

Go slow Union members deliberately take their time in performing tasks.

When a dispute reaches deadlock the Trade Union Congress (TUC), a body which represents most unions, might step in and offer help in bringing both sides together. If both parties agree the services of ACAS the Advisory, Conciliation and Arbitration Service, may be sought.

ACAS is an independent body established by the **1975 Employment Protection Act** to help improve industrial relations. In a situation of stalemate 2 services can be offered. Conciliation – where an independent person or persons will talk to both sides and try to bring them together to negotiate again. Arbitration – where independent people listen to the case put by both sides in the dispute and then suggest what can be considered a fair settlement.

Government control of trade unions

Throughout the late 19th and 20th centuries trade unions have gained the right to organise strikes and individuals the right to strike without being responsible for the losses due to those strikes. This is known as **trade union immunity**. Many people felt that the circumstances where this immunity applied had widened too much over the years. The 'balance' of power between trade union and employers has changed recently with the introduction of three main Acts of Parliament:

- the Employment Act 1980
- the Employment Act 1982
- the Trade Union Act 1984

Before looking in some detail at these Acts, some terms must be explained:

Picketing Trying to peacefully persuade non-

Fig 6.3   Picket outside The Sunday Times, *Gray's Inn Road*

striking workers to join a strike or striking workers to work. There is no legal 'right to picket' but peaceful picketing has long been recognised as lawful.

Secondary picketing Trying to persuade non-striking workers from a different employer to join the strike.

Secondary action Industrial action taken by workers in a firm not directly involved in the dispute.

Blacking A form of secondary action – not handling goods from a firm in dispute.

Closed shop An agreement between an employer and one or more trade unions which requires certain employees to be members of a trade union or one of a number of trade unions.

Employment Act 1980

This Act

- made money available to unions to help pay for the secret balloting of members on such issues as starting or ending strikes, electing officers, changing union rules etc.
- amended Section 15 of the Trade Union and Labour Relations Act 1974 providing basic rules for picketing:

1 may only be undertaken in contemplation or furtherance of a trade dispute

2 may only be carried out by persons attending or near their own place of work; (a trade union official may accompany a member of his or her union)

3 its only purpose must be peacefully obtaining

or communicating information or peacefully persuading a person to work or not to work

- removed legal protection from any new closed shop agreement unless 80 per cent workers affected voted in favour
- issued Code of Practice on the conduct of picketing (17 December 1980). This suggests a limit to the number of pickets of six at any entrance to a workplace, for example, and further guidance on 'good practice'.

Employment Act 1982

This Act

- removed protection from **all** closed shop agreements unless 'approved' in a secret ballot (80 per cent workers affected, 85 per cent of those voting, indicating they wish to keep it) within two years of the Act becoming law. If not approved any worker dismissed for **not** belonging to a trade union would be unfairly dismissed under the 1978 Employment Protection (Consolidation) Act. Even in an approved closed shop – that is, one which has voted yes in the manner mentioned above – workers can refuse to join if they have genuine objections on grounds of conscience or for a number of other reasons listed in the Act. (A Code of Practice on Closed Shop Agreements and Arrangements came into effect 18 May 1987)
- banned 'union labour only' contracts and makes industrial action against non-union businesses illegal.
- reduced trade union immunity against civil damages, to only those for action taken in furtherance of a **lawful trades dispute**
- reduced lawful trades disputes. Do not now include those where the employer and employees are not in disagreement. Only disputes between employer and employee (that is most industrial disputes) are considered lawful.

Trade Union Act 1984

This Act was introduced to increase democracy within unions. It:

- introduced secret ballots for all voting members of union executives at least every five years

- made all forms of industrial action illegal unless a majority of those due to take part in the action have voted yes in a secret ballot, held not more than four weeks before the action is due to start
- made unions with political funds (part of the membership fee given to a political party) ballot their members at regular intervals to determine whether the members wish their union to continue to spend money on party political matters.

CASE STUDY

The 1988 Ford UK dispute:

Ford UK employs 32 500 manual works who belong to 12 unions, the largest of which is the Transport and General Workers Union. February 1988 saw the first all-out strike at Ford UK for more than a decade. In this case study we shall look at the reasons for the stoppage and consider the consequences.

Negotiations for the 1988 settlement began in November 1987 with the management offering a 4.25 per cent pay rise which, in typical negotiating manner rose progressively to 6.5 per cent by the New Year. The difference in this case was that the Ford offer contained two further proposals. First, it was to be a three year deal, with pay rises in line with the rate of inflation for 1989 and 1990. Second, and much more important, the unions were asked to accept five major changes in working practices at the Ford plants. They would however, gain higher pensions and full pay in the event of lay-offs. The membership rejected this offer and voted in secret ballots 88 per cent in favour of strike action. On Wednesday 27 January the unions called for an indefinite all-out strike to begin on Monday 1 February.

The five management conditions

1 *Introduction of Japanese style 'Quality Circles'.* Workers of all levels in teams meeting regularly to set targets and review performance.
2 *Reduction of differences between skilled and semi-skilled workers.* Skilled maintenance workers could be asked to work on the assembly line alongside semi-skilled colleagues whilst not engaged in repair work.
3 *Changes in role of foremen.* Routine shopfloor management undertaken by 'Group Leaders'

recruited from semi-skilled or skilled men heading a 'production team'. The foreman's role to be upgraded to a management role recruited from not only supervisors, as now, but middle management and technical staff.
4 *Harmonisation of white and blue collar employment conditions* – leading to a totally unified workforce by 1990.
5 *Ability to recruit part-time workers to help reach production peaks.*

The background

For some time British car manufacturers had lagged behind European and Japanese competitors in terms of efficiency. It takes 65 per cent more man hours for Ford to build a car in the UK than in Germany, and 250 per cent more than the Japanese. To overcome this lack of efficiency, Ford for some time have argued that they need a more flexible workforce. In the UK it was common practice to have the workers divided into different skills or jobs and agreements that only a person with the right job title should be able to carry out a specific task. This is known as demarcation. It can lead to over-manning and loss of time. Agreements in 1985 reduced the number of manual job descriptions at Fords to 52. At the Nissan factory in Sunderland there are only two manual job titles and each day starts with a five-minute quality meeting. It is interesting to note that Nissan produce 21 cars per worker per year whilst Fords only 16. The workers pointed out, however, that Ford UK reported record pre-tax profits of £109m, and were the most successful British car manufacturers.

Last minute improvements – rejected.

On January 28th the management increased the pay offer to seven per cent in the first year and inflation plus two per cent in the following two. In addition the company was prepared to drop conditions 3 and 5 above.

Four hours before the strike was due to commence the Unions called off the action and recommended acceptance of a new deal. In this the Company had offered seven per cent this year and inflation plus 2.5 per cent in the following two. This slight improvement was coupled with agreement to refer the controversial five conditions to plant level negotiations with problems to be decided in national negotiations.

It came as some surprise to the union leaders to find that by 4 February secret ballots indicated that the membership was still 60 per cent against the offer and wished to proceed with the strike.

(Although the majority of Ford plants voted in favour of the revised offer – 11-10 under the Government's legislation (1984 Trade Union Act) – because the majority of members were against, the strike could, legally, go ahead whereas under Ford's old agreements it would not!).

From Monday 8 February, the strike commenced. Although 40 per cent of the workers had voted in favour of accepting the revised offer, and therefore against the strike, at all 21 plants the action was solid. For example, in Southampton (where Transit vans are made) the workers had voted 2-1 against the strike but none of the 2740 employees worked. This very quickly caused problems in Ford's European operations. Within a week the Sierra line at Genk, Belgium, was closed causing 8500 workers to be laid-off due to the lack of British-made body reinforcement brackets.

By the second week of the strike the Ford management made a new offer: this, made on 16 February reduced the agreement to just two years and offered seven per cent in 1989, the same as 1988 and back-dated the 1988 offer to November 1987. As with the previous offer, all controversial conditions are to be decided at plant level negotiations. Union members voted in secret ballots 67 per cent in favour of accepting this offer (20 plants in favour 1 against – Dagenham). Workers return to work on Monday 22 of February.

Ford claims the ten day dispute cost them around £20m. (The firm did not have to pay wages or incur any variable other costs but lost two weeks production.)

Strike timetable

Nov 1987–Jan 1988	Negotiations. Offer raised from 1st year 4.5 per cent to 6.5 per cent. Second & Third years inflation + five employment conditions. Unions reject.
Jan 26	Union calls indefinite all-out strike from 1st Feb. 88 per cent support in secret ballot.
Jan 28	Increased pay offer. Two conditions dropped. Unions reject.
Jan 31	Increased pay offer. All conditions subject to negotiation. Unions accept. Strike called off.
Feb 4	Secret ballot result rejects offer and Unions' recommendation. Strike called for 8th Feb.
Feb 8	Strike commences. All 32 500 manual workers out.
Feb 9	2000 workers sent home at Genk.
Feb 16	Ford revised offer. Two year only. Unions accept.
Feb 19	Members vote in favour of acceptance
Feb 22	Full return to work.

Information adapted from the *Independent* and *Sunday Times* 26 January–21 February.

Exercise

1 What made the Ford 1988 offer significantly different to previous offers?

2 Why did the union membership have to vote in a secret ballot before they could commence industrial action?

3 Why might foremen and skilled maintenance workers not agree to the changes in conditions of employment proposed by Ford UK in the original offers?

4 What evidence is there to show that Ford UK factories are less efficient that those in Europe? Give one cause for this.

5 What is a demarcation? How might it reduce efficiency?

6 How might the opening of the Nissan factory in Sunderland have affected the attitude of Ford UK management?

7 Why were the union leaders embarrassed by the outcome of the second secret ballot of members? Why might the UK Government have been embarrassed by the outcome of the second secret ballot?

8 Why were Ford Belgium workers laid-off within one day of the commencement of the UK strike? How could it have been avoided?

9 How much did the ten-day strike cost Fords? Why was this so low?

10 Why do you think workers at the new Nissan plant in Sunderland were prepared to accept conditions of work very similar to those Ford wish to impose on its UK workforce but that workers at Dagenham still reject them?

Tasks ▬▬▬▬▬▬▬▬▬▬▬▬▬▬

1 Draw a flow-chart to show the wage bargaining process using the description above.

2 For each of the forms of industrial action discussed on page 79 think of one occupation where it would be appropriate and effective and one where it would not.

Give reasons for your choice.

3 Which of the following occupations would not be able to negotiate a productivity deal? State your reasons for each answer.

car workers	school teachers
coal miners	bricklayers
nurses	bus drivers
waiters	shop assistants
social workers	managing directors

Days lost through Industrial Action 1973–1985 (United Kingdom)

Year	No. of disputes beginning	People involved	No. of days lost
1973	2873	1 513 000	7 197 000
1974	2922	1 622 000	14 750 000
1975	2282	789 000	6 012 000
1976	2016	666 000	3 284 000
1977	2703	1 155 000	10 142 000
1978	2471	1 001 000	9 405 000
1979*	2080	4 583 000	29 474 000
1980	1330	830 000	11 964 000
1981	1338	1 499 000	4 266 000
1982	1528	2 101 000	5 313 000
1983	1352	573 000	3 754 000
1984**	1206	1 464 000	27 13 5 000
1985	887	7 91 000	6 402 000
1986	1050		1 923 000

* 17 863 000 days are accounted for by the 1979 industrial action of the Engineering Unions.
** 22 483 000 days are accounted for the coal miners' dispute.
Source: Department of Employment Gazette

4 (*a*) Given that the working population of the UK is 26 million what proportion was involved in industrial action during 1985?

(*b*) Which dispute accounted for the loss of over 22 million working days in 1984?

(*c*) In 1982 281 million days were lost through sickness (long term only, *not* short periods of up to five days). How many times greater than the days lost through strikes are the days lost through long term sickness?

(*d*) What has been the general trend of industrial disputes over the last ten years?

The Trades Union Congress (TUC)

TUC is one of the best known abbreviations in Britain, but many people have little or no idea of what the Trades Union Congress actually is or indeed what it does. Some think it is a union which it is not; others a Government body, which it is not. Some even think that it is a political party, which it is not.

In 1868 individual trade unions joined together to form a club or organisation which could be a spokesman for all trade unions. This we call the TUC. Today 87 of the country's 200 unions belong to (or are affiliated to) this central organisation. The TUC has its own head office and staff and is divided into seven main departments. These gather information which is used in discussions with Government and to help member unions. Although less than a quarter of all unions belong to the TUC most of the larger ones do which means when the elected leaders of the TUC speak with Government they are representing the views of over 9.5 million workers.

In order that the leaders of the TUC know what member unions feel about current issues and problems (and indeed so that those leaders might be elected) the member unions each send delegates once a year to an annual conference. Unions send one delegate for every 5000 members in their union and have one vote for every 10 000 members. Individual unions put forward motions which are discussed in formal debate and are then voted upon. If a motion is carried it becomes TUC policy. Between conferences the day-to-day running of the Congress is left in the hands of a General Council which has 44 elected members representing all industries and types of employment. Four seats are also reserved for women. The Congress has an elected General Secretary who is the figurehead and voicepiece of the TUC.

It is also affiliated to a large number of international organisations and nominates representatives to various government and public bodies including the National Economic Development Council (NEDC) and ACAS.

Employers' organisations

Employers often join together to form organisations based upon industries. For example, the

British Hotels', Restaurants' and Caterers' Association. These organisations represent the member companies in that industry in negotiations with trade unions on wages and conditions of work and the Government when discussing standards etc. They will also give advice to members on legal matters. Some, such as the British Carpet Manufacturers' Association perform a dual role since they not only undertake the work mentioned previously but also act as Trade Associations which means promoting their product and helping to sell it.

The Confederation of British Industry

The CBI was formed in 1965 by the amalgamation of three smaller organisations and is now the largest central employers' organisation in Britain. It represents about 300 000 companies and defines its role as:

'. . . an independent, non party-political body financed entirely by industry and commerce. It exists primarily to ensure that Governments of whatever political complexion, and society as a whole, understand the needs, problems and intentions of British business, and the contribution it makes to the prosperity of the country.'

Members of the CBI come from five main areas:

1 Individual industrial companies
2 Individual commercial companies
3 Public sector – nationalised industries/public corporations
4 Employers' organisations and trade associations
5 Commercial associations – like local Chambers of Commerce.

CBI policy is determined by its members. The governing body of the CBI is the Council which has 400 members drawn from regions and member organisations. All policies must be approved by the Council. For the last few years the CBI has held a delegate conference which acts as a forum for debate.

Like the TUC the CBI nominates representatives to government and public bodies and belongs to international employers' organisations. The CBI also provides many services for its members. By employing specialists it is able to give advice on such things as taxation, overseas trade and legal problems.

ASSIGNMENTS

1 You have been made President of the local branch of a trade union. Part of your responsibilities include speaking to local workers in your field and trying to recruit new members. Write a five minute speech you might make to try to convince people to join your union.

2 With reference to a current dispute, or one about which you have learnt, describe and explain the process of **collective bargaining**.

3 The trade union official most workers come into contact with is the **shop steward**. If you were to become a shop steward what would you consider to be your main duties and responsibilities as an official of a trade union?

4 When you start work you may well join a trade union.

(*a*) How could you as an individual member influence the running of your union?
(*b*) Explain fully three benefits you as a member would expect to gain which non-members would not gain.

5 The Government has changed the law regarding picketing.

(*a*) What is **picketing**. Why and when is it employed?
(*b*) Why and how the Government recently changed the law regarding picketing?
(*c*) Why do the unions, in general, oppose such changes?

SUMMARY EXERCISE

1 Trade unions are concerned with anything which affects the material well-being of their members. With reference to the TGWU case

study on page 74 list four such areas of concern for the modern British trade union.

2 Small craft unions such as the National Union of Basket, Cane, Wicker and Fibre Furniture Makers of Great Britain and Ireland are often said to be bad for industry and the trade union movement. Give two reasons why such small craft unions are criticised.

3 Give three examples of **industrial unions**. What advantages are there for the employer if he negotiates with one industrial union rather than several smaller craft unions?

4 The Transport and General Workers Union is the largest union in the UK with nearly two million members. It is an example of an open, general union. Give two reasons people join such large unions.

5 The Association of Scientific, Technical and Managerial Staff (ASTMS) is an example of a **non-manual union**. (Sometimes called **white collar** unions because the jobs undertaken by members are so clean.) In recent years such unions have grown. 44 per cent of all non-manual workers are now union members. Give three reasons for this growth.

6 The work place representative is an ordinary worker who is elected by fellow union members to represent them on the shop floor. Name two other duties the work place representative performs for the union.

7 List three factors a union might bear in mind when considering a pay claim.

8 A strike, groups of workers collectively withdrawing their labour, is one form of industrial action. List three further forms of industrial action and give examples of where such action has recently been used.

9 The Advisory Conciliation and Arbitration Service is an independent body which can be requested to help in a dispute between employers and trade union. Assistance can be given in the form of: (*a*) arbitration and (*b*) conciliation. Distinguish between these two terms and indicate situations where either would prove useful.

10 Why are some unions in some occupations considered more powerful than others? What effect does this have upon their members' wage rates?

7 Mass Production and Automation

Most goods and services are **mass produced**. This does not refer to the size of the product; very small items can be mass produced. Mass production means making a large number of identical products. This process can be made extremely efficient: each worker is given a specific task to perform as the product moves past on an assembly line. Raw materials and components are delivered at one end of the factory and finished products emerge from the other. The process is quick and reduces unit costs. This process is most noticeable when applied to something as large and complex as a modern motor car.

The story of this most sophisticated car dates back to before the turn of the century when William Morris, an Oxford bicycle repairer, started making cars. After the First World War he produced some 367 cars with the help of 150 workers at Cowley.

Fig 7.1   Body assembly line (Courtesy: Austin Rover)

Six years later Morris Motors employed 14 000 people and produced 52 000 cars. The names Morris and Cowley had become famous.

The Cowley plant is where the Rover 800 is produced today. The company is now Austin Rover. Morris remained a separate company until 1951 when it merged with rivals Austin.

In the early days of motor car manufacture many small firms either merged or were taken over by larger rivals. Originally, Morris bought in many components for the manufacture of his successful Morris Oxford. Engine, gearbox, etc were all produced by small engineering firms in the Oxford area. Morris gradually bought up these companies in order to secure supplies during the depression of the 1920s. Morris learnt about the advantages of mass production techniques from Americans when he visited the Ford plant in Detroit. These methods were introduced at the Cowley plant. The assembly process was broken down into separate, timed jobs: each worker therefore contributed very little to the overall output. The cars were on a continually moving track, with the workers on either side. Components were delivered to the assembly line by trucks. These techniques increased output and

reduced unit cost. The Morris cost £390 in 1919 but the much improved equivalent was only £162 in 1930.

The principle of mass production is the same today. Cars move along tracks and the production workers complete a simple task on each car as it passes. Today, however, many of the tasks are undertaken by machines, automatically.

Austin Rover use computers in the styling, design, engineering and production of cars and the Rover 800 is the most advanced yet. Rover call this computer integrated engineering. It is more efficient, flexible and produces a car of much higher quality. The computer allows the designers to test ideas before the first prototype is built.

It takes 400 individual panels to build the body of the Rover 800. These are held together with 4000 welds. 45 per cent of these welds are made by automated equipment using a total of 58 robots.

There are four body types with 13 derivations; these can pass along the production line in any sequence. The computers adjust to each type. If one robot should break down the others automatically carry out all the welds. Each completed body shell is checked by 62 laser

Fig 7.2   Automatic body framing station (Courtesy: Austin Rover)

Fig 7.3   Windscreen fitment by robot (Courtesy: Austin Rover)

cameras to make sure it is exactly the right size.

Even the windscreen is fitted by a robot using laser cameras. Such techniques allow a superbly engineered car with a high degree of luxury to sell at highly competitive prices throughout the world. It has meant that fewer people are now employed in the motor car industry in general and at Austin Rover in particular.

1 Morris merged with its greatest rival Austin in 1951. What is this type of integration called? What advantages would the new, larger company have?

2 (a) Austin Rover use many robots – list down as many jobs as you can that are undertaken by robots in a car plant.

(b) Write down one job at Austin River which could not be undertaken by a robot (do not write down tea-lady as they use drinks machines!).

3 What effects has the use of robots had on employment at Austin Rover.

4 Austin Rover speak about the 'cycle of benefits' which new technology brings to both company and customer.

(a) Give an example of one of these benefits for the customer.

(b) Give an example of one of these benefits for the Company.

5 Mass production techniques can lead to boredom. How could this affect the company's output?

6 Austin Rover claim that the use of robots brings benefits to the employee. Name one benefit.

7 Quality is most important to Austin Rover. How do robots help to increase quality?

8 What evidence is there that robots are flexible?

Advantages of mass production techniques

Mass production increases output and reduces unit costs because:

- practice makes perfect
- less training needed for each employee
- machinery introduced which is: faster, more accurate and more powerful than manual production.

Problems associated with mass production techniques

Mass production is here to stay. Most of the goods we take for granted in the western world would be far too expensive for the average person if they were not mass produced. It is not without problems, however – these are:

- boredom for unskilled workers: there is little variety as simple tasks are repeated many times
- less skilled workers are needed
- risk of unemployment – machines replace workers
- greater interdependence – each production stage is dependent upon the last
- slow workers have difficulty keeping up.

Producers take these problems very seriously as they can lead to an unhappy workforce, absenteeism, shoddy work and a high job turn-over. In trying to avoid these problems some firms employ such methods as job rotation giving workers a greater say in the running of their section, and even playing piped music.

Limits to mass production

Not all goods are mass produced. For some this may be because the demand for the product is too low. Formula One racing cars are an excellent example. It is technically possible to mass produce these in just the same way as the Rover 800. It would not be worthwhile; even if the price were reduced, very few people would buy such a car since it can only be used for racing.

Some services cannot be mass produced due to their nature – doctor's consultations, for example.

Automation

The use of automatic machinery, like the robots at Austin Rover, goes hand in hand with mass production. This brings even more advantages.

- further increase in output
- reduced costs
- boring jobs can be done by machines

In 1980 Austin Rover produced 5.9 cars per worker per year; by 1987 this had increased to 14 cars per worker per year. Although some of this improvement is due to better use of the workforce and the ending of restrictive working practices, much has been due to the introduction of automatic machinery.

The process leads to more unemployment; **technological unemployment** – the replacement of workers by machines. It is noticeable in a modern factory just how few workers there are. Technology is having an impact on the way we live and work. The number of hours worked each week has fallen over the century and this is likely to continue. People have a greater amount of leisure time and leisure industries are consequently growing. As machines replace jobs people need to be more flexible, and the country needs more retraining schemes. Technology is changing so rapidly people cannot expect to stay in the same job for their entire working life but will experience periods of work, leisure and retraining. Perhaps schools should train people for leisure. Certainly it has reduced the average working week.

The working week

| Year | Hours worked per week by | |
	Men	Women
1969	45.7	37.9
1974	44.0	37.2
1979	43.2	37.2

When you think that our grandfathers probably worked a 55-60 hour week we can see what a dramatic change there has already been. Will this trend continue? Will you be working a 30 or 25 hour week?

Task

In groups of six design a simple paper cube which can be made with scissors, glue, ruler, pencil and paper.

Conduct an experiment.

Let everyone in the group produce their own paper cubes to the agreed design. Work like this for an agreed time – say 30 mins, then count up the number of cubes made. What problems did the group have? How many pairs of scissors, rulers, pencils and glue sticks did your group require? Calculate the output per person.

Repeat the experiment but this time construct a simple production line. Split the process into several tasks. Drawing, cutting, folding, sticking. You will probably need more people drawing and cutting than folding and sticking. Work for the same length of time – 30 min. At the end count the number of cubes made? How many pairs of scissors, rulers, pencils, glue sticks etc. did you need? Was there an increase in output? What problems did you encounter?

ASSIGNMENTS

The assembly line at Austin Rover is auto-mated.

1 What is meant by automation?
2 What advantages may arise from increased automation for the following?
   (*a*) the customer
   (*b*) the company
   (*c*) the employee
3 What problems may arise for the country from increased automation?

SUMMARY EXERCISE

1 The main advantages of mass production are that they reduce costs and increase output. Explain why this is true.
2 If you were to work in a factory using mass production techniques state two characteristics you would expect your work to have.
3 Does mass production *always* cause unemployment? Explain your answer.
4 What is meant by the term **interdependence**? Give your own example to explain this.
5 Give an example of a good, other than riding hats, for which the demand is so low that it is not produced using mass production.
6 Services like hair-stylists are not mass produced. Can you think of three more examples?
7 Some skills like typing are needed in many different industries. Can you think of two other examples.
8 We are told mass production can lead to boredom. Can you think of two ways in which a firm can try to prevent its workers from becoming bored? Explain why the firm would want to prevent boredom.
9 Define **automation** and give an example of industries where it can, and cannot be introduced.
10 Can you give one example of each of the following:
   (*a*) A car produced with little or no mass production techniques
   (*b*) A car produced using mass production but little automation
   (*c*) A car produced using fully automated production.

8 The Question of Location

One important decision to be made by any entrepreneur is where they should locate a new plant or factory. This is true whether it is a small one-man business or large public company. Entrepreneurs want to make the largest profit they can. The choice of site will be very important, for some types of business, in determining just how large this profit will be. It would be very foolish to open a travel agency in a small back street out of town. People would not be prepared to search out such a service and one could not rely on passing trade. Far better would be a unit in a busy shopping centre in the middle of town. This would be convenient for people and give you a chance to catch the eye of the passer-by. Let us consider two firms whose names are known all over the world: British Petroleum and Ford Motor Company. If we take a major factory for each and ask why the site was chosen we can perhaps learn important lessons.

CASE STUDY

Ford Motor Company, Dagenham, Essex

Ford cars were first produced, or at least assembled, in British as long ago as 1911, not at the Dagenham site, but in a small factory in Trafford Park, Manchester. After the First World War the demand for cars began to grow and the Manchester facroty, although capable of producing well over 6000 cars a year, was still too small so that by 1925 the Dagenham site was chosen. As you will see later, work did not start on the site until 1929, however, and the first vehicle, the Model AA truck, rolled off the production line in October 1931. Dagenham was to become world famous, the major production site for Ford and a most successful factory.

It must at first have seemed a rather strange choice since much of the 500 acre site was lowlying marsh into which engineers had to sink 22 000 concrete piles 400 feet deep. The factory was therefore neither cheap or quick to construct and a special share issue was required to pay for it. (Much of the technical details can be seen in the newspaper article which follows on page 95.)

The map (Fig 8.1) which follows and the aerial photograph of the site clearly show why Dagenham was chosen.

Here is a summary of the chief reasons:

Transport facilities
- Deep-water wharf – The photograph clearly shows the factory right on the River Thames. The factory was constructed with its own wharf capable of berthing ocean going ships of up to 10 500 tonnes cargo carrying capacity. The site can therefore export finished cars (often in kit form for reassembly in foreign countries) and import raw materials by sea which is a cheap method of transport. Henry Ford thought this to be most important and even turned down a site in Rotterdam because it did not have these facilities.
- Railway – Ford were able to construct their own sidings from existing railway lines and, by using the specially designed rolling stock shown on the map, were able to deliver finished cars throughout the UK.
- Road – The site is adjacent to the A13 and full use is made of road transport. Car transporters, like those shown, and lorries delivering rolls of sheet steel for body pressings are familiar sights in and around Dagenham.

Labour supply
- The LCC (later known as the GLC, now disbanded) was at the time constructing a huge estate next to the village of Dagenham. This and its proximity to London guaranteed a large labour supply.

Fig 8.1

Size and cost of site

- It was a large site, suitable for expansion and being of poor quality relatively cheap.

Close to Greater London

- As we have seen being close to London meant a ready labour supply but it also meant being close to a large number of small engineering firms. Such firms still flourish on the outskirts of London and could therefore supply components. The capital with its vast population also represents a large market.

Study the aerial photograph on page 93 carefully. In the foreground is, of course, the River Thames.

Notice the company's own wharf complete with cranes but alas, in this shot, no ships! The building immediately behind the wharf is the original plant where today engines of all sizes are built. To the right is the foundry. As you look, follow the company road on the left, over the man-made lake – all that remains of the marsh – to the railway sidings where there are whole lines of full transporter trucks. The building on the left behind the rail lines is the body shop and on the right the assembly shops; the two being linked by a bridge through which the completed body shells glide to meet up with their chassis and engine after several coats of paint. In the background you can see the old Dagenham council estate with a few modern tower blocks.

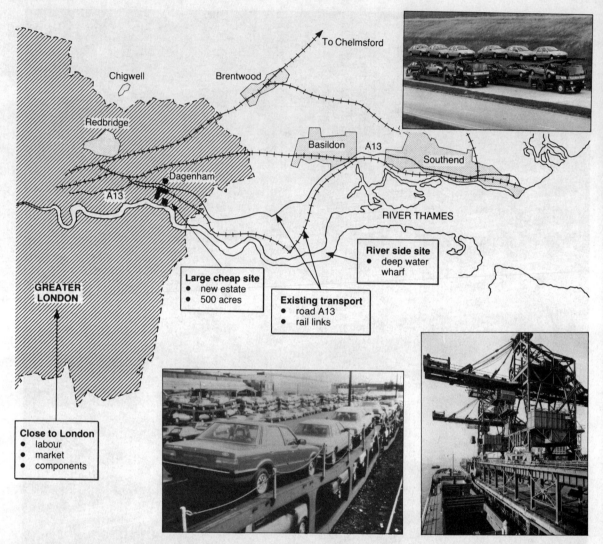

Chigwell

Brentwood

To Chelmsford

Redbridge

Basildon

A13

Southend

Dagenham

A13

RIVER THAMES

River side site
● deep water
  wharf

Large cheap site
● new estate
● 500 acres

Existing transport
● road A13
● rail links

**GREATER
LONDON**

Close to London
● labour
● market
● components

Fig 8.2   The location of the Ford Dagenham site

ASSIGNMENTS

1 Draw in your notebooks a sketch-map of Dagenham to show the main reasons for the choice of site.

2 Read this article from the *Ilford Recorder* 3 May, 1929.

THE RECORDER, FRIDAY, MAY 3, 1929.

THE FORD FACTORY.

Start To Be Made This Month.

A GIGANTIC SCHEME.

Employment For Local Men.

DAGENHAM WORKS TO COST THREE MILLION.

An industrial development of immense magnitude, and one that will provide employment for thousands of workpeople in the south, is foreshadowed by the announcement that a start will be made on the new Ford factory, at Dagenham, on May 16th.

It is computed that for the first two years from 3000 to 4000 men will be employed in laying down the necessary plant. The number will be increased to 15 000 when the factory is fully in action.

The whole scheme, it is estimated, will cost between two and three millions sterling, and its completion will mark the most important landmark in the industrial history of the district.

The official announcement that a definite start is to be made on the erection of the new Ford factory – the advent of which has for so long been rumoured – on May 16th, was made at a meeting of the Dagenham Council on Friday.

What such a factory means to Ilford and Dagenham it is, at this early stage, difficult to visualise. One thing that is certain, however, is that it will bring to the towns, and their environs, a measure of prosperity that will be the envy of other communities.

This week, in a special interview, Major Caink, of Ford Motors (England), Ltd., who is responsible for the arrangements in connection with the Dagenham developments, gave the 'Recorder' an outline of the magnitude of the scheme. He quoted figures, which, by their immensity, are almost incomprehensible but which convey an idea of the vastness of the undertaking. The works, when completed, will be enormous.

THE PROPOSALS

'How many men will be employed?' Major Caink was asked by our representative.

'For the next couple of years,' he replied, 'three to four thousand men will be employed in laying down manufacturing plant. When that work is completed, we shall employ about 15 000 men.

'The rate of production is estimated at 500 cars a day, but about two and a half years will elapse before we can start producing the cars.'

Asked what work will be first put in hand, Major Caink replied that already he had given out contracts for the levelling of the ground and the laying of the railway tracks. 'Then,' he added, 'there would be bridges to build, followed by the erection of assembling sheds.'

A COOL £60 000

'Will the men employed on this work be local men?' – 'Yes, as far as possible Dagenham men will be employed.'

Major Caink said that a river wall would have to be built, as well as two jetties, before operations could begin in earnest.

"What will be the cost?" was our representative's next question.

'Oh,' replied our informant, 'the levelling, the laying of the track, the building of the river wall and so on will only cost about £60 000. Of course, the whole scheme will cost much more; probably between two or three millions.'

Seeking further information about the new Ford enterprise, our reporter interviewed Mr. Francis, the surveyor to Dagenham Council.

AN AGREEABLE SUBJECT.

'You've come to see me about Ford's,' he said, proffering a cigarette.

'Yes,' replied the reporter.

Mr. Francis appeared to enjoy talking of Ford's and he soon warmed to his subject in a smokefilled room. After describing an imaginary picture of a future Dagenham, he discussed the preliminary arrangements that have already been made for the starting of the project.

'Well, Major Caink and Mr. Brooks saw me last week on behalf of Sir Percival Perry, the chairman of Ford Motors (England), Ltd. They told me that there would be a ceremony on May 16th. Mr. Edswold Ford is to cut the first sod on that day.

CUTTING THE FIRST SOD.

'They propose to erect a big marquee inside which a portion of the ground will be roped in, and here the first sod will be cut. The remainder of the marquee will be set aside for refreshments for the guests.

'A fleet of 15 Ford cars will be sent to Valence House at 11.45 a.m. to take the councillors to the site. They are also making special arrangements for the transportation of the representatives of the L.C.C., P.L.A., and Essex Country Council.'

'Mr. Edswold Ford,' he continued, 'will make a speech outlining the proposals of the firm, and his speech will be followed by one from Sir Percival Perry.

'Councillor C. Dellow (chairman Dagenham Council) will respond on behalf of the district.'

IMMEDIATE PREPARATIONS

'What plans have you had in for approval?' asked the reporter.

'The information which we have in regard to the immediate proposals is that they will put down three assembly sheds, 300 ft. wide by 1000 ft. long. There will be a railway loop-line serving all sheds. A reinforced concrete riverside wall and a private road are to be constructed, the latter from Rippleroad, opposite Marsh Green Farm, down to the riverside crossing Dagenham Breech.

'That's all I can tell you,' concluded Mr. Francis.

Do you think that everybody in the community would greet the news of a giant factory on their doorstep with the same enthusiasm shown in this article? If you read the newspapers or watch television news programmes you would probably have seen reports about such groups as Greenpeace and the Ecology party Many people today are worried about the environment and the way we are polluting it. You are a reporter on your local paper and a new car plant is to be built very close to your school. Write a short article about this decision bringing out both good and bad points.

CASE STUDY

BP Oil, Llandarcy Refinery Ltd, Neath, West Glamorgan

Until BP (then the Anglo-Persian Oil Company) started refining crude oil in 1921 at their South Wales site such refining was carried out close to the oil fields. For several reasons, however, BP decided that it would be better to refine the crude oil actually in the British Isles, some 6000 miles away from the oil fields in Persia, but in the marketplace for the finished product.

This not only meant more profit but greater security of supply for the consumer. It is not only petrol for the motorist that comes from such refining but also high grade lubricants, fuel oils and chemicals for industry. Having decided to refine in the UK the company had to look for a site. After looking at several the 650 acre site at Skewen, near Swansea in South Wales was chosen. Look at the map (Fig. 8.3) and then read the summary of reasons for the choice that follows it.

Transport facilities

- Crude oil is, as we all know, shipped in large special ships which need a special terminal to unload safely. BP were able to sign a 99 year lease for the south side of Swansea's Queen's Docks, for this purpose.

Labour supply

- Adequate labour supply was available in the area both to build and staff the refinery. When one considers that is now employs 1600 workers it shows how important labour is.

At the time the South Wales area are suffering from very high levels of unemployment due to contractions in traditional local industry like coal mining.

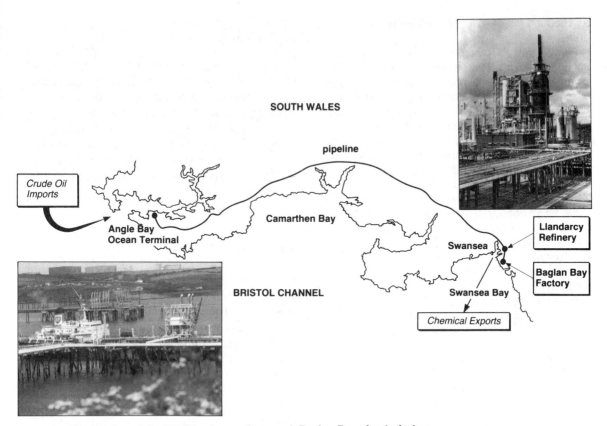

Fig 8.3   The location of the BP Llandarcy refinery and Baglan Bay chemical plant

Land

- Adequate cheap land was available, at the time only waste land.

During the late 1940s and early 1950s it became possible to build very large tankers to ship crude oil from the Middle-East. Unfortunately the Swansea docks were not capable of taking such large ships but it was so much cheaper for the company to transport oil in this way that a new larger terminal was needed. In August 1960 the Ocean Terminal at Angle Bay on Milford Haven was opened. This site was capable of dealing with ships of up to 250 000 dwt.

The crude oil is pumped from the ships into storage tanks, cleverly landscaped into the beautiful countryside of the Pembrokeshire National Park, and from there underground by pipeline 62 miles down the coast to the old Llandarcy refinery. It would have been impracticable to move a giant refinery but in this way BP have been able to use the largest oil tankers.

Similar pipelines carry one of the refined products,

naphtha, a little further down the coast to the BP Chemicals Ltd plant at Baglan Bay. Here, with other raw materials, the company manufactures chemicals for the world's plastics industry. Baglan Bay, opened in 1963, was chosen because it is so close to its main supply of feedstock (raw material) and because of its supply of land. This was a 500 acre site with a prime coastal position making waste disposal possible through a $2\frac{3}{4}$ mile pipe out into the Bristol Channel. The export of chemicals via an extended Queen's Docks was also possible. Added to this adequate labour supply in the area made it a logical choice of site. Another related factor was that South Wales was (and still is) a **development area**. This means that Central Government provides grants to companies moving to these areas to help with such things as building costs etc.

It must be stressed that BP take pollution of the environment very seriously and do not just dump waste out at sea. The waste is treated and the company has a full-time environmental control team which samples water in the Bristol channel as well as checking the atmosphere and noise levels in the area.

From this development of BP we can learn two important lessons. First, when a large established plant finds that one or more of the original reasons for choosing the site no longer apply it will often continue to produce there. We call this **industrial inertia**. It is obvious that once built, once the original location decision has been made, particularly with heavy, capital intensive industries like the petro-chemical industry, it would be very difficult and expensive to close down and move. This is, of course, not so with our original example – the travel agency. If we rented a shop in the wrong district it would be easy to move. We could even take all our fixtures and fittings.

Secondly, and perhaps more importantly, once the refinery was established other chemical factories followed. This is not only true for Baglan Bay. Other chemical companies now operate in the South Wales area. In this way an area develops a reputation and becomes associated with a product.

Exercise

Answer the following questions in complete sentences.

1 In 1925 Henry Ford found it necessary to look for new British premises. Why was this?
2 Many people would have found the choice of Dagenham strange for the construction of the Ford manufacturing plant. Why was this and how were the problems of the site overcome?
3 Can you think of at least two raw materials imported into the Dagenham area by Ford?
4 What three types of modern transport method does the Dagenham site enjoy?
5 Can you think of one type of modern transport for which the Dagenham site is not ideally situated? Does this matter?
6 Why, before the BP Llandarcy refinery was built, was crude oil usually refined close to the oil fields?
7 Can you see two reasons which attracted BP to Llandarcy which are similar to those which attracted Ford to Dagenham?
8 Why, when super-tankers were introduced did BP not move or close down the Llandarcy refinery?
9 BP still use the Queen's Docks in Swansea. What for?
10 Why was the Baglan Bay site chosen for chemical production by BP?

Location factors

In the case studies three common factors emerged which had influenced the choice of site – **land, labour** and **transport facilities**. There are many other factors which might affect this choice, but this will depend upon the type of firm. Some firms may need to be close to their markets or to sub-contractors, other may need special waste disposal facilities.

Here we shall look at these factors in a little more detail.

Land

The term land refers to all naturally occuring factors of production e.g., the actual land, the climatic conditions, the minerals and raw materials under the ground. For some industries such as oil, the position of raw materials will decide the location. Agriculture is obviously dependent upon the type of soil and the climate but in a country as small as Britain this will not have too great an influence. Some industries are dependent upon agriculture themselves and will thus be in certain areas, like jam making and sugar beet refining. Manufacturing industry will just want good, cheap building land often with room for expansion.

Labour

All industry needs labour and it is expensive to move people around. Labour intensive industry, like clothing manufacture, will tend to locate close to large centres of population. Sometimes a firm has to move the labour, such as with North Sea oil wells.

Transport costs

Some firms might cause raw materials to lose weight during the productive process. That is they start with heavy or bulky inputs and end up with a much lighter finished product. These **weight or bulk reducing** firms will clearly be able to minimise transport costs if they are sited close to the raw materials since it would be silly to pay for the transport of waste. An example would be the production of pig iron from iron ore where much of the weight of raw material goes up the chimney in smoke. Such firms are often called **material orientated**. In this country this can mean being sited close to a port since we have so few raw materials. The opposite to this would be a firm which adds weight during the productive process, for example brewing as the majority of beer is water. Why pay to ship water around? For this reason breweries are found around most centres of population. Such firms are often called **weight gaining** and tend to be **market orientated**.

It is difficult to think of too many examples of firms where transport cost are very important to us here in the UK since this is such a small country and has such good communication networks. In general transport costs will be more important to firms which produce cheap, heavy goods as opposed to light, expensive goods since, for the latter, transport costs represent such a small proportion of the final cost. Consider the difference between brick manufacture and diamond cutting.

Market

Some firms, weight or bulk gaining firms, will reduce transport costs by situating themselves close to their markets. There are a further two types of business which will tend to be close to the market for the product. Firstly, it would be foolish to mass produce a product like bread in just one area and transport it to other areas to sell – it would arrive stale. Even in a relatively small country such as the UK some goods, **perishable goods**, will need to be produced as close to their place of consumption as possible. In fact, there has been a return to small retail bakers producing their own bread on site. (Hot oven bread can now be smelt in most high streets and even inside some famous supermarket chains.) The second type of market orientated good is, in fact, not a good at all but a service. **Service industries**, like hairdressers, are spread out all over the country in every town and city. You would not travel miles just to get your hair cut, would you?

Waste disposal and safety

Considerations about these two factors can be very important for such firms as chemical manufacturers. One important waste of an atomic power station is heat so that these buildings are usually located on the coast. They are also kept well away from large centres of population because of potential danger.

Sub-contractors and other acquired advantages of an area

If an area attracts a large number of firms from the same industry it will change or acquire additional advantages which will often attract still further firms. Sub-contractors offering specialised services will set up in the area together with component manufacturers. Educational facilities, such as specialised training in local colleges, will make the area of greater importance to the industry. Special transport facilities and even markets may be constructed. In the end the area will become famous for that product and the name will help to sell the product, e.g. Sheffield steel, Northamptonshire shoes etc. This will often mean that the acquired advantages of the area become more important than the original advantages of the area so that if these original advantages disappear firms will stay where they are. As we have seen this is called **industrial inertia**.

Personal influences

Often none of the factors looked at will decide the location for an entrepreneur. The choice of site will depend simply upon the personal likes or dislikes of the entrepreneur. It could well be the area in which they were born and live which is chosen and no other reason at all.

Industrial location

We have looked at the factors which influenced the choice of sites for the Ford, Dagenham plant and BP refinery and chemical plants at Llandarcy and Baglan Bay. Figure 8.4(a) however shows the location of car assembly plants and oil refineries throughout the UK. It can be seen that they are spread out over the country. This is because no one area is uniquely suited to this type of production. It is possible to produce cars and refine oil in a variety of different locations. Costs are not minimised in just one area. This is true for the majority of industries. These are called **scattered or dispersed industries**.

For a few industries however, for various reasons, not all sites are equally attractive and many firms from the same industry tend to congregate in a few areas. These industries are called **concentrated** or **highly localised**. Examples include the textile industry, coal mining, ship building and to a lesser degree iron and steel. With some smaller industries it may be due to historical reasons, for others it will be because of the natural uneven spread of raw materials throughout the country. Ship building will need deep, safe estuaries and centres of population close to steel production. Iron will need to be close to one or more of the heavy raw materials or a port for imports. Figure 8.4(b) shows the location of ship building and iron and steel.

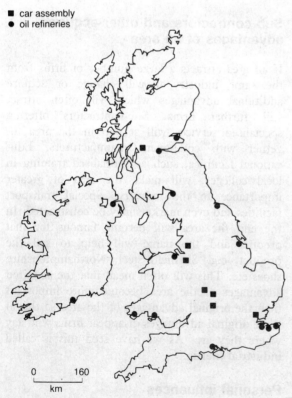

■ car assembly
● oil refineries

0   160
km

The location of major car assembly plants and oil refineries

Fig 8.4 (a)

● ship building
■ iron and steel

0   160
km

The location of major ship building and iron and steel works

(b)

Government influences on location

Some areas become dependent upon a very few industries. Newcastle on ship building, Corby on steel, Nottingham on textiles for example. Although this might restrict the choice of careers in such areas, and perhaps lead to pollution, so long as the industry survives the area will prosper and attract firms in similar and allied fields. If the industry were for any reason to collapse then the area would fall into decline as well. It would not only be the people who were employed in the declining industry who would be affected. Component manufacturers, service industries and even the public sector would be faced with falling demand, unemployment and decline. This we call **regional unemployment**. Three of Britain's most highly localised industries: textiles, ship building and iron and steel have been in decline due to foreign competition for many years now. When one considers that at the end of the Second World War textiles represented over 30 per cent of our exports by value and now forms just three per cent you can see how this industry has declined in importance. Look at the map below and you can see how uneven unemployment is.

Notice the figure for Northern Ireland – more than twice the unemployment of the South East. The problem is not as simple as this. Within some areas there are unemployment black spots like

Regional unemployment January 1987 (% of working population)

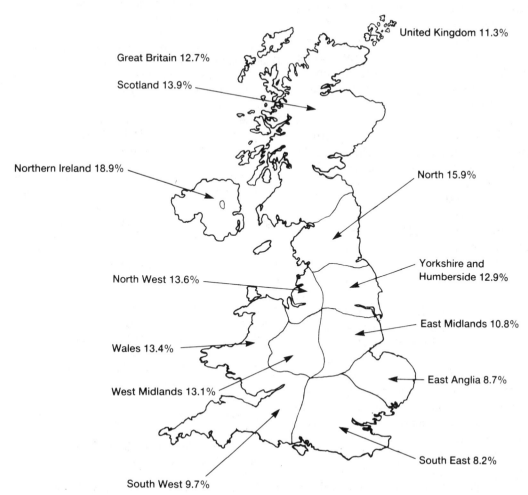

Fig 8.5 Regional unemployment, January 1987 (Source: Department of Employment, 1987 HMSO)

Corby in the Midlands due to the closure of the British Steel plant. Even within cities there are run down areas perhaps due to high rents/rates which have forced firms out to the cheaper sites. What can be done to remedy regional/localised unemployment such as this?

It is clear that firms left to make their own rational decisions will choose the cheapest site. For the new expanding industries this will not necessarily be the areas which suit the older declining industries. If nothing were to be done this would leave wasted factors of production. Land would be wasted; and there would be empty industrial estates. Capital would be wasted; roads unused, factories closed down. People in these areas might be unemployed for months, even years, which not only means wasted labour but also hard times and a low standard of living for the families concerned.

The only body which can do anything to help is the Government. There are two alternatives for the Government: move the people who are unemployed to where there are jobs *or* move new industry to the unemployed people.

The first alternative can be rejected since not only would it be very impractical and perhaps cause emotional upset for families who would be split up, but it would also leave whole areas of the country wasted. Schools and hospitals would lie empty in, say, Newcastle but there would be overcrowding in, say, London.

The Government has therefore for many years now tried to encourage industry to move to areas of high unemployment. With the public sector this is easy since such industries are controlled by the Government. (I find that my income tax inspector works in Bootle although I live in Northants. I pay my car tax to Swansea along with my television licence and the National Giro Bank is in Bootle. These sites were chosen by the Government to provide employment.) The private sector industry, however, needs to be persuaded and the most effective method is to make areas of high unemployment financially attractive. Paying something towards the cost of moving and setting up a factory in areas of high unemployment will in the end save the Government money since they will not have to pay unemployment benefit to the people who now find work.

CASE STUDY

Nissan

In March 1984 the Japanese giant vehicle group Nissan announced that it was to build a car plant in Washington New Town, Sunderland. Initially this plant was to be a 'pilot' assembly plant producing kits imported from Japan. The site was chosen for several reasons:

- *size:* it was a large site (800 acres) which allowed for future expansion,
- *transport*: it was close to docks for importing the kits from Japan,
- *finance*: as an assisted area it qualified for British Government grants.

The plant opened in 1986 after an initial investment of £390 million and more than £100 million in British Government grants. Many in the UK motorcar trade were surprised at this generosity since by 1988 the Bluebird cars produced in Sunderland would count as British made and not be subject to the 11 per cent maximum market share voluntary quota agreement with the Japanese. In December 1987 Nissan agreed a further development plan at Sunderland with the government. It was announced that Nissan would be investing an additional £216 million to build a new small car to replace the Micra model at the Sunderland factory. This would mean an additional 1400 jobs at the plant and bring the total direct employment to 3500 by 1992 in one of the UK's worst unemployment blackspots. In the deal signed by Lord Young, Secretary of State for Trade and Industry, and Mr Takiashi Ishihara, Chairman of Nissan, the British Government agreed to provide a further £25 million financial assistance. The expansion could also create up to 3000 additional jobs with UK component suppliers since Nissan plan to spend £450 million a year on locally produced components. Within 18 months of starting production the new car will have 80 per cent local component content. Under this agreement Nissan is promising to export 60 per cent of the 100 000 cars to be produced at each year.

Financial assistance in assisted areas

Areas of very high unemployment are designated **assisted areas**, of which there are two types:

1 *Development areas*: areas of very high unemployment, e.g. Liverpool, Newcastle, Glasgow.

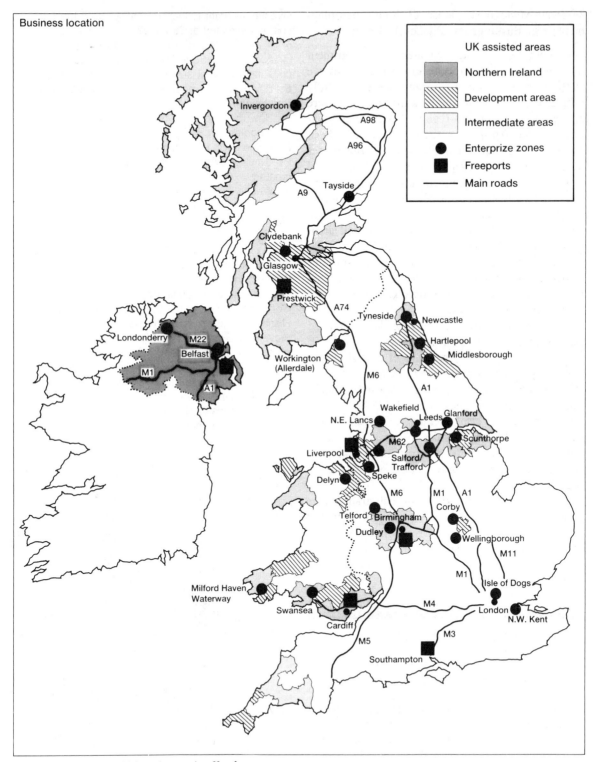

Fig 8.6   Areas for which assistance is offered

2 *Intermediate areas*: areas of high unemployment, e.g. Birmingham, Plymouth, Cardiff.

In both types of assisted area the government gives grants to firms to encourage them to move to these areas. A system of grants can successfully influence the choice of site by a firm and therefore create employment in a region of high unemployment. Since April 1988 these grants have been known as *regional selective assistance*. Businesses must satisfy the Department of Trade and Industry that the planned investment in the assisted area would not go ahead without government support. Small and medium sized firms (500 employees or less) operating in the assisted areas or urban development areas are also entitled to grants of up to two-thirds the cost of consultancy advice in six areas of management. (Medium sized firms not in these areas will only receive grants of up to half of such costs.)

Small firms (those employing less than 25 people) in development areas receive;
(*a*) *Investment grant*: 15 per cent of capital expenditure (up to a maximum of £15 000);
(*b*) *Innovation grant*: 50 per cent towards costs of innovations (up to a maximum of £25 000).
The government also operates a *contract preference scheme* where companies in the assisted areas are given preferential treatment if they tender for contracts to supply the government of nationalised industries.

In the past regional development grants have gone to large firms which many believe would proceed with new factories irrespective of government inducements. Today funds are directed towards small firms and overseas investors in Britain like Nissan.

Tasks

(You may need to use a calculator for some questions)

1 Find out the current average level of unemployment in the UK and the current local level of unemployment. Explain any differences.
2 Explain how the government policy of assisted areas aims to reduce regional unemployment.
3 Explain why the government does not give grants to the unemployed in 'blackspots' to help them to move to areas of high employment.
4 A small firm employing 20 people wishes to build and equip a new workshop in Glasgow. What size investment grant is the firm entitled to if the total cost is estimated at £80 000?
5 A medium sized firm employing 400 people located in Cardiff spends £12 000 on business consultancy. What size grant is the firm entitled to?
6 What reasons made Nissan choose Washington, Sunderland?
7 How many jobs did the original Nissan development create?
8 If this initial development cost the government £100 million, what was the cost per direct job created?
9 What will be the cost per direct job of the second phase of the Nissan development?
10 What indirect employment is likely from the Nissan development?
11 Lord Young said of the announcement, 'This is very good news for the North-East and the UK'. Why do you think he said this?
12 Mr Hal Miller, chairman of the House of Commons Motor Industry group, warned that Nissan's decision would herald a further Japanese move into Europe and put further pressure on British producers. What does Mr Miller mean by 'pressure'?
13 In 1986 44 per cent of new car registrations were British produced cars. How will the new Nissan plant effect these figures?
14 If the Nissan plant and the new small car are successful how might it effect employment in Oxford?

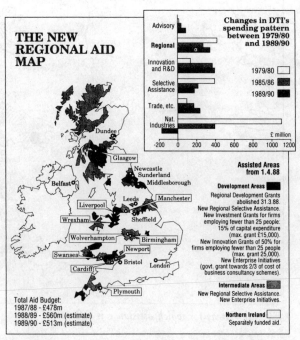

Fig 8.7

Agencies providing assistance

1 Training Agency (formerly MSC) offers expert advice and assistance on training needs and can help companies with recruitment of new personnel. The Training Commission also offers the **Enterprise Allowance** Scheme to those who have been unemployed for more than 13 weeks and who wish to start their own business. The scheme pays £40 per week for up to a year, thus providing a regular income until the new business is established.

2 European Community (EC)

(a) The European Investment Bank (EIB), a part of the EC, provides loans at very favourable rates of interest – sometimes three per cent less than normal rates – for up to half of the fixed capital cost of any project. Large loans (amounts over £4.25 m) are dealt with by the EIB direct and can be offered over 12 years. Smaller amounts (anything between £15 000 and £4.25 m) are organised through other organisations, like Investors in Industry (*see* below) on a local basis.

(b) The European Coal and Steel Community (ECSC) also grants loans for up to 50 per cent of the cost of a project for redundant coal or steel workers. The loans are normally offered over eight years with a 'grace period' of two years on the repayment of the principal (the amount borrowed). Also offered by ECSC are Coal Conversion Loans for companies wishing to convert from oil or gas to coal, anywhere in Britain.

3 Investors in Industry (3i)

3i provides companies of all sizes with long term funds through loans or equity capital to finance a range of projects including business start-ups, relocations and management buy-outs.

3i is also a major source of finance from EIB, ECSC and the Government Loan Guarantee Scheme, so that local industries can benefit. It is also keen to offer risk capital in new business ventures, especially high-technology projects.

4 British Technology Group (BTG)

A Government-sponsored body the BTG specialises in supporting projects related to new technology by offering long term finance for up to half the funds required. Interestingly, the BTG aims to recover its investment through a levy on sales resulting from the investment. Such a scheme involves both parties in a partnership approach to ensure that the project is successful.

5 Enterprise Zones

The Department of the Environment has established 25 Enterprise Zones throughout the UK. Their prime aim is to stimulate activity of private businesses and encourage them to relocate. The Enterprise Zones will last for ten years and offer a combination of incentives, including, for example, tax privileges, exemption from local authority rates (but not water rates), and the speeding up of administrative controls, like planning permission for company extensions.

Furthermore, for capital spending on the construction, extension or imporvement of industrial and commercial buildings there is an initial tax allowance of 100 per cent. If, therefore, a company extended an hotel in an enterprise zone at the cost of £100 000 the full sum could be used to reduce the amount of tax that the company may have to pay on its profits for that year. Alternatively, the initial allowance can be reduced in whichever form the owner chooses. For example, if 50 per cent is claimed initially (in the first year) them the company can claim the rest in allowances of 25 per cent for the next two years.

Each Enterprise Zone has a simplified planning scheme which allows certain types of development to take place without applications being necessary; only a development proposal is required. Most enterprise zones have a set target of about 14 days to process any proposals submitted.

Special arrangements for businesses within Enterprise Zones are regularly accepted, particularly with reference to services like gas, electricity, sewerage, telecommunications and roadworks.

6 Freeports There are six freeports in the UK: Belfast, Prestwick, Liverpool, Birmingham, Cardiff and Southamptom. The freeport offers freedom from VAT, Customs duty, and EEC levies and quotas. It is regulated by HM Customs and Excise, controlled by port police and patrolled by private security. Consequently it can boast one of the most secure business environments in Britain. This has led to reduced insurance premiums for some companies. A company importing fabrics from the Far East to be made into bed linen and hence exported to Europe and North America can perform all the tasks within the freeport and thus save on handling costs and time. In addition, all of them have direct access to motorway and rail networks.

7 Business parks The idea of business parks has been borrowed from the USA; they are sometimes known as 'science parks'. The key to their success is the **environment**. Buildings and offices are designed to a high standard, grounds are land-scaped (some even have golf courses) while leisure facilities for employees such as squash and tennis courts are considered necessary amenities. Location is all-important: sites are normally close to major conurbations and major communication networks.

Other than the Cambridge Science Park, a fine example of a Business Park is to be found at Heathrow. This is London's first business park. It is ideally situated, being close to Central London as well as motorway and air links. It is set in 100 acres of fully lanscaped grounds with a further 250 acres of lakes, parkland and an 18-hole golf course. There is also a wide range of sporting, banking, shopping and catering facilities.

SUMMARY EXERCISE

Answer *all* of the following questions in complete sentences as fully as possible.

1 For what products are the following areas famous:
    (*a*) Sheffield
    (*b*) Coventry/Midlands
    (*c*) Stoke-on-Trent
2 What areas are famous for these products:
    (*a*) Coal mining
    (*b*) Ship building
    (*c*) Textiles
3 The answer to questions **1** and **2** above give examples of industries which are carried out in just a few areas. These are called **concentrated** or **localised** industries. Can you think of one or two more examples?

4 The opposite to a concentrated industry is called a **dispersed** or **scattered industry**. These industries are carried out all over the country. Can you think of three examples?

5 Give an example of an industry which would need to be close to a good transport system and an example of an industry where this would not matter.

6 There are three types of industry which need to be close to their market. These are often called **market orientated** industries – give an example of each type.

7 A **weight-losing** industry such as pig iron manufacturing is usually located close to at least one of its raw materials. Can you explain why?

8 An industry may well continue producing in an area even though the reasons which made it move there in the first place have long since gone. This is called **industrial inertia**. Why does the industry remain there?

9 Take any one of your answers to question **2** and question **4** and explain why one industry is **concentrated** and the other is **scattered**.

10 Why, when trying to solve the problem of regional unemployment, does the Government not give grants to people to help them move to areas with employment?

ASSIGNMENTS

1 Describe clearly the location of a factory that you have studied giving at least four factors which influenced the choice of this site.

2 Why are some industries said to be **scattered** whilst others highly **localised** or **concentrated**? What problems do you think can arise for (*a*) the country and (*b*) the area from the concentration of some industries?

3 Describe how the Government is trying to cure the problem of regional unemployment.

9 International Trade and Payments

If you look at your family's weekly shopping to see where the goods were made or grown you will soon notice that a great deal of what we buy is not made in this country. Look at your school car park and you will see cars from Japan, Germany, Sweden and France as well as the UK.

The UK exports 29 per cent of all that is produced in a year and imports about the same value of goods. This chapter examines why countries trade with each other and how this benefits a country. It also looks at British trade in detail and asks how this trade is financed.

Why countries trade

Countries trade with other countries for a variety of reasons:

- There are goods which some countries cannot make or grow in commercial quantities. For example, the UK cannot grow citrus fruits.
- If a country produces far more of a product than the home market requires the industry might be able to enjoy economies of scale and so produce that product more efficiently and sell it at a lower price. For example, wheat from the USA.
- Some countries have a natural advantage in producing a product such as raw materials, climate etc, or they have acquired an advantage over time and now have an experienced labour force and special machines and equipment. This will mean that such countries can produce goods and services more cheaply than others. They therefore **specialise** in certain products. For example, Brazil and coffee or the UK and insurance.
- By importing goods which they *can* produce a country can enjoy greater choice and variety.

The people are able to benefit from research and development undertaken in different countries in such things as cars, televisions, new drugs, and even films and television.

Exercise

1 There are some goods the UK *cannot* produce in commercial quantities; citrus fruit for example. List ten examples of products which must be imported into this country.
2 List as many goods as you can that are produced in Britain of which a large percentage are exported.
3 Some countries have a natural advantage in producing goods and have specialised in producing them. Can you match these products with the following countries?

Kuwait	Sugar
New Zealand	Tea
Denmark	Oil
Australia	Bacon
Sri Lanka	Lamb
Mauritius	Butter

4 Give two further examples of countries which have specialised in the production of a product, stating the product *and* country.
5 List ten goods currently imported into this country in large numbers but which we could produce ourselves.

Specialisation in trade

In Chapter 2 we saw that people have different abilities, and likes and that the economy gains if people specialise in those jobs in which they have natural ability. The same applies to countries and the gain from specialisation and trade can be demonstrated very easily with a simple hypothetical example or model.

Model to Demonstrate the Gains from Specialisation and Trade

In this model it is assumed there are two islands close to each other. They both produce two crops, sugar and tea. To produce anything the factors of production – human, natural and man-made are needed. For the purpose of this exercise it is assumed that each island has the same amount of resources.

Before specialisation and trade each island devotes half of their resources to each crop with the following results:

Position before specialisation and trade	Sugar output ('000 tonnes per annum)	Tea output
Island A	500	50
Island B	300	200

If each island specialised in the product in which it has an advantage then it could devote all of its resources to this product and double production as follows:

Position after specialisation	Sugar output ('000 tonnes per annum)	Tea output
Island A	1000	–
Island B	–	400

If they were now to trade at a rate of exchange of one tonne of tea for five tonnes of sugar and Island A were to buy 100 000 tonnes from Island B it would 'cost' 500 000 tonnes of sugar:

Position after trade	Sugar consumption ('000 tonnes per annum)	Tea consumption
Island A	500 (1000)	100 (–)
Island B	500 (–)	300 (400)

Compare this with the original position without specialisation and it can be seen that both countries have gained from specialisation and trade. Island A has now gained 50 000 tonnes of tea per annum and Island B 200 000 tonnes of sugar and a further 100 000 tonnes of tea per annum. How much each country will gain depends upon the agreed rate of exchange.

Work through the above example but with an exchange rate of one tonne of tea to three tonnes of sugar. If Island A sells 300 000 tonnes of sugar, what is the gain to each country?

A country therefore can gain from specialisation and trade. In Chapter 8 you were asked to pick out countries which have, to a certain extent, specialised in a product. It is rare to find a country which is totally dependent upon one product. When people specialise there are dangers of boredom and the risk of unemployment. These are also problems for a country as the following case study shows.

ASSIGNMENT

To see just how much this country imports of a certain product, conduct a survey using the motor car industry. Make a note of the different cars in your staff car part or ask the pupils in your school what car(s) their families own. Produce a list which could then be converted into a pie chart. Remember your survey is very limited and could be distorted. A school in Dagenham might find very different results to one in Luton. Why? Think about your results and write a conclusion including your ideas on possible distortions.

CASE STUDY

Sweet and Sour

Mauritius, a member of the Commonwealth, is a small island in the Indian Ocean as you can see from the map. It is about 130 times smaller than the UK with a population of just 940 000. Although the island was known of before the 10th century it was not inhabited until Dutch explorers settled on the island in 1598.

During the 18th century it was occupied by the French who used it as a staging post for their ships on route to attack the British in India. The British captured the island in 1810 and it remained under British control until independence in 1968.

Mauritius is a volcanic island, or rather what is left after volcanic activity. It is shaped like a saucer with plains in the north and a plateau in the centre of the island bordered by mountains (all that remains of

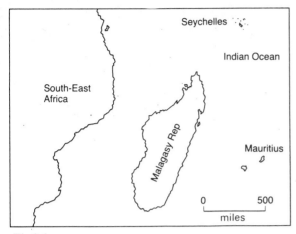

Fig 9.1

the volcanoes). The soil is composed of finely ground igneous rock (produced from the volcanoes), fairly fertile although rocky. The climate, known to geographers as 'maritime subtropical', has two seasons. Between May and October it is cool (25 °C). For the rest of the year it remains hot (31 °C). Rainfall is high averaging from 900 millimetres per annum on the west coast to over 1500 millimetres per annum on the south coast. The air is humid with strong winds blowing most of the year and with the risk of cyclones during the hot periods. The British changed the nature of the country from being a staging post to a plantation colony. Using slave labour from East Africa they built sugar cane plantations to take advantage of the climate. With the liberation of slaves in 1835 Indian workers were employed on these plantations. Today Mauritius is an example of a **monoculture economy**. The island has specialised to a great extent in the production of just one product – sugar – and in spite of efforts since the war to change things, the country is still dependent upon this one cash crop as can be seen from the chart opposite.

Mauritius remains poor, however, with income per head being only £645 as compared to £4851 in the UK. A country dominated by one product finds that the fortunes of that product determine the fortunes of the whole economy. If sugar prices are as high as they were during 1970–76, Mauritius prospers but if the world price of sugar falls or if the crops are ruined by cyclones as they were in 1980 then the whole country suffers. Much of the sugar is now refined from beet which can be grown in more temperate climates like Britain. Also many other countries grow the cane. Mauritius is forced therefore to take whatever price it can get. Being a

member of the Commonwealth used to mean special agreements with Britain to buy sugar – now the country has an agreement with the EC which buys 500 000 tonnes a year at a fixed price (above world prices). Even so, the income from sugar has not risen as quickly as the prices of essential imports like oil. This has led to major problems as you can see:

Mauritius trade 1982

	$ million
Exports	363.3
Imports	393.1
Trade balance	−29.8

A typical year was 1982. The country bought more from abroad than it was able to sell. This meant they were forced to borrow from the International Monetary Fund (IMF).

The people of Mauritius are only too well aware of the problems and have tried to find a solution to the problem. They have tried to diversify (introduce new and different industries). Some have aimed at reducing imports. Vegetables are planted between the rows of sugar cane and in this way the island can produce 70 per cent of their requirements. Also brewing, plastics, paint and packaging industries have been formed. The residue left after the sugar cane has been milled, (called bagasse), is already used to produce half of the electricity for the island. A further new power station was opened in 1984.

Tourism has been encouraged also, with the building of a new airport and the Government has introduced an export processing zone, with tax incentives for new exporting industries such as knitwear, diamond cutting and electronics.

Being dependent upon one crop left Mauritius extremely vulnerable. If this dependence can be reduced changes in the world price of sugar or bad weather will not affect the economy so badly.

For the reasons shown in the Mauritius example and others, countries do not specialise in the production of just one product but a range of products.

It would be ridiculous for any country to concentrate, say, on the production of housing bricks since however cheaply they could be produced the cost of transporting them to another country would make them far too expensive. For this reason most countries produce bricks.

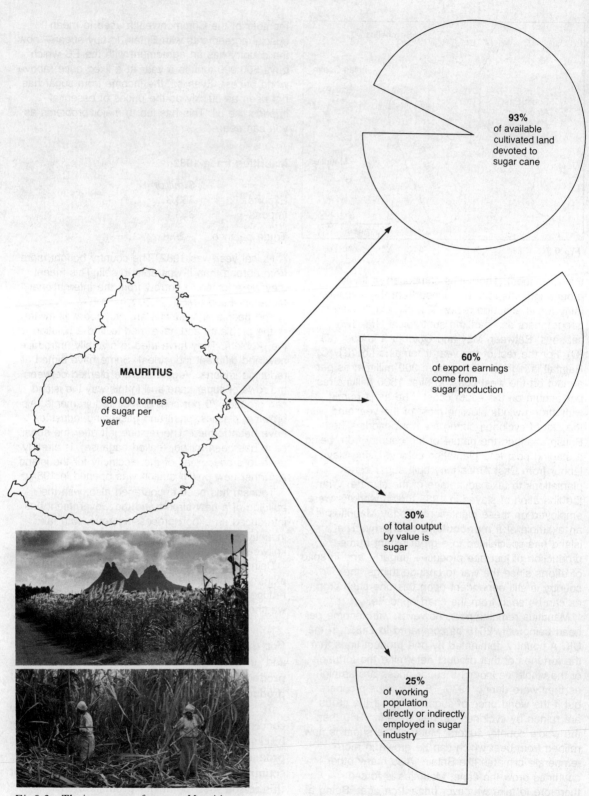

MAURITIUS

680 000 tonnes
of sugar per
year

93%
of available
cultivated land
devoted to
sugar cane

60%
of export earnings
come from
sugar production

30%
of total output
by value is
sugar

25%
of working
population
directly or indirectly
employed in sugar
industry

Fig 9.2   The importance of sugar to Mauritius

A country like the UK can produce a limited quantity of agricultural products very efficiently. The UK could not specialise in these products because it does not have the land available to do so. It might be unwise also for a country to become too dependent upon supplies of vital goods from a foreign country in case of war or political disagreement. (South Africa for example distils oil for petrol from coal in a very expensive process because other countries will not sell her crude oil.)

We have learnt why countries trade with each other and also why they try not to overspecialise and the consequences of this, but some countries try to deliberately reduce or even stop some trade by creating barriers.

Exercise

1   What natural resources first encouraged the British to turn Mauritius into a sugar plantation economy?
2   What agreement about sugar exports has Mauritius with the EC and what do you think would happen to the Mauritius economy if this agreement was to be discontinued?
3   If the Mauritius people were able to produce more sugar would they necessarily prosper? If not, why?
4   What disadvantages from specialisation in one product does this example illustrate?
5   What disadvantages would you find from living in a country dependent upon one product?

The barriers to trade

There are several ways in which a country can reduce or even prevent trade with other countries:
Tariffs   One way of reducing imports is to impose a tax or tariff on imported goods as they enter the country. The importer has to pay the tax before he can sell the goods and therefore is likely to charge more for the goods in order to reclaim the tax. The imported goods therefore are offered to the public at a higher price and this hopefully deters them from buying them. As a member of the EC the UK has no tariffs between itself and all of the other members but it has a small tariff,

as do the other member countries, which applies to all other non-EEC countries. This **common external tariff** as it is called at present stands at 6.4 per cent. (Source: *Europe without frontiers. EC periodical 4 1987.*)

Subsidies   The opposite way of reducing imports to tariffs would be to try and make home-produced goods cheaper. To do this a country can give a grant to a home industry so that the goods produced by that industry cost less which encourages people to buy them in preference to dearer imports. This grant is called a **subsidy**. Many would argue that help given to British Leyland and the British ship building industry in recent years would fall into this category.

Quota agreements   By this method the price of imports is not altered but the quantity of imports is limited to a certain number per year or month.

Other methods   Some goods are considered to be dangerous like drugs and these are strictly controlled and in some circumstances trade with another country is made illegal. This is called an **embargo** and is used as a political weapon.

CASE STUDY

Japanese Video Tape Recorders (VTRs)

In February 1983 Japan agreed to restrict the number of VTRs exported to the EC. At that time Japanese VTRs were being produced and sold at lower prices than European VTRs. For this reason European manufacturers were operating at below their full capacity. (1.2 million units per annum instead of 1.4 million.) The Japanese agreed to limit video exports to the EC to 4.55 million units in 1983 and to charge higher European prices on those sets. The reason behind this agreement was to allow the three European manufacturers of VTRs, Grundig, Philips and Thopson-Brandt, an opportunity to increase production so that they could obtain the economies of scale enjoyed by their Japanese competitors, and as a result reduce their prices to compete on an equal footing with the larger Japanese companies. This seemed unlikely however, since the total estimated market for VTRs in 1983 was thought to be well below five million. Also several Japanese companies had assembly plants in Europe which received VTRs in kits from Japan and then assembled them in Europe allowing them to stamp 'made in EC' on them. Since these plants put another 600 000 sets a year on the market there seems little room for a European manufacturer anyway. The same agreement also limited the number of large colour television tubes Japan would export to the EC in 1983 to 900 000. This again might at first have looked like a good thing for EC industries but within three months it had caused problems. Many firms, including British firms such as Thorn-EMI rely upon Japanese large tubes as their only source of supply. Faced with this restriction they announced the scrapping of expansion plans!

Exercise

1 What type of trade restriction does this case study illustrate?
2 What argument was used to justify it?
3 Why was it unlikely to help EC industry?
4 How would it have been possible to make sure it helped EC industry?
5 Why did the restriction of colour tubes stop planned expansion in the UK?

Why countries try to restrict trade

Many reasons are given for the reduction of trade by the imposition of barriers. Here are a few:

1 **To protect a young, growing industry** As seen in the case study a small firm that has just started production cannot enjoy the same economies of scale as an older, larger, well established firm in another country. For this reason the young firm will need to charge higher prices. If there is a cheaper foreign alternative people will choose it and the firm will never survive. If the cheaper foreign alternatives are kept artificially expensive while the smaller firm grows then it will be able to compete fairly.

2 **To allow an old, declining industry to do so slowly** A country may well be flooded by cheap foreign goods which will lead to the collapse of a traditional industry. This will cause unemployment. To allow time for workers to find new jobs the flood of cheap foreign goods could be slowed by some form of restriction.

3 **To prevent dumping** *Dumping* is a term used to describe foreign goods sold in a country at below the cost of production. Here a home industry could be ruined by ridiculously cheap imports and they can be prevented by some form of restriction.

4 **To help with a temporary balance of payments problem** Sometimes a country will import too much, more than they can really afford (as we saw with Mauritius). Restrictions on imports can help to reduce these imports so long as other countries do not retaliate and restrict their imports!

International trade and the United Kingdom

International trade is important to the UK, with exports and imports accounting for nearly 30 per cent GDP at market prices.

The composition of the United Kingdom's imports and exports

As we have discussed, a country will specialise in producing those goods in which it has an advantage and will import those things it lacks or cannot produce commercially. In most cases it should be possible to predict the composition of the imports and exports of any country.

Exercise

Copy out the following table and complete for the United Kingdom.

	Those resources we have in abundance	Those resources we lack
Natural	coal	copper
Human	large skilled	large cheap unskilled
Man-made	factories	computer controlled machines

From the above exercise you ought to reach some conclusions about imports and exports to and from the UK.

Table 9.1 Commodity Composition of Trade 1986[a]

	Exports (f.o.b.)		Imports (c.i.f.)[b]	
	£ million	per cent	£ million	per cent
Non-manufactures	**16 208**	**22.2**	**21 349**	**24.8**
Food, beverages and tobacco	5 478	7.5	10 067	11.7
Basic materials	2 046	2.8	4 988	5.8
Fuels	8 683	11.9	6 294	7.3
Manufactured goods	**54 595**	**74.8**	**62 833**	**73.0**
Semi-manufactures	20 671	28.3	22 673	26.3
of which: Chemicals	9 692	13.3	7 346	8.5
Textiles	1 712	2.3	3 163	3.7
Iron and steel	1 867	2.6	1 796	2.1
Non-ferrous metals	1 552	2.1	1 836	2.1
Metal manufactures	1 465	2.0	1 644	1.9
Other	4 383	6.0	6 888	8.0
Finished manufactures	33 925	46.5	40 160	46.7
of which: Machinery	18 314	25.1	19 395	22.5
Road vehicles	3 954	5.4	7940	9.2
Clothing and footwear	1 396	1.9	3 122	3.6
Scientific instruments and photographic apparatus	3 128	4.3	3 078	3.6
Other	7 133	9.8	6 625	7.7
Miscellaneous	**2 206**	**3.0**	**1 884**	**2.2**
Total	**73 009**	**100.0**	**86.066**	**100.0**

Source: *Monthly Review of External Trade Statistics.*[a] On an overseas trade statistics basis. (This differs from a balance of payments basis because, for imports, it includes the cost of insurance and freight and, for both exports and imports, includes returned goods.)[b]c.i.f. = cost, insurance and freight, that is, including shipping, insurance and other expenses incurred in the delivery of goods as far as their place of importation in Britain. Some of these expenses represent earnings by companies resident in Britain and are more appropriate to the invisibles account.
Note: Differences between totals and the sums of their component parts are due to rounding.

The composition of UK trade is shown in Table 9.1.

Exports

As I am sure you predicted the UK exports manufactured goods, chemicals, machinery and vehicles (being most important). Looking at the figures for just one year, however, does not let us see the whole picture. Certainly, since the industrial revolution the UK has imported raw material and turned them into manufactured goods which have been exported but the type of manufactured good has changed considerably. Just before World War II, for example, textiles represented nearly 25 per cent of all UK exports; today as you can see it is less than three per cent. Iron and steel is another product which has fallen as a percent-

age of our exports. These have been replaced by machinery and the other high technology products mentioned above. A further change can be seen in the non-manufactures. Fuels have increased to 13.6 per cent of exports because of the growing importance of North Sea oil. The UK still imports crude oil but today in value terms is a net exporter of oil. In the past the UK exported coal.

Imports

This is a little more difficult to predict. Looking at what this country has and has not got one would expect imports in the main to be raw materials and foodstuffs. This is true up to a point. Over one third of UK imports are in this category but surprisingly the rest are manufactured goods, products which could be manufactured here. Since the war, as the country has grown in prosperity people have not wanted more and more food, but better manufactured goods with more choice and greater variety. This has meant that much of the growth in world trade has been in manufactured goods.

Just as there are plenty of British motorists who believe that you cannot buy a better car than a Renault – there are just as many French motorists who love to drive a BL Metro. The UK still imports a lot of foodstuffs (although British farms have become more efficient) but the growth of imports of manufactures has been very dramatic and leaves food as a smaller percentage of the total than before the war.

Invisible trade

The trade considered latterly is known as **visible trade** – that is trade which can actually be seen (goods being loaded onto and off ships and planes etc). The UK earns much foreign currency by selling services to other countries. We call this **invisible trade**. Gross earnings from invisible exports are usually equal to about half the earn-ings from visible exports but, unlike visible trade, the UK always earns a surplus on invisible trade.

Table 9.2 divides invisible trade into three groups. **Services; interest, profits and dividends** and **transfers**.

The **services** are a large positive item and are just as they sound. For example, if a German flies to America on a British Airways Concorde it appears as a positive earning under civil aviation. If, on the other hand, a British firm imports some grain on a Greek ship the freight charge would appear as a negative payment under sea transport. The largest earning is that of financial and other services carried out by our banks and insurance companies in the City of London. General government refers to the costs of keeping embassy staff abroad. Transfers refer to direct transfers of money abroad. For individuals such transfers might arise due to emigration but for the Government they include membership fees paid to such organisations as the EC and aid given to under-developed countries. **Interest, profits and dividends** refers to the earnings from money lent to foreign firms or reward for owning foreign shares. In 1984 it was a large positive item.

Table 9.2 Britain's Invisible Transactions 1984

£ million

	Credits	Debits	Balance
Services	**21 327**	**17 342**	**+3 985**
Private sector and public corporations			
of which. Sea transport	20 854	15 946	+4 908
Civil aviation	3 235	4 386	−1 151
Travel	3 016	2 547	+469
Financial and other services	4 169	4 617	−448
General government	10 434	4 396	
	473	1 396	+6 038
			−923
Interest, profits and dividends	**50 744**	**47 440**	**+3 304**
Private sector and public corporations	50 128	45 542	+4 586
General government	616	1 898	−1 282
Transfers	**3 808**	**6 061**	**−2 253**
Private	1 438	1 601	−163
General government	2 370	4 460	−2 090
Total invisible transactions	**75 879**	**70 843**	**+5 036**

Source: *United Kingdom Balance of Payments 1985 Edition.*

The direction of UK trade

It is not surprising that the chief market for UK exports and source of imports are her trading partners in the EC. Over half of UK exports and well over half of her imports are with European countries. This has not always been the case. Just before World War II, European countries only accounted for about 25 per cent of UK trade. Nearly half was with Commonwealth countries, that is countries which in the past had formed the British Empire but now, although retaining links with the UK have their independence, countries such as Australia, New Zealand as well as India and many developing countries. The reasons for this change in the direction of UK trade and the relative importance of these different trading partners has already been seen. It is due to the growth in the post-war period of trade in manufactured goods. Since the war the developed countries have traded in finished manufactured goods and semi-manufactures and although the UK still purchases

raw materials from developing countries and of course manufactured goods from countries like Hong Kong and Singapore, the main growth in trade has been with European countries like Germany, which is now the most important exporter to this country with over a 10 per cent share. North America (which includes Canada) is still an important market for the UK and supplies important imports such as cereals, tobacco and metal ore as well as modern machinery like computer technology.

The pie chart on page 116 singles out the oil exporting countries. These developing countries, like Kuwait, Saudi Arabia, Nigeria and Libya, became important during the early 1970s when they increased the price of oil rapidly. For several years this meant that since the UK had no oil at that time, she had to purchase the same quantity of oil at these higher prices. This meant the UK imported far more (from these countries) than she exported to them and now with North Sea oil and export drives to these countries the chart shows that the UK exports more to these countries than she imports in oil from them.

Table 9.3 Britain's Main Markets and Suppliers 1986[a]

	Value (£ million)	Share (per cent)
Main markets		
United States	10 380	14.2
Federal Republic of Germany	8 542	11.7
France	6 210	8.5
Netherlands	5 443	7.5
Belgium/Luxembourg	3 833	5.3
Irish Republic	3 558	4.9
Italy	3 472	4.8
Sweden	2 308	3.2
Spain	1 905	2.6
Canada	1 698	2.3
Main suppliers		
Federal Republic of Germany	14 139	16.4
United States	8 468	9.8
France	7 349	8.5
Netherlands	6 616	7.7
Japan	4 933	5.7
Italy	4 658	5.4
Belgium/Luxembourg	4 084	4.7
Norway	3 265	3.8
Irish Republic	3 054	3.5
Switzerland	2 989	3.5

Source: *Monthly Review of External Trade Statistics*
[a] On an overseas trade statistics basis. Exports are f.o.b.; imports c.i.f.

The balance of payments:

The balance of payments is a record, kept by the Government, of all movements of money into and out of this country during the course of a year. Exporters and importers have to provide the Department of Customs and Excise with information.

Note: Importers will report the cost of imported items to them – that is, including transport and insurance costs. When such figures are quoted they have c.i.f. after them to indicate they include credit, insurance and freight. Exporters on the other hand will report the value of exports which they receive – not including these other items. Figures quoted in this manner have f.o.b. after them (free on board). Clearly free on board figures are those we wish to use.

There are two money flows between countries: that which finances trade; and that which finances investment. These two different movements are treated separately in the balance of payments accounts.

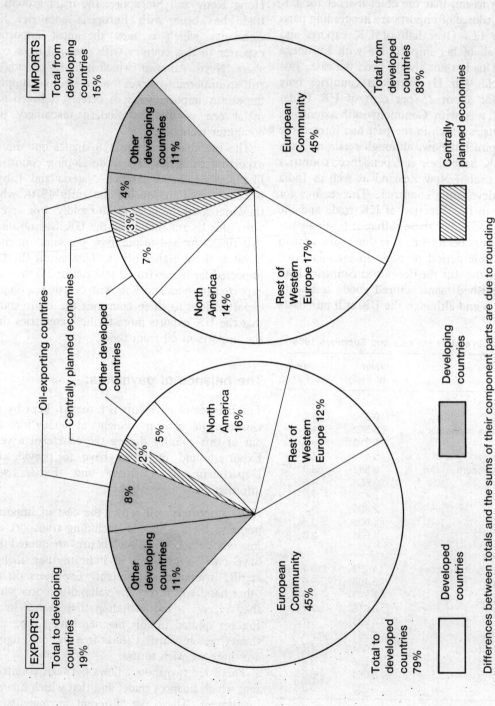

IMPORTS

Total from developing countries 15%

Total from developed countries 83%

Other developing countries 11%

4%

3%

7%

North America 14%

Rest of Western Europe 17%

European Community 45%

Centrally planned economies

Oil-exporting countries

Centrally planned economies

Other developed countries

EXPORTS

Total to developing countries 19%

North America 16%

5%

2%

8%

Other developing countries 11%

Rest of Western Europe 12%

European Community 45%

Total to developed countries 79%

Developed countries

Developing countries

Differences between totals and the sums of their component parts are due to rounding

Fig 9.3   (Source: Monthly Review of External Trade Statistics)

Current account

This shows all monetary movements arising from trade. This is usually split into visible and invisible trade.

Visible exports – visible imports = Balance of trade.

Although the Balance of Trade was positive in 1980, 81 and 82 it has since then been negative. Thus:

Invisible exports – invisible imports = invisible balance

The invisible balance is always large and positive. The UK over the last few years has imported **goods** to a greater value then it has managed to export but, has exported **services** to a greater value than it has imported.

When these two balances are added together the **current account balance** is achieved. It is this balance, when negative, to which the media refer when they speak of a balance of payments deficit. Technically, as you will see, the balance of payments accounts always balance – a balance of payments deficit cannot exist but a current account deficit can and frequently does in the UK. It can be seen that in the years 1983, 1984 and

1985 the invisible balance was large enough to leave the current balance positive. In 1987, however, the current account balance was −£1560 m!

Capital account

As mentioned above money will flow between countries for reasons other than to finance trade. Private individuals and companies buy shares in foreign companies for example and governments lend to each other. These are known as **capital flows**. Each year the total capital flows into the UK are taken away from the capital flows from the UK and the Balance of investment and other capital flows in calculated. As you can see; since 1980 this has been large and negative. It must be noted that this is not a bad thing since some of these flows will bring invisible earnings into the country in the future.

At the bottom of the table is the Balancing Item. This is the difference between the information collected from importers and exporters and that recorded by the Bank of England. In 1984 the Bank of England recorded that £1040 m more entered the country than had been recorded so it was added on in the Balancing Item.

Table 9.4 Britain's Balance of Payments 1980–84

£ *million*

	1980	1981	1982	1983	1984	1985
Current account						
Visible trade balance	+1 361	+3 360	+2 331	−835	−4 101	−2 068
Invisible transactions balance	+1 739	+3 168	+2 332	+4 003	+5 036	+5 831
Current balance	+3 100	+6 528	+4 663	+3 168	+935	+3 763
Investment and other capital transactions	−1 503	−6 972	−3 199	−4 865	−3 291	−3 207
Allocation of Special Drawing Rights	+180	+158	−	−	−	−
Net transactions with overseas monetary authorities	−140	−145	−163	−36	−	−
Foreign currency borrowing (net)	−941	−1 587	+26	+249	+408	+959
Official reserves[a]	−291	+2 419	+1421	+607	+908	−1 758
Balancing item	−405	−401	−2 748	+877	+1 040	+243

Source: *United Kingdom Balance of Payments 1986 Edition.*
[a] Drawings on (+)/additions to (−).

Looking at the figures for 1985:

Balance of trade ....   £
                                    −2 068 m

Invisible balance .... +5 831 m

Current account
Balance .... +3 763 m
                                           ADD
Investment & Other
Capital flows .... −3 207 m
                                           ADD
Balancing Item .... +243 m

Total currency flow   +799 m
(Known as the Balance for
official financing)

In 1985 £799 m more entered the UK than left. The final entries in the Balance of Payments account show what was done with the surplus funds (as in this case) or where the funds came from. Surplus funds can either be added to the Country's reserves (shown in Table 9.3) or used to pay back past borrowing. A negative balance can be financed through additional borrowing from foreign countries and organisations such as the IMF or by reducing or drawing on the Country's reserves.

In 1985 we have seen above that a £799 surplus had to be dealt with. In fact, an additional £959 was borrowed which allowed reserves to increase by £1758.

It can therefore be seen that the Balance of Payments will always balance. A total currency flow out of a country will be financed by borrowing and drawings on official reserves and a total currecy flow into the country will be used to pay back borrowing and build up official reserves.

As we can see it would be very surprising for the value of a country's imports to be exactly the same as exports, that is for the current account balance to be zero. After all, decisions to import are made by a different set of people than decisions to export. A country cannot keep on importing more than it is able to export. To do so would require heavy borrowing from organisations like the IMF. We saw in our case study that Mauritius was in this position. When a country has a series of current account deficits it is often referred to as

Exercise

For each of the following, state where on the UK balance of payments statistics they would occur and whether they are visible or invisilbe, export or import, current account or capital transfer etc. For example, if a German flies to America on British Airways Concorde this would be:

   Invisible Export – on the current account

Try to categorise the following:
(a) A French farmer buys a Ford tractor manufactured at the British Basildon plant.
(b) The UK Government repays a loan to the IMF.
(c) The British Post Office pension fund managers buy shares in an American computer manufacturing firm.
(d) British troops, stationed in Germany, take their wives out for a meal in a German restaurant.
(e) A friend's father purchases a brand new Japanese motor car.
(f) An Arab businessman buys all of the shares in an ailing British company.
(g) An American airline company insures a new Boeing 747 with British insurance underwriters based at Lloyds in London.
(h) The UK Government makes its contribution to the EEC funds for the year.
(i) British Leyland purchase German computer controlled 'robot' welding machinery.
(j) British Leyland send a number of technicians to Germany to learn how to service the robots they have just bought.

a **balance of payments deficit** or **balance of payments crisis**. To try and cure such problems a Government might undertake a number of measures:

Deflation If the Government increases taxes and makes it difficult for people to borrow they will be forced to reduce their spending. This will mean less imports and more goods produced at home available for export. The problem with such measures is that if they last for any length of time they tend to increase unemployment.

Trade barriers A Government could increase tariffs to reduce imports and as we have already seen encourage exports by the use of subsidies. As the UK is signatory to the *General Agreement on Tariffs and Trade* which aims to reduce trade barriers, we could not use such policies for long, although in the short run other members of GATT might be sympathetic.

Currency deflation The example below shows that the price of imports and exports depends upon the value of a nation's currency. When you go abroad you have to buy foreign currency to spend in the shops. If a UK importer wishes to buy Japanese cars he must pay for them in yen which have to be bought. If the value of a country's currency falls, foreign currency will cost more and the price of imports rise. Since a foreigner can now purchase more of that country's currency for the same amount our exports appear to cost less.

In this simplified example the prices in the USA and UK of a product produced in the UK – whisky – and a product produced in the USA – wheat are analysed. It is assumed that a case of whisky costs £48 in the UK where it is manufactured and a tonne of wheat costs $100 in the USA where it is grown. Ignoring *all* taxes, import

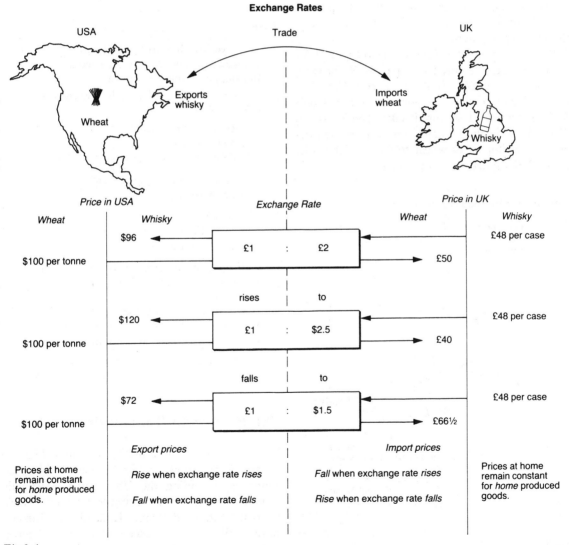

Fig 9.4

duties and transport costs the effects of changes in the exchange rate on prices of these two goods can be shown.

If the exchange rate were £1 to $2, then to buy a case of whisky an American would need to convert dollars into pounds. Since it cost $2 for every £1 it will cost $96 to buy £48. On the other hand for the British importer of wheat he will need $100 which will cost £50.

If the exchange rate were to rise to £1 to $2.50, the American has to pay $2.50 for every £1. So to buy £48 would now cost $120. However, the British importer of wheat receives $2.50 for every £1 so now it only takes £40 to buy $100. A rise in the exchange rate therefore causes the price of the UK import of wheat to fall but the price of the UK export to rise.

If the exchange rate were to fall to £1 to $1.50, then the American only has to pay $1.50 for every £1. So to buy £48 would now cost $72. The British importer of wheat however, receives only $1.50 for every £1 so now it takes £66.50 to buy $100. A fall in the exchange rate causes the price of the UK import of wheat to rise but the price of the UK export – whisky – to fall.

Currency deflation and a current account deficit

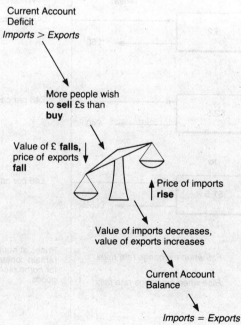

Fig 9.5

Whether or not a fall in the value of a currency will reduce a deficit on the current account of the balance of payments will depend very much upon how sensitive consumers are to changes in the price of that country's imports and exports.

In the past exchange rates have been fixed but now they are allowed to fluctuate on the exchange markets. If people want to hold a currency its price will rise. This solution is to a certain extent automatic since a deficit on the current account of the balance of payments would mean that less people required that currency than wanted to sell it. The price or exchange rate would tend to fall therefore and exports would become cheaper.

Exercise

1   Three British tourists travel abroad for their holidays. One goes to France, a second to Holland and a third to Norway.

A three course meal costs the following in each country:

45 Guilders (in Holland)
96 Francs (in France)
110 Kroner (in Norway)

Who is buying the cheapest meal if the exchange rates are as follows?

£1 to 4.5 Guilder
£1 to 12 Franc
£1 to 11 Kroner

2   If the exchange rate for the French Franc were to fall to £1 to 10 Francs would your answer be the same?
3   Under which heading on the UK balance of payments would meals bought abroad by tourists from this country appear?

The European Community (EC)

The European Community (or Common Market) is an organisation to which many European countries, including the UK belong. Originally it was a group of six countries: France, West Germany, Italy, Belgium, Holland and Luxemburg. Following the success of an earlier agreement between these countries on the price and output of coal and steel they negotiated the terms of a far more comprehensive agreement called the **Treaty of Rome** which they all signed in March 1957. This established the EC which started to operate from 1 January 1958. It is an organisation of cooperation with regard to trade between the member nations. Within 10 years of establishment all tariffs and other barriers to trade between member countries had been removed and a common external tariff of 9.3 per cent (later reduced to 6.4 per cent) had been established around them all. Any good arriving from a non-member country faces this common external tariff but any goods bought and sold between member countries do not. This should encourage trade and growth between member countries.

From the very beginning the EC was far more than the customs union just described. The six countries meet regularly to discuss economic and social problems they share and to come to agreement upon how to jointly solve them. They have, therefore, common policies on agriculture, transport, regional development, energy and foreign trade.

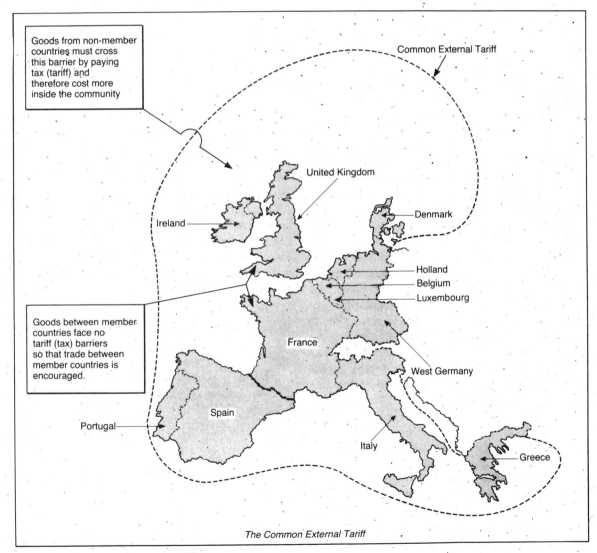

Goods from non-member countries must cross this barrier by paying tax (tariff) and therefore cost more inside the community

Common External Tariff

United Kingdom

Denmark

Ireland

Holland
Belgium
Luxembourg

Goods between member countries face no tariff (tax) barriers so that trade between member countries is encouraged.

France

West Germany

Spain

Portugal

Italy

Greece

The Common External Tariff

Fig 9.6   The common external tariff

The organisation has its own administrative centre called the European Commission which employs over 10 000 civil servants to help put these common policies into practice. Each member country contributes money to a common fund which the Commission spends on these common policies. The members aim to allow a free movement not only of goods and services between themselves but also the free movement of people who wish to work in other member countries and entrepreneurs who wish to establish businesses in other member countries.

At first the UK did not wish to belong to the EC since much of her trade was with the Commonwealth – countries like Australia from whom we bought butter and New Zealand from whom we bought lamb. We had special agreements with these countries dating back to the 1930s called the **Commonwealth Preferential Trading Agreements** where the UK guaranteed not to prevent imports from the Commonwealth by use of barriers like tariffs. During the 1960s the UK made a similar agreement, to reduce certain tariffs, with a further eight European countries to create the **European Free Trade Area**. This was purely a trading arrangement which left member countries free to retain their own existing additional agreements with non-member countries.

During this period UK trade developed far more with European countries many of whom were members of the EC. Also the original six members of the EC were growing faster than the UK and had less inflation and unemployment so that many people in the UK felt that we had made a mistake in not joining. So, after one unsuccessful attempt in 1962 the UK became a full member of the EC on 1 January 1973 together with Ireland and Denmark.

Our membership of the EC meant many changes. To be a member we agreed to accept all of the common policies and put them into practice. The major one was the **Common Agricultural Policy (CAP)** which was a very different system to ours. Until we joined the prices of agricultural produce were kept low since we imported so much from the Commonwealth. To help UK farmers the Government gave them a grant to bring the price they received up to a price it was

agreed they need to stay in business. Under CAP, higher prices are maintained for the European farmer by placing tariffs on cheaper imported foodstuffs and buying excess production from the Community funds. You may have heard of the 'butter mountain' which refers to butter bought by the Community in order to keep prices high. (Some has been sold cheaply to Eastern European countries.)

The Common Agricultural Policy has been very successful; it has encouraged farmers to produce more and more food. The purchase and storage of excess production has, however, taken an increasingly large proportion of the EC budget – and today uses two-thirds of the EC's £30 million budget. This has annoyed many people in the UK which is not an agricultural nation and contributes more to the EC funds than it receives in EC payments. After negotiations these contributions have now been reduced.

At a summit in February 1988, the EC Council of Ministers decided to put a stop to excessive agricultural spending. Limits are now put on *all* agricultural output and if farmers exceed these ceilings it results in automatic cuts in the guaranteed prices paid to farmers. In August 1988 the first of these cuts was imposed – a 10% reduction in vegetable prices was announced following a vegetable harvest which exceed the ceiling by 20 per cent.

The Treaty of Rome had a vision of a united europe:

'Resolve to ensure economic and social progress of their countries by common action to eliminate the barriers which divide europe.'
but 30 years after the original six countries signed this historic document, many barriers still existed. The removal of customs barriers did not produce a single market. For this reason, in 1985 the Council of Ministers asked the Commission to put forward concrete proposals to achieve a single market in Europe by 1992. These proposals are currently being carried out in a systematic way so that by 1992 there will be a single European market:

"an area without internal frontiers in which the free movement of goods, persons, services and capital is ensured . . . ."

The programme aims to remove three types of barrier:

1 physical barriers – customs barriers, passport controls etc
2 technical barriers – different product regulations and standards, safety standards, health and environmental standards and standards of consumer protection etc
3 fiscal barriers – different rates of VAT and duties. (it is proposed these will not be collected in the present time consuming manner which holds up trade but will still be collected!)

Since the UK became a full member the community has grown to include Greece, Spain and Portugal and now has 12 member countries.

In 1979 the **European Parliament** became the first internationally elected body. It sounds very grand but has limited powers.

The European Parliament can dismiss the Commission with a two thirds majority. It can also reject the Community Budget (its spending plans for the coming year) as well as being consulted in the process of Community law-making. As you can see above, however, the most important decision-making body is the **Council of Ministers.**

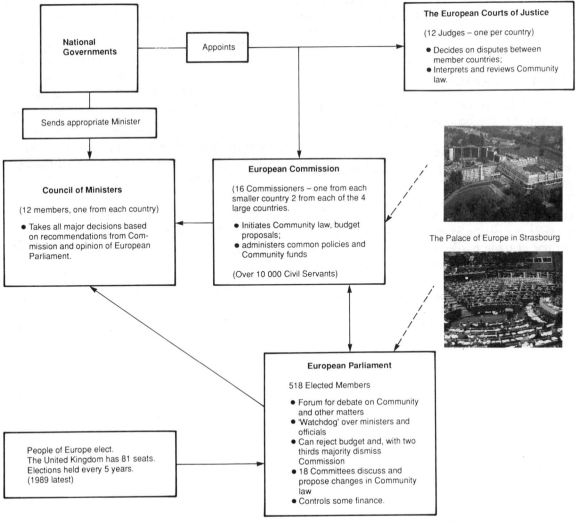

The Palace of Europe in Strasbourg

Fig 9.7

This is where the appropriate Minister from each member country's Government meets to agree policy put forward by the Commission. The **Commission** is run by 16 Commissioners, one from each of the smaller countries and two from the four larger countries (including the UK).

This is the main administrative body for the EC. The 10 000 civil servants who work for the Commission not only have the task of putting into practice all of the agreed Community policies but are also responsible for suggesting new laws and budget proposals each year. The Commission consults with the European Parliamentry Committees who scrutinise proposed Community law and suggest alterations and improvements.

Each member country appoints a Judge to sit on the **European Court of Justice** to interpret Community law and settle disputes between member countries.

SUMMARY EXERCISE

1 The UK depends upon international trade. Can you list four benefits we gain as a country by such trade?

2 Give three reasons why countries do not specialise totally in the production of just one product.

3 Name three types of **barriers to trade** currently used by the UK.

4 Give one reason given by countries to justify the use of **trade barriers**.

5 What is the difference between **visible** and **invisible** trade?

6 Give an example of an **invisible import** that you or your family might undertake.

7 Which two countries joined the EC with the UK in 1973?

8 The UK often has a **balance of trade deficit**. What is meant by this statement?

9 Which body takes the major decisions in the EC?

10 Give one power that the European Parliament has.

ASSIGNMENTS

1 'It is important for Britain to trade with other countries.'

  (a) By mentioning at least two of the advantages of international trade show why the statement is true.

  'In spite of these advantages Governments still set up barriers which reduce or even prevent trade.'

  (b) Take three of these barriers and say what each one is called and state why and how they reduce or prevent international trade in each case.

2 Many people own a foreign car; perhaps you own or will soon own a foreign motor bike. Both are examples of visible imports into this country.

  (a) Explain the difference between **invisible** and **visible imports** using your own examples.

  (b) Give four types of invisible exports from this country, with examples of each.

  (c) In what ways might a country try to prevent foreign imports from entering the country?

10 Economic Development and Aid

The world can be divided into those countries which enjoy a very high stardard of living and those which do not. Malnutrition is the biggest killer in the world today. 500 million people are regularly undernourished, and every day 10 000 people die from lack of food.

The North-South divide

The capitalist and communist worlds – the 'North' or 'developed' world consumes the majority of the world's wealth – 85 per cent – but is home to only 30 per cent of the world's population. The rest of the world – the 'South' or 'developing' world, sometimes called the 'third world' is poor in comparison. Over 100 countries accounting for 70 per cent of the world's population sharing between them only 15 per cent of the world's wealth. About two-thirds of the world's poorest people live in four countries: Bangladesh, India, Indonesia and Pakistan.

Within third world countries there are great differences. One way of measuring poverty is by

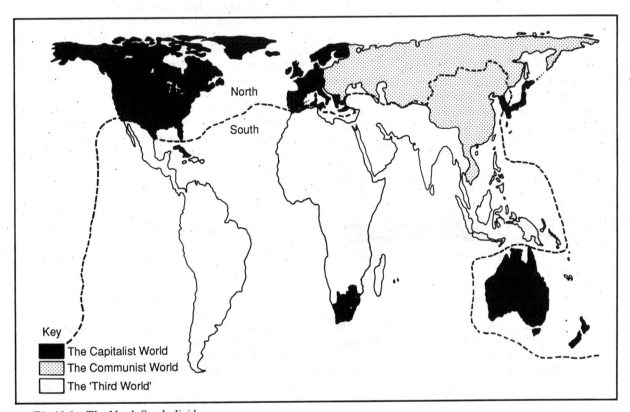

Key
- ■ The Capitalist World
- ▒ The Communist World
- □ The 'Third World'

Fig 10.1   The North-South divide

looking at the level of gross domestic product per head (*see* page 10). In some of the relatively 'richer' third world countries in South America, for example, GDP per head is relatively high and growing rapidly. This does not mean that there is not still very real poverty in these countries. Brazil, for example is seventh largest economy in the world and the fifth most important advertising market. At least one third of Brazil's population, however, suffer extreme poverty and malnutrition. Most remaining third world countries can be called 'low-income' countries. In these countries even if resources were evenly distributed it would be insufficient to adequately support their populations.

Gross National Product per capita (1984)
Selected Countries:

	US$
UK	8570
Brazil	1720
Peru	1000
Sri Lanka	360
Mozambique	230

Typically such countries have the majority (66 per cent) of their population engaged in agriculture and rely heavily upon exporting one or more raw material to the developed North. Because of their very low incomes such countries are ill-equipped to deal with natural disasters such as drought or flood and experience high infant mortality rates. Low income leaves little for education and health care – the bulk of their populations remain illiterate and prone to disease.

CASE STUDY

Sudan – 'The breadbasket of the Arab world'

Sudan, situated in Eastern Africa is the largest country in that continent, bordered by Ethiopia, Kenya, Uganda, Zaire, Chad, Libya and Egypt. The Sudanese eastern boundary is formed by the Red Sea and the River Nile runs through the country from North to South. Sudan suffered badly from the effects of the African droughts in the mid 1980s and, by a cruel irony, the capital Khartoum and surrounding area suffered from flooding during the

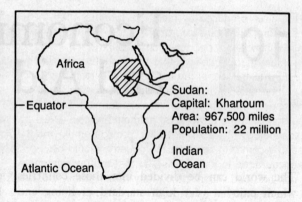

Sudan:
Capital: Khartoum
Area: 967,500 miles
Population: 22 million

rainy season in August 1988, when it received two years' expected rainfall in 15 hours.

The majority of people in Sudan are poor subsistence farmers – they provide food for themselves and their families by working on the land. Sudan is not without considerable agricultural reserves. Sudan is a former British colony: during the early part of this century, Britain began an impressive irrigation scheme – the largest of its type in the world – on the Gezira plain leading to two million acres of rich farm land. The plan was to grow cotton which would be converted into cloth in the mills of Lancashire. Cotton prices fell dramatically during the 1970s and so the independent Sudanese Government switched to food production on the Gezira and irrigated further large areas, in an attempt to make Sudan self-sufficient in food and with sufficient surplus to export ('food first'). At the same time many expensive development projects were started with the help of foreign investment. A huge sugar refinery was built, for example, the £400 million Kenana Sugar Scheme, but world sugar prices fell before the plant was opened and it was unable to compete with other countries.

The World Bank, the world's largest development agency, has lent much to Sudan. It expects a 10 per cent return on investments, however, and was unhappy about the use of the Gezira plain for food. There was, therefore, a partial return to the cotton cash crop. Many people believe that the modern intensive farming techniques used are partly to blame for the famine. People with no land claims are forced to farm marginal land which quickly turns to desert. A staggering 85 per cent of Sudan's fuel is charcoal. This tempts poor farmers to cut down trees which increases the problem. Even man-made water-holes do not help the situation since they lead to over-grazing. The poor farmers are unable to buy the grain produced by merchant farmers when their own crops fail due to drought.

Is there any hope for such a country?

Many people believe that there ought to be a return to traditional farming techniques with the help of international aid. Such farming is in many respects the opposite of Western farming relying, as it does, on many workers, animals and low levels of technology. It would, however, provide employment and income. In addition, the country should be encouraged to industrialise so that the raw materials can be used within the country rather than exported and re-imported as expensive finished products.

Task

1 Sudan's story is a catalogue of errors. What mistakes were made which have led to such immense problems?

2 Why did the British irrigate vast areas of the Gezira plain at the beginning of this century?

3 Why was it a mistake for Sudan to rely upon one 'cash crop'?

4 Why do you think multi-million pound investment projects in the 1970s were a failure?

5 Why was the World Bank unhappy about the 'food first' programme of the 1970s?

Third world problems

The Sudan story illustrates some of the major problems faced by the third world.

1 Poverty

Low income countries suffer from a 'cycle of poverty' from which they cannot break out. Poverty leads to poor education and health care, a lack of social capital – roads, schools, hospitals. This in turn leads to high population growth, more mouths to feed and poor crops – once, and if, the expanding population has been fed there are little or no surpluses to sell – this leads to a lack of funds for investment in better production techniques and education – poor crops follow and the cycle goes on.

2 Resource problems

Many third world countries lack energy sources – or the capital to exploit their own. They may, in addition, lack other resources. Many suffer from poor natural resources, unreliable climate, poor soils etc.

3 Dependence upon cash crop/or mineral

Often the legacy of a colonial past, many countries hope to export one 'cash' crop. This causes problems when the demand for that crop or mineral falls. Sudan suffered from falling cotton prices, Mauritius from sugar etc.

4 Foreign debt problems

Brazil, for example, owes $100 billion, the cost in interest and repayments being $15 billion per year. (In 1988 the richest countries of the developed world agreed a package of relief for much of the third world's debt).

Most people now agree that the problems facing the third world are a matter of concern for the whole world and that measures ought to be taken to help the third world. There is no problem with food production – the North often has huge surpluses – but with distribution.

The Brandt report stated this problem clearly when it pointed out that just one-half of one per cent of one year's world military expenditure would pay for **all** the farm equipment needed to increase food production and approach self-sufficiency in food-deficit low income countries. This influencial report therefore, not surprisingly, recommended greater aid from the affluent North for food production, an emergency programme for the very poorest countries, programmes to reduce population growth and the convertion of arms production into civilian production. It also recommended that new ways of financing development ought to be adopted to avoid the debt problems and that the third world countries should be helped to industrialise by the reduction of tariffs and other forms of protectionism.

Some people argue that the South ought not to be dependent upon the North as it will not encourage those countries to sort out their own problems. Aid is also critised in that, as you will see, it has strings attached and helps the donor country as much or more than the receipient.

Types of aid

The countries of the North collectively give much to the South in the form of aid. The UK is no exception.

There are three types of aid:

1 official aid
2 commercial support
3 voluntary agencies.

1   Official aid

(a) *Bilateral aid* This is where one country helps another directly – often by the support of specific projects such as power stations or water supply schemes. In the UK these are either agreed directly between our Government and the recipient country or are organised by the Commonwealth Development Corporation. Bilateral Aid accounts for 62 per cent of UK Official Aid and in 1985 amounted to £822m. This is spent on financial aid and technical co-operation (TC). The largest recipient was India which received £106.5m, of which a large amount went to purchase 21 British-made military helicopters! Northern countries like bilateral aid as it can be 'tied' so that the donating country's industry must be used.

(b) *Multilateral aid* This is were a large number of Northern countries give funds to international aid agencies who distribute the aid to developing countries. Such bodies include:

(i) EC – handles the European Development Fund, the official instrument of aid and technical cooperation between member countries and African, Caribbean and Pacific countries.

(ii) World Bank, which consists of the following organisations
• International Bank of Reconstruction and Development (IBRD) – lends on commercial terms (as seen)
• International Development Agency – lends on concessional terms
• International Finance Corporation – lends to private enterprises in third world

(iii) United Nation Agencies such as:
• UNICEF – United Nations Childrens' Fund (New York); provides funds for mass health campaigns, child welfare and education.
• WHO – World Health Organisation (Geneva) helps to control disease and improve health and nutrition.
• UNDP – United Nations Development

Programme which co-ordinates several types of TC programmes.
• UNESCO – United Nations Educational, Scientific and Cultural Organisation (Paris), which aims to promote international collaboration through education, science and culture.
• UNIDO – United Nations Industrial Development Organisation (Vienna) which aims to promote the industrialisation of developing countries. (Funds from UNDP above)
• FAO – Food and Agricultural Organisation, which aims to increase the efficiency of the production and distribution of all food and agricultural products; to improve the condition of rural populations and to raise levels of nutrition.

(iv) Regional Development Banks (RDBs). These are similar to the IBRD and aim to invest money and skills in projects for economic and social development of member countries. There are three continental banks serving Africa, Latin America, and Asia.

In 1985 the UK gave £495m (38 per cent) in multilateral aid.

Table 10.1

Britain's gross public expenditure on Overseas Aid

	1983 £m	1984 £m	1985 £m	1985 %
Multilateral agencies				
European Community	189	226	235	17.8
World Bank Group	205	197	128	9.7
UN agencies	57	66	84	6.4
Other	29	42	48	3.6
Total multilateral aid	**480**	**531**	**495**	**37.6**
Bilateral country programmes				
Financial aid	372	397	429	32.6
Technical co- operation	133	138	154	11.7
Total country programmes	**505**	**535**	**583**	**44.3**
CDC loans	56	108	79	6.0
Institutional TC	99	102	124	9.4
Total other programmes	**155**	**210**	**203**	**15.4**
Administrative costs	33	35	36	2.7
Total gross aid	1173	1311	1317	100.0

The Organisation for Economic Co-operation and Development (OECD) is not an aid agency, but it has a Development Assistance Committee which aims to co-ordinate aid policies and programmes amoungst members.

Table 10.2

Britain's bilateral aid by region

	£m 1983	1984	1985
Africa North of Sahara	11	18	21
Africa South of Sahara	226	248	285
America	68	58	70
Middle East	9	11	10
South Asia	208	237	193
Far East	27	57	52
Europe	9	10	34
Oceania	25	27	22
Unallocatable by region	111	115	134
Total bilateral aid	**694**	**781**	**822**
	percentages		
Commonwealth	73	73	65
Non-Commonwealth	27	27	35

Tasks

1 What proportion of Britain's bilateral aid went to Commonwealth countries in 1985?
2 Draw a suitable graph to illustrate Britain's bilateral aid in 1985
3 To which international agency did the UK contribute most in 1985?

2 Commercial Support
This refers to the commercial involvement of private enterprise from developed economies, such as the UK, in third world economies. It takes two forms: direct involvement and indirect involvement.

(a) *Direct involvement* Large multi-national companies like BP and Unilever will invest in a third world country. For example in 1976, the Benso Oil Plantation Limited was set up as a joint venture between Unilever and the government in Ghana. To build this plantation, forests had to be cleared and roads constructed. 4000 hectares of oil palm were planted and harvesting commenced in 1981. A palm oil factory has also been built within the plantation and Ghanaians have been trained to run the plant. The scheme has provided three new

villages, social clubs, a shop, a canteen, a clinic, and a school.

Such a scheme benefits Unilever as well. It secures supplies of palm oil for soap making in Europe at low costs. Some people feel that it is the multinational company which gains the most from such direct involvement. They are able to pay low wages and are accused of destroying cultural diversity by 'westernising' small parts of the third world for their own profit.

(b) *Indirect involvement* Most British bilateral aid is 'tied', i.e. it must be spent in the UK. In this way both countries gain. The developing country gains the aid and UK firms gain valuable orders. British firms can also tender for contracts to supply multilateral aid packages. In 1985 the UK contributed £495m to multilateral agencies but UK businesses gained £600m orders from multilateral aid agencies.

In 1977 the Aid and Trade Provision (ATP) was established in the UK to help UK firms gain such contracts. Long term loans are arranged to the developing country at low rates of interest through banks. ATP finances the difference between the rate charged and the internationally agreed fixed rate for that particular country, with the Export Credit Guarantee Department (of the DTI) providing the difference between this fixed rate and the prevailing commercial rate. Since 1978 exports totalling £1.9bn have been secured with £410m from ATP.

3 Voluntary Agencies
Voluntary agencies like Oxfam work both independently and in co-operation with the British

Table 10.3

Income of major overseas donor charities 1984/85

Charity	Voluntary donations £000	Total income (inc. Grants. Sales etc.) £000
Band Aid	56 500	69 000
Oxfam	49 533	57 430
Save the Children (SCF)	35 469	42 678
Christian Aid	17 374	20 357
Tear Fund	11 019	11 790
Action Aid	10 500	11 317
Catholic Fund for Overseas Development (CAFOD)	10 115	11 882

Government through the Overseas Development Administration (ODA).

The public in the UK give most generously which enables these major charities to both respond to emergencies in the third world – such as the 1988 floods in Sudan, and to develop long-term projects with workers in the field providing irrigation schemes, clean water pipes, schools, clinics etc. It is in the financing of these long term schemes that the ODA and voluntary agencies co-operate. Some schemes are jointly financed with ODA contributing 50 per cent of the cost.

World population growth

In the United Kingdom, as you saw in Chapter 5, births and deaths roughly balance each other and for several years, in common with most of the developed world, our population has remained fairly stable at 56.5 million. The United Nations currently estimate that this situation will occur over the whole world in just over 100 years time, 2100, when the world will have a total population of 10.2 billion (over twice its present size).

The majority population growth will be in the third world – those very countries less able to cope with the extra mouths to feed. Countries in the third world tend to have higher fertility rates: whereas in the UK women on average have 1.8 children, women in sub-Saharan Africa have an average of 7 children, in North Africa 6 and Asia 4.5.

Tasks

Using the Table 10.4:

1 (a) Which country in the table has the highest proportions:
  • under 15
  • over 60
(b) Explain why this might be so.
(c) What problems might this cause each of these countries?

2 Calculate the percentage increase in population between 1961 and 1985 for:
(a) United Kingdom
(b) Italy
(c) Brazil
(d) Zimbabwe

3 Look back at the population pyramid for UK on page 59. Use the data above to sketch a population pyramid for a typical developed country and typical developing country alongside each other, using the same scale to enable comparison.

SUMMARY EXERCISE:

1 Name three developed countries and three developing countries.
2 How many times greater is the GDP per head in the UK than in Mozambique (approx)?
3 Name three characteristics of a developing country.
4 Why does poverty lead to poverty?
5 For what historical reasons are some third world countries dependent upon one 'cash' crop or mineral?
6 What problems does the dependence upon one cash crop or mineral give a developing country?
7 Why is foreign debt a problem for developing countries?

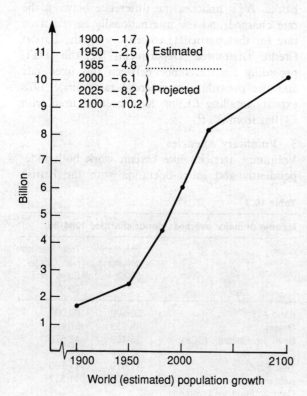

```
          1900  – 1.7  )
    11 –   1950  – 2.5  } Estimated
          1985  – 4.8  ).....................
    10 –   2000  – 6.1  )
          2025  – 8.2  } Projected
     9 –   2100  – 10.2 )
```

Fig 10.2 World (estimated) population growth

Table 10.4

Population and population structure: selected countries

	Estimates of mid-year population (millions)						Percentage[1] aged		Expectation of life at birth[1] (years)	
	1961	1971	1976	1981	1984	1985	Under 15	60 or over	Males	Females
United Kingdom	52.8	55.6	55.9	56.4	56.5	56.6	19	21	71.4	77.2
Belgium	9.2	9.7	9.8	9.8	9.8	9.9	20	19	68.6	75.1
Denmark	4.6	5.0	5.1	5.1	5.1	5.1	20	20	71.4	77.4
France	46.2	51.2	52.9	54.2	55.0	55.2	22	18	70.4	78.5
Germany (Fed. Rep.)[2]	56.2	61.3	61.5	61.7	61.2	61.0	17	20	70.2	76.8
Greece	8.4	8.8	9.2	9.7	9.9	9.9	22	17	70.1	73.6
Irish Republic	2.8	3.0	3.2	3.4	3.5	3.6	31	15	68.8	73.5
Italy	49.9	54.0	56.2	56.5	57.0	57.1	21	18	69.7	75.9
Luxembourg	0.3	0.3	0.4	0.4	0.4	0.4	19	18	66.8	72.8
Netherlands	11.6	13.2	13.8	14.2	14.4	14.5	22	16	72.7	79.3
Portugal	8.9	9.0	9.7	9.9	10.1	10.2	26	15	65.1	72.9
Spain	30.6	34.1	36.0	37.8	38.3	38.6	26	16	70.4	76.2
European Community[3]	281.5	305.2	313.7	319.1	321.2	322.1	..	..	..	..
Sweden	7.5	8.1	8.2	8.3	8.3	8.4	19	22	73.0	79.1
Turkey	28.2	36.2	41.1	45.4	48.3	49.3	39	5	53.7	
Australia	10.5	12.9	13.9	14.9	15.6	15.8	25	14	71.4	78.4
USSR	218.0	245.1	256.7	267.7	275.1	278.6	36[5]	13	64	74
Egypt	26.6	34.1	37.9	43.5	47.2	48.5	40	6	51.6	53.8
Tanzania	10.6	13.6	16.4	19.2	21.1	21.7	46	6	47.3	50.7
Zimbabwe	4.0	5.5	6.3	7.4	8.0	8.3	51	3	51.3	55.6
China	671.0	840.0	908.3	1 011.2	1 049.7	1 059.5	34	8	62.6	66.5
India	439.0	551.3	613.3	676.2	745.0	750.9	39	6	46.4	44.7
Japan[4]	94.0	105.7	112.8	117.6	120.0	120.8	23	14	74.2	79.7
Canada	18.3	21.6	23.0	24.3	25.1	25.4	22	14	71.9	78.9
USA	183.8	206.2	215.1	230.0	236.7	239.3	22	16	70.5	78.2
Brazil	71.8	95.2	109.2	124.0	132.6	135.6	38	6	57.6	61.1
Peru	10.3	13.8	15.6	17.8	19.2	19.7	41	5	52.6	55.5

1 Latest available year.
2 Includes West Berlin.
3 Includes United Kingdom, Irish Republic, Denmark, Greece, Portugal, and Spain throughout.

4 Includes Okinawa.
5 Under 20.

Source: Government Actuary's Department; Demographic Year Books and Monthly Bulletin of Statistics, United Nations

8 For what economic reasons ought a developed country be concerned about the plight of developing countries?

9 Why might a developed country prefer to give bilateral aid as opposed to multilateral aid?

10 Why are birth rates so much higher in developing countries than developed countries? What effect will this have upon the distribution of population by the year 2100?

11 The Means of Exchange

If you were to empty all your pockets you would probably find some cash; coins and banknotes which we all know as **money**. In this chapter this strange idea of money will be considered.

This chapter is entitled 'the means of exchange' as this is one of the most important functions of money. It provides a mechanism for changing what people have into what they want. Your teacher sells his talents to the local education department in order to buy those goods and services he desires. Although, if asked, we would all probably admit to wanting more money, it would not be the actual notes and coins we desired but those extra goods and services for which this money could be exchanged. Imagine a bank robber who obtains £1 million from his crime and flies away in a light aeroplane to avoid capture. If the plane were to crash land on a desert island although he may be very rich in terms of cash he would probably starve since you cannot eat banknotes and coins.

Legal Tender

Exercise

Here are pictures of two coins worth one pound. One is an ordinary one pound coin, the other fits a car wash machine at a garage and we shall assume costs one pound.

Copy this table into your book filling in the gaps. For some of the answers you will have to make an intelligent guess.

		£1 coin	Car wash token
1	Manufactured by?	The Royal Mint	
2	Manufactured from?	Cupro nickel (cheap hard wearing metal alloy)	
3	Cost of manufacture?		A few pence
4	Distinguishing features?		Groove which fits machine and prevents copies
5	Available where?	From Bank of England through banks	
6	Exchangeable for?		One car wash

Now answer these two questions

1 Which of these two coins would you prefer to be given
2 If the price of a car wash were to increase to £2 which of these two coins would you prefer to be given and why?

From the above exercise we can see that these two coins are not that different. They both are made cheaply from a hard-wearing metal alloy. They are about the same size and have special markings to prevent forgery and are a standard weight to operate machines. Most people would probably prefer to be given a £1 coin, however, because this coin is 'money' and can be exchanged for anything priced at £1. The car wash token can only be exchanged for one car wash and is *not*, therefore, money.

Many different commodities over the years and in different societies, have been recognised as money. Such objects as shells, sharks teeth, cattle, salt and of course gold and silver. They all have at least one thing in common. When they were used as money they were generally accepted, that is most people in that society would accept them in payment for goods and services.

Today our cash, the notes and coins, have no value in themselves. They are almost worthless but by law people must accept them in payment for goods and services because they are **legal**

Fig 11.1   A printing press used to print £10, £20, and £50 notes

tender. Legal tender is any means of payment which must be accepted by law in settlement of a debt. In this country Bank of England notes and Royal Mint coins are legal tender. Although anyone selling goods and services must accept these notes and coins in payment they can insist on the exact money and they are protected from being given large quantities of small change since coins are only legal tender up to these amounts:

Bronze coins (1p and 2p) up to 20p
Cupro nickel coins (5p and 10p) up to £5
50p coins and 20p coins up to £10
£1 coins up to any amount
Banknotes (£1, £5, £10, £20, £50) up to any amount

Exercise

All of the following can be used to buy certain goods and services but only three are legal tender. Can you pick out which?

(*a*) A book token
(*b*) A postal order
(*c*) A cheque
(*d*) A money-off voucher from a newspaper.
(*e*) A commemorative Crown
(*f*) A 16½p stamp
(*g*) Trading stamps
(*h*) A 10 pound note
(*i*) A one pound coin
(*j*) An old silver sixpence

Which of the three you picked are you unlikely to spend and why?

Bank deposits

Most of the money we use in a modern society is not in the form of notes and coins. Many people have **bank accounts**. Often wages are paid straight into a bank account. Rather than going to the bank every time you wish to buy something and drawing out your money you can use this money to buy goods and services without drawing it out, in fact you can do so hundreds of miles from the bank. As we shall see in the next case study it is becoming easier to use these deposits as if they were cash.

In May 1988:

	£m	
Notes and coins in circulation with public	13 579	(13½%)
UK Private sight sterling deposits with banks		
non-interest earning	34 267	(34½%)
interest earning	51 352	(52%)

We consider bank deposits as money since they are generally accepted in payment for goods and services. As you can see they represent nearly three quarters of the money held by private individuals.

CASE STUDY

A cashless society?

Barclays Bank took one step nearer a cashless society with the introduction of the 'Connect' card in the summer of 1987 – the first DEBIT card in the UK. When introduced the system used vouchers similar to VISA CREDIT cards but the amount spent was deducted from the customers current account much like a cheque. As more and more electronic machines are introduced in retail outlets at point of sale so the voucher system will be phased out to be replaced by automatic authorisation and debiting when the customer's card is 'wiped' through the electronic till. Within a year most clearing banks had introduced similar multi-purpose cards.

Cheques

Today the most common way of using bank deposits as money is the cheque. In 1983 about 2 500 000 000 cheques were written and each cheque costs about 50 pence to process.

A cheque is a written instruction to your bank asking them to transfer money from your account to the account of someone else. It must be remembered that the cheque is not money or legal tender. It is merely a formal letter to a bank asking them to transfer money from one account to another. The *money* is the bank deposit. Figure 11.2 shows a correctly completed cheque. At the top is the address of the bank and the date. It asks the bank to pay the person whose name appears in the space *or* do anything they order the bank to do. There is space for the amount to be written in words and figures to avoid confusion and a space to sign. The numbers identify the cheque, the branch and the account and can be read by electronic sorting machines. The two vertical parallel lines mean that the cheque is crossed and must therefore be paid into the account of the person named on the cheque. It is possible to have uncrossed or open cheques which can be exchanged for cash at the branch upon which they are drawn. An open cheque is clearly not very safe since it could be lost and cashed by anyone who finds it. A crossed cheque is very safe since it can only be paid into an account.

Most banks give their customers a **cheque card**. This encourages shops to accept cheques written by such people. If someone writing a cheque has a valid cheque card which has the same signature as the cheque and the same bank number as the cheque, then anyone accepting such a cheque can simply write the cheque card number on the back and the bank promises to pay any amount up to £50 – even if the customer does not have £50 in their account! A cheque can be written on any scrap of paper. In the past people have written cheques on hens eggs, the side of a cow and even on a shark! Banks have to deal with so many cheques each day, however, it helps them if we all use a standard form, so customers are given a cheque book containing blank cheques whenever they need them.

Fig 11.2 A cheque

CASE STUDY

The amazing three-day journey of a cheque

Peter Griffiths has a bank account with National Westminster Bank at South Woodford. His wages are paid straight into his account each month and he uses the cash dispensing machine once a week to draw out any cash he needs for buying small things. This week after drawing out his cash he has a balance left in his account of £189.90.

On Saturday he travels to Central London to do some shopping. In a sale he notices a jacket he likes at a price too low to miss – £46.75. He has only a few pounds on him but he does have his cheque book and cheque card. The shop accepts the cheque Peter writes and he leaves for home. The story of his cheque is only just beginning.

The shop has an account with Lloyds Bank. Peter's cheque asks his bank to take £46.75 from his account and give it to Lloyds Bank so that they can add this amount to the shop's account. This is how it happens. It is called the **cheque clearing system.**

Step 1 The shop pays Peter's cheque into their bank – probably on Monday morning.

Step 2 Lloyds Bank instructs its computer, which keeps records of all accounts, to add £46.75 from Peter's account, along with all other cheques paid in by the shop, to the shop's account. This it will do but this money cannot be spent since it has not yet been received. The amount – £46.75 – will be printed by a special machine along the bottom edge of the cheque in magnetic ink so it can be automatically read.

Step 3 At the end of that day all the cheques paid into that branch of Lloyds Bank would be sent to Lloyds Bank head office in London and sorted into different banks. Peter's would be in the National Westminster pile along with hundreds of others.

Step 4 On Tuesday morning Lloyds head office would have received piles of cheques from all of its many branches. These piles would be put together. Now Peter's cheque would be one of thousands and their combined total would represent the total amount owed that day by National Westminster Bank customers to Lloyds Bank customers.

Step 5 During Tuesday, Lloyds Bank representatives will take all these cheques to the **Bankers' Clearing House**. This is a building owned jointly by all of the high street banks where they can present each other with the various piles of cheques. The Lloyds Bank representatives will pass over the piles of National Westminster Bank cheques and in effect say this is what your customers owe our customers. At the same time the National Westminster Bank representatives will have similar piles of Lloyds Bank cheques which in total will show how much Lloyds Bank customers owe National Westminster Bank customers.

By subtracting one amount from the other it is possible to find the net amount owned by one bank to the other.

Step 6 Peter's cheque, along with all the other cheques picked up at the clearing house, would be taken back to the head office of National Westminster Bank and electronically sorted into different branches and at the same time the amount of each cheque and the account from which it must be taken is stored in the memory of the bank's computer. The cheques are then sent to their branches. (Peter's to South Woodford.)

Step 7 Peter's cheque would arrive in South Woodford on Wednesday and, along with other cheques, would be checked. A clerk would make sure it was not a stolen cheque and had been properly completed. If all was in order it would be stamped 'paid'. (Any improper cheques would be stopped and the bank's computer, via the branch terminal, would be instructed not be deduct the amount. The cheque would be sent back to the person to whom it was paid with a reason for it not being paid. Since it goes straight back to the person who paid it in it is said to **bounce**. They would have their account deducted by this amount.) Peter's account would automatically be reduced by £46.75 leaving him a balance of £143.15. The shop, having not been advised that the cheque was to be stopped, would be able to use this £46.75. Also on that day the net amount owed by Lloyds to National Westminster or vice-versa from Tuesday's exchange of cheques would be made by a simple adjustment of each bank's account at the Bank of England.

We have followed just one cheque through the system. Remember this is just one of four million cheques which pass through this incredible system every day. People can use the money they have in their bank accounts without having to draw it out in the form of cash.

On 9 February 1984, the clearing banks launched a new fully automated electronic sameday payments system called CHAPS (Clearing House Automated

Payment System). This was designed for companies and individuals who need to tranfer money very quickly. Peter's cheque took several days to complete its journey and therefore transfer the money. Using computers the CHAPS system allows a customer to contact his bank and ask for money to be transferred that same day to any other bank account. This replaces the old 'town clearing' which used cheques (which had to be drawn on banks in the City of London) and was operated in a similar way to the general clearing but much faster. It is hoped that the system will be expanded to cover more payments.

Exercise

> Using your own example draw a flow diagram to show a three-day journey of a cheque. Look carefully at the **steps** in the case study.

The functions of money

There are various functions money can carry out:

- It helps people **exchange** what they have into what they want. It is sometimes called **a medium of exchange**.
- It is a convenient way to **store wealth**. It is possible to save money in a bank account which is safe and to a certain extent a good way of maintaining its value.
- It can be used as a standard **unit to measure value**. Money places a value upon objects which everybody understands. If we describe an object as being worth £10 then automatically we can compare it to other objects worth £10 and have a real idea of its value.
- It enables people to **borrow, lend** and **pay for things later**. If people relied upon bartering, that is directly swapping objects, it would be impossible to pay for things in the future. You could not, for example, swap a pig for a goat if you did not have the pig; since quality and size etc could vary. One could, however, buy a goat for £50 by offering £15 now and £5 a week for the next 7 weeks. The seller would know that the quality and value of the money would be constant. Money in developed economies therefore has no value in itself. It is only

a token, but it is made generally acceptable in exchange for goods and services by the weight of law. Most of our money is kept not in the form of cash (notes and coins) but in bank deposits which can be used to settle debts by the use of various methods to transfer amounts from one bank account to another. The most popular current method is the cheque, although technology will soon change this!

Exercise

1 The direct swapping or exchanging of goods without the use of money is called **barter**. Suppose you live in a society which has no money and you are asked to swap a pig for a plough at the local market. Write down two problems you might encounter.

2 The BBC ran a television programme for children on Saturday mornings called *Swap Shop*, perhaps you remember it. Amongst other things children were encouraged to take toys they had outgrown or did not want to an outside broadcast location where they could swap them. Very little swapping ever appeared to take place. Write down why you think this was so.

3 Why are the banks, British Telecom and IBM spending so much money on inventing a new way of spending bank deposits? What is wrong with the cheque clearing system?

4 We define **money** as 'any kind of material or object that has come to be accepted within society as a normal means by which people pay for their purchases'. Before our token money and bank deposits people used gold and silver coins. Before this societies used real commodities like cattle as money. In this chapter, four others have been mentioned. Write down two further commodities which have been used as money and, for each, state at least one problem such money might have.

5 Which of the four functions of money is being fulfilled in each of the following examples:

(a) James puts £100 into a Building Society account.

(b) Mrs Bright buys a washing machine on hire-purchase.

(c) Jane buys a record.

(d) Mr Smith calculates the value of his house contents for insurance purposes.

ASSIGNMENT

Look carefully at the two groups of advertisements. Copy out and fill in the following table:

	Old Price	New Price	% Increase or Decrease	Quality better/ worse/ same as today
Gents Watch				
Radio	£34			

Now answer these questions:

1 Which of the items increased by the greatest amount over the 30 or so years?

2 Which of the items fell in price? Can you think why?

THE P53
WILL
CALL
AT
ALL
STATIONS

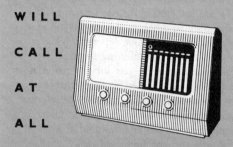

Switch on your Model P53 — and YOU will be a traveller to distant places, enjoying the music, news and entertainments of all the world! Perfect in performance and tone, elegant and distinctive in appearance — the P53 is today's finest investment in top-quality radio.

Ask your Dealer

for a demonstration!

MODEL P53
5-valve, 8-waveband bandspread superhet for A.C. Mains.

£34 TAX PAID

News Chronicle, 1951

Fig 11.3

Precision with Elegance

5 YEARS' WRITTEN GUARANTEE

416 | **414** | **846**

No. 416.
Gents' model in 9-ct. gold case. Plain dial, £15.19.6 inc. postage. Luminious dial 5/- extra.

No. 414.
Ladies' model in 9-ct. gold case. Plain dial, £14.2.6 inc. postage. Luminious dial 5/- extra.

No. 846.
Gents' model in 9-ct. gold case. Plain or, luminous dial, £20.15.0 inc. postage.

Each watch shown has a 15-jewelled, Swiss lever, bench-tested, movement.

To secure any of the watches illustrated write your name, address and. the model number required on a postcard. Further supplies will be available shortly, but as stocks will be limited, order now. Do not send any money until you are advised that your watch is ready for dispatch. A limited variety of other models is also available, send 1d. for illustrated leaflet.

Woman, 1945

£33·99

£22·99

£35·00

1984 advertisements

Fig 11.4

The value of money

The value of money, the number of goods and services we can buy with a certain unit of currency, does not remain the same. Prices change. If there is a general increase in prices then we can buy less with the same amount of money. This is called **inflation** where prices have risen and the value of money fallen. The trouble is that although prices change they do not all change by the same amount nor even in the same direction as the previous case study showed.

In general, prices rise over time and the UK has been through a prolonged period of rapid price rises. Between 1976 and 1986 prices rose on average by 146 per cent. Put another way you needed £2.46 to buy roughly the same basket of goods in 1986 as £1 would buy in 1976.

Some prices such as for housing and eating out rose more sharply than the 146 per cent. Others such as clothing and household goods rose less sharply. Since prices change for different goods at different rates it is very difficult to measure these price changes accurately. It is only possible to estimate the rate of inflation. This is done using the calculation known as the **retail price index**.

Each month 130 000 separate prices on 600 different goods and services are collected by the Department of Employment. These are turned into an average increase in prices which is quoted in the newspapers and on television. It is not a straightforward average of the 130 000 prices however. Some price increases are more important to the average family than others and these are given greater importance by a statistical operation called **weighting**.

Inflation and earnings

Prices rose by nearly 150 per cent between 1976 and 1986. Fortunately for the average family, average earnings rose by nearly 190 per cent during the same period. In 1976 average weekly earnings were just £64.40. To be able to buy the **same** amount of goods and services in 1986 as £64.40 would have bought ten years earlier, that same average family would have required £158.42. In fact average earnings were £184.70 in 1986. Thus average family in 1986 were better off by some £26's worth of earnings and they were paying less direct tax!

The problems of inflation

From the previous paragraphs it could be assumed that inflation is not a problem. If wages and prices increase at the same rate nobody seems to suffer. This is not quite true however. Some people did not fare as well as the average couple above. People on fixed incomes, for example, would see their spending power fall. Also, if prices in this country rise more rapidly than those in other countries it might make it difficult to sell our exports and lead to a balance of trade deficit.

Governments try to prevent prices from rising too rapidly. Sometimes they will try to stop wages from rising by agreement with the trade union movement and even pass laws to prevent prices from rising. This is called a **prices and incomes policy**. Other governments have tried to reduce the rate of growth of our money. If people cannot borrow money they are unable to spend, less goods are sold so producers are only able to sell goods by reducing their price. It is a very complicated problem.

Banks

When considering money in this chapter banks have been mentioned many times since the deposits or accounts that are kept with the high street banks are money. For the next few pages we look in detail at these banks.

Exercise

For 20 years the Ford Cortina proved to be one of the most popular cars in Britain. During its history it sold 4 279 079 cars and had four different body shapes.

These four body shapes are shown here. Beside each picture is the year of introduction and the price of the most basic model.

Mark I Cortina 1962–66
September 1962
1200 cc basic
£639

Mark II Cortina 1966–70
October 1966
1300 cc basic
£669

Mark III Cortina 1970–76
August 1970
1300 cc basic
£909

Mark IV Cortina 1976–82
September 1976
1300 cc basic
£1950

Model	Year	Price	Average Weekly Manual Wage	Price ÷ wage	No of weeks
Mk I	1962	£639	£15.86	40.29	40
Mk II	1966	£669	£20'30½	—	—
Mk III	1970	£909	—	—	—
Mk IV	—	—	—	—	—

Using the graph below showing the average wage for manual workers calculate how many weeks' wages would be needed for the average manual worker to be able to buy the basic Cortina in each of the four years. This would be best undertaken in a table:

1 By how much did the price of the basic Cortina increase from September 1962 to September 1976?

2 Did the ability to buy the basic Cortina for the average manual worker increase or decrease from 1962-1976?

3 Did the quality/size/performance of the Cortina improve or deteriorate between 1962-1976?

4 What evidence is there to suggest that the standard of living for the average manual worker improved during the 1960s and 70s?

5 Which group of people might not have enjoyed this improvement in standard of living?

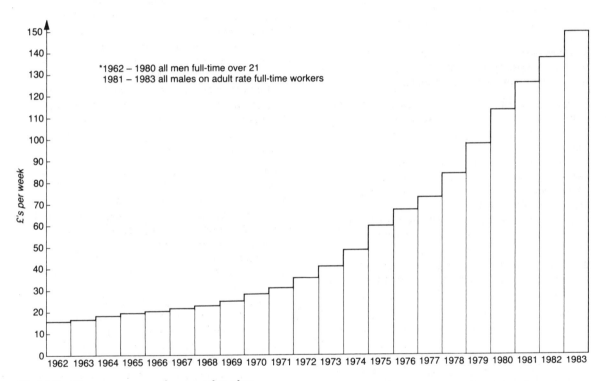

Fig 11.5 The average wage for manual workers
(Source: Dept of Employment)

CASE STUDY

Simon and Michelle

Simon and Michelle are married. Simon, who is 22 years old, has worked as a trainee manager for a large food retailing chain since leaving school at 18. Michelle is 2 years younger and left school at 16. After several jobs she took a post as secretary at the same store as Simon. Last year they were married and live in a rented flat near the store. At about this time Simon completed his training and was made assistant manager. This meant that he became part of the salaried staff and, instead of receiving a weekly pay packet with cash, he received a monthly pay cheque. It was a crossed cheque so he needed to open a bank account. After talking to his manager he discovered that he could have his wage paid straight into a bank account every month and just receive a pay slip telling him how much he had been given.

Simon and Michelle chose a bank close to the store; it happened to be a branch of the National Westminster Bank. Opening an account was very easy. Simon and Michelle filled in a form, paid in £10 to open the account and gave the name of their manager at work to act as a referee (that is confirm that they were who they said they were). They decided to open a **joint current account**. This meant they would both receive cheque books and be able to spend their money this way. Soon Simon and Michelle's wages were both being paid straight into their account and they both had cheque books. Simon and Michelle have both been surprised at just how many services their bank will undertake for them and most of them free of charge! In just a few months they have used all of these:

1 On the wall of their bank is a 24 hour money dispensing machine called a **service till**. Simon and Michelle have a plastic card and secret code number which enables them to draw out money whenever they need it. Recently they had a weekend in France as a sort of late honeymoon. They returned on Easter Sunday and had no cash (having spent more than they anticipated on duty free drink and perfume). The bank did not open again until Tuesday but the service till allowed them to draw out all the cash they needed. This machine also lets them order a new cheque book and statement (a sheet showing how much they have in their account and what they have spent).

2 Regular bills like rent, rates, electricity and gas are now paid automatically by the bank. Simon and

Fig 11.6

Michelle just completed and signed a form for each. Where the amount and frequency of payment remains unchanged they use a **standing order**. They order the bank for example to pay their landlord the rent for the flat on the 26th of every month. Where the amount varies they use a **direct debit** which instructs the bank to allow certain organisations, like the local authority who collect the rates, to ask for payment which the bank will then make – unless Simon or Michelle instruct the bank not to.

3 When they were planning their weekend in Paris, Simon and Michelle were able to order all the **foreign currency** (in this case French francs) from the bank. Next year they plan a holiday in Spain but they will take travellers' cheques which again they will order through their bank. These are much safer than cash. When they collect them at the bank they sign them. Then, while abroad, they will be able to exchange as many as they wish when they wish into foreign currency at the hotel or in shops, garages or banks. If they have them stolen they will be able to claim the money back.

4 Simon and Michelle do not want to live in rented accommodation all of their married lives. Recently they went to see the bank manager about buying a house. He was very helpful and explained that they would need to borrow a large sum of money over as many as 30 years paying back a small amount each month plus interest. This is called a **mortgage**. At National Westminster they have a special scheme where young couples like Simon and Michelle can open an account called a **mortgage saver account**. They agreed to put £150 per month from their current account into this special account. They have no cheque book for this account and will not spend the money they save, but the bank will pay them interest which will be added to their account. In two years they will have saved £3600 plus interest and will be able to borrow up to £30 000 to buy a house or flat. Both Michelle and Simon were surprised that the bank manager could talk about lending them so much money without batting an eyelid.

5 This month Simon and Michelle were able to open an **access account**. They were sent a card like the one opposite. With this they can pay bills very simply. A special form, together with the access card, is put in an imprinter machine, and Michelle or Simon sign the completed form. At the end of each month they receive an account from

Access which shows how much they have spent in this way and they can either settle at once by sending one cheque or send a small amount and pay off the rest in future months. If they only pay a small amount they will have to pay interest. Simon and Michelle are planning to buy a video in this way next month.

This couple have certainly used their bank since opening an account. These are just a few of the hundreds of services that large banks, like National Westminster, can offer their account holders.

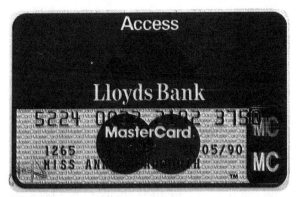

Fig 11.7

Exercise

1   Why did Simon and Michelle open a **joint current account**?
2   Name three ways in which the bank enables Simon and Michelle to pay bills without using cash.
3   In what two ways do Simon and Michelle hope to borrow money from the bank?
4   In what way did the bank help Simon and Michelle by giving advice?
5   Why do you think the manager seemed happy to lend Simon and Michelle money?

Some people think that a bank is an expensive way of holding money or paying bills. At Simon and Michelle's bank this is not so. As long as they keep a credit balance or £500 cleared average balance they do not pay bank charges. This means that the cheques, standing orders, direct debits etc are free. If they were to fall below this amount then the charges are very low. Cheques and direct debits only cost 28 p each. The annual charge for keeping the account is only £12. Most people who

CHARGES FOR CURRENT PERSONAL ACCOUNTS				
	Minimum balance for free banking	Transaction charge	Rate of interest authorised overdrafts	Rate of interest unauthorised overdrafts
Barclays	Credit or £500 cleared average balance	Debits 29p, credits nil, quarterly charge £3	3–7% over base rate	15% over base rate
Lloyds	Credit or £500 cleared average balance	Debits 25p, credits 25p, monthly charge £1	19.5% apr.	29.8% apr
Midland	Credit balance	Autodebits and direct debits 27p, cheques and s/orders 30p, credits nil, quarterly charge £3	19.2% apr.	Up to 26.2% apr
Nat West	Credit balance or £500 cleared average balance	Debits 28p, credits nil, quarterly charge £3	3–7% over base rate	25% branch std rate
TSB	Credit or £500 cleared average balance	Debits 29p, credits nil, quarterly charge £3	Usually 5% over base	13.5% over base rate
Yorkshire	Credit balance	Debits 29p, credits nil, quarterly charge £3	Negotiable	13.5% over base rate
Nat Girobank	Credit balance	Debits 85p, credits nil	11.5%	None
Co-op Bank	Credit balance or £500 cleared average balance	Debits 36p, credits 36p, quarterly charge £3	5% over base rate	17.5% over base rate
Nationwide Anglia	N/A	None	23.1% apr	34.4% apr
Abbey National	N/A	None	19.5% apr	29.8% apr

Fig 11.8   (Taken from The Independent *22.05.88)*

hold bank accounts do not pay charges because they have credit balances. There are special schemes for students and young couples which allow them free banking. Recently most banks have started paying low rates of interest on credit balances held in current accounts.

Banks like the National Westminster are public limited companies. This means they are owned by shareholders and are in business to make a profit. How can they manage to do this if they do so much for nothing? The clue to this is contained in your answer to question 5 of the last exercise. Banks make a profit by lending out the money that customers deposit with them to other customers who need to borrow. Banks are careful and will only lend to people who they are sure can afford to pay back the loan and the interest charged. In this way they are able to make a profit. The more money people and companies deposit with them the more they can lend out, and so the larger the profit they can make. For this reason each bank tries to offer a large range of useful services for their customers so as to attract as many customers and accounts as possible.

Summary of bank functions

1 Accept deposits Individuals and companies can deposit money with a bank by opening an account. There are many different types of account. **Current** or **cheque accounts** offer the customer the ability to pay bills using cheques and other devices (soon electronic) and reward the customer with low rates of interest and if the balance (amount in account) falls below a certain minimum they may have to pay charges. **Deposit** and **savings accounts** do not allow the customer to pay bills. They are not given a cheque book for example. They are rewarded with interest which is a certain percentage of the amount held in the account paid every six months. In general, the harder it is to take the money out, for example if the customer agrees to leave it in the account for two years as Simon and Michelle did, then the higher the interest the bank will pay.

2 Agents of payment For customers with current accounts banks will pay those people or companies to whom the customer owes money. This is done by transferring money from one account to another on the instruction of the customer using a cheque, standing order, direct debit mandate etc.

3 Lenders of money Banks lend money in several ways but they all cost the customer who borrows. They must pay back the loan with interest (a percentage of the loan added to the amount borrowed) and it is in this manner that banks make a profit. There are various types of loans:

(*a*) *An overdraft* Here a customer is allowed to write cheques for more than they have in their current account. They only pay interest on the amount they are overdrawn which can be any amount up to an agreed minimum. They can be overdrawn for just a few days or many months. It is a flexible way of borrowing. Very useful for a small businessman.

(*b*) *Personal loan* Account holders, over 18 and who can demonstrate their ability to pay back are able to borrow a lump sum for such large items as a new car, house repairs and improvements, holidays and expensive household items like televisions. Most banks make it very easy to borrow in this way and it probably means just a form to fill in. The sum borrowed is fixed as is the length of time. The interest is added on and monthly repayments made. It is not as flexible as an overdraft but in general a little cheaper.

(*c*) *Credit card* Access and Barclaycards allow customers to pay for items at the end of the month with one cheque and simply using one plastic card when shopping. They also allow the customer instant credit since when the account is sent at the end of each month the card holder does not have to settle in full. They can pay a small minimum amount and then the rest over a period of time. This is perfect for those last minute decisions where there is not enough time to negotiate a loan. They are expensive however, with a much higher rate of interest.

(*d*) *Mortgage* This is a special form of long-term loan given to people who wish to buy a house. The sum borrowed is so large that the house being bought remains the property of the bank until the

The Role of the Banks

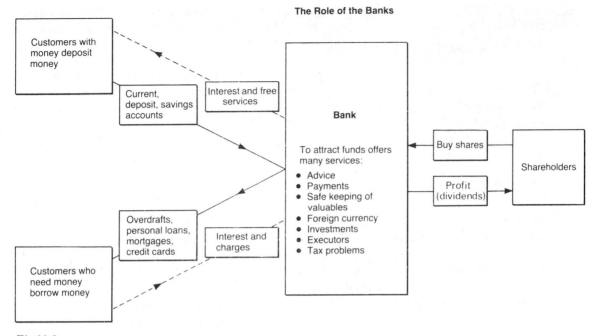

Fig 11.9

payments are complete. A monthly repayment is made which contains the interest and part of the sum borrowed.

(*e*) *Loans to businesses* Banks also lend millions of pounds per year to businesses. They have special schemes such as the National Westminster Business Development Loans which lends £2000 to £100 000 for one to ten years, or Farm Development Loans where up to £250 000 can be borrowed for up to 25 years. Large businesses and small one-man operations can also borrow. There are even special schemes for students who have long expensive training like medical, law and dental students.

Looking at the functions of banks like this it can be seen that the services offered by banks attract customers so that they will deposit money which can be lent out at a high rate of interest.

As shown in the advertisement, banks are quick to point out their ability to lend.

Here are a few more of the services on offer at a typical bank:

- **Income tax advice**
- **Investment management** – look after investments in stocks and shares, normally for amounts of more than £20 000
- **Stockbroking services** – will arrange for the buying or sale of shares
- **Insurance advice**
- **Unit trusts** – scheme to buy shares for large numbers of small savers.
- **Safeguarding valuables** – safe deposit boxes to lock up valuable documents or jewellery
- **Night safes** – shopkeepers or owners of expensive items can drop money or valuables into a special safe using a door in the bank wall to which they have a key
- **Executors and trustees** – can appoint the bank in your will to carry out your wishes after you die
- **General financial advice**
- **Many special services for business customers** – For example, up-to-date profiles of foreign countries to help exporters from this country. (Much of the information in the Mauritius case study came from a National Westminster country fact sheet.)

ASSIGNMENTS

1 Visit a local bank and find out the rate of interest they pay for:

   current accounts
   deposit accounts
   savings accounts

Also find out how much they will charge in interest for:

   a personal loan
   an overdraft

2 Using the information you have gathered explain how banks make a profit.
3 You have a family member who runs a small business but does not believe in banks. Write a letter using the information above trying to convince them to open a bank account.

Finance companies

One of the most common ways of borrowing is to buy goods on HP – **hire purchase**. When a person buys a car or washing machine over a number of months they have in fact borrowed from a special type of bank called a **finance company** (or **finance house**).

With a hire purchase agreement the purchaser is hiring a good while they pay for it. Of course they are able to use that good from the beginning of the agreement but it is not legally theirs until it is fully paid for. Until the last instalment has been paid the good belongs to the finance company which has paid the retailer and now collects the repayments. These repayments will include the interest and part of the original price of the article. Towards the end of a hire purchase agreement the purchaser might well be paying a very high rate of interest. This is because the rate of interest is often a fixed amount per month but by the end of the agreement the amount owed is very small since so much has been paid back. For this reason the **Consumer Credit Act (1974)** requires that all agreements over £30 should specify the **Annual Percentage Rate** of interest (APR). It will be found that in most cases hire purchase is a very expensive way of borrowing.

Example

If a person took out a hire purchase agreement to buy a motorbike at £1000 and the rate of interest was 10% and repayment period two years he would need to repay:

£1000 (loan) + £200 (interest 10% × £1000 × 2) = £1200 or £50 per month

After the first year this person would have repaid £600 or £500 (half) of the loan plus £100 interest. In the following year they would pay:

£500 (loan) + £100 (interest)

The interest is now 20%, this percentage growing as the months pass.

If a person cannot keep up with repayments the finance company can reclaim the goods if they have a court order but will often extend the terms if someone is in trouble. It is illegal to sell goods which are being bought on hire purchase.

The finance company lends out money which savers have deposited. Normally only large amounts for long periods of time are accepted by the finance company which pays a high rate of interest to the saver.

Building Societies

Since 1 January 1987 most Building Societies have been able to offer a full range of services similar to those of banks (pages 144–5). They remain the chief source of loans for house purchase, however (pages 196–7).

Banking Services at the Post Office

The **National Girobank** was established some 20 years ago to offer a cheap banking service through the Post Office. Anyone over 15 can open a Giro account with just £1. The Girobank offers some of the services of the high street banks but not all. It is cheaper than the high street bank in that no charges are made as long as an account is in credit.

Unlike some building societies who keep you waiting for a mortgage, **NatWest don't.***

 NatWest The Action Bank

P R E S S   F O R   A C T I O N

Here are the main services:

- Cheque book and card (for those over 18)
- Standing orders/direct debit
- Free statement
- Deposit accounts
- Personal loans
- Thomas Cook travellers' cheques and foreign currency

There are post offices in most villages (20 000) and they are open longer hours than banks.

Exercise

Compare a current account at a high street bank with the National Girobank cheque account.

For what sort of customer would a Giro account be preferable to a bank account and for what sort of person would the opposite be true?

The Bank of England

The Bank of England was formed in 1694 although in the early early days it was just like any other bank. In those days it did lend a large amount to the Government and this started a long association with the Government which led to control by Parliament and eventual nationalisation. Today the Bank of England is a very special bank, called the **Central Bank**. It is in control of the money system of this country.

Today the functions of the Bank of England include:

Note issue All banknotes are printed in Debden in Essex and circulated through the Bank of England.

Government's banker All taxes are paid into the Government's accounts and all Government spending passes through the accounts at the Bank

of England. Our Government borrows vast sums of money and the Bank of England is responsible for this debt.

Bankers' bank All banks keep at least one per cent of their deposits in their accounts at the Bank of England. At the end of each day if one bank owes another bank money due to the cheque clearing system the debt is settled by a transfer of funds from one account to another.

International cooperation The Bank of England represents the UK on such international monetary bodies as the IMF.

Government monetary policy If the Government wishes to reduce the money in circulation – to control inflation – it is the Bank of England that is responsible for putting this policy into effect.

SUMMARY EXERCISE

1 Explain clearly what is meant by **barter** and **commodity money**. Give two disadvantages of both as a system of exchange.

2 We have in this country a token money system where our cash is worthless. Why then do people readily accept this in payment for goods and services?

3 'A cheque is *not* money but a **bank account** is.' Explain this statement.

4 If a country experiences a period of rapid inflation what happens to the value of its currency?

5 For what reasons is **inflation** often considered a bad thing for the economy of a country?

6 Explain in detail the difference between a **personal bank loan** and an **overdraft facility**.

7 The high street banks offer most of their services freely to customers. How then do they make such large profits for their shareholders?

8 Name one service offered by the high street banks but *not* offered by the National Girobanks.

9 Give one advantage of holding a National Girobank account rather than a high street bank account.

10 The high street banks all have accounts with the Bank of England which holds about one per cent their total deposits in these accounts. How do these accounts help in the operation of the cheque clearing system?

ASSIGNMENTS

1 You discover that an old relative keeps all of her money in a shoe box under the bed because she does not like banks. Write down all the points which you would mention to her in order to change her opinion of banks. Be sure to include the different types of account and all the standard banking services which would be of use to her.

2 Some people have odd notions about banks. Those who have never been inside one tend to look upon them as cold, aloof and mysterious. Nothing could be further from the truth. Banks are friendly places, staffed by men and women whose desire is to help. Other people talk scathingly of banks – as scathingly as Mark Twain who claimed that 'a banker is a fellow who lends you his umbrella when the sun is shining and asks for it back the minute it starts to rain'. These people forget that a banker is handling other people's money and has to be just as careful with it as if it were his own.

Source BIS Booklet No 1, Page 1

(a) List four services provided by banks for their customers which convince you that they are indeed '. . . friendly places staffed by men and women whose desire is to help'.

(b) Mark Twain obviously thought of banks as places which do not like lending money to people. Of course banks do like to lend . . . they have to – why?

(c) Describe two ways in which banks lend money so as to show the difference between these two ways.

3 There are said to be four main functions of money in a modern society. Take each one of these functions in turn and with examples show how they are performed.

4 You probably have a few coins in your pocket or purse at the moment. If you lived in a primitive society you might not use money to trade. You might still **barter**. Describe what is meant by **bartering** and show why it is no good as a system of exchange in our highly developed society.

12 Incomes

The main source of 'money' for most people is the reward they receive for making a contribution to production, their **wages**. In Chapter 1 we learnt about the circular flow of income.

People specialise in a certain occupation or job and are paid a wage in the form of money. Some people, known as entrepreneurs, undertake a very special type of work. They bring together other types of resource and create businesses, produce goods and services and satisfy wants. These individuals either acting alone or in groups, receive **profit**.

Once individuals have money they are able to exchange it for goods and services by spending. This we call **consumption**. It is also possible for an individual to keep some of this money to be spent at a later date. This is known as **saving**.

Once individuals have earnt money they are faced with several choices – to spend, save, where to spend etc.

Since most people do not have enough money to be able to satisfy all of their wants they are faced with these choices. If they are to act sensibly they must consider the opportunity costs of using their scarce money in one particular way rather than another. If the individual decides to spend some money on shoes they might not be able to buy a coat.

Gross and net income

When someone finds paid employment they receive a **wage**. This can sometimes be paid

	Gross pay	A person's **earnings**
	less	
Collected by the employer for the Government	Income Tax	— Money taken by the Government to provide public and merit goods
	less	
	National Insurance	— Money taken by the Government to provide a State pension and benefits
	less	
Collected by the employer for the worker	Pension Contributions	— Money taken by the firm in order to provide a larger pension than the state
	less	
	Voluntary Payments	— Money taken at persons request to pay for trade union membership, or to save for holiday etc
	equals	
	Net pay	A person's take-home pay

weekly in the form of cash or a cheque or it might be paid monthly with a simple transfer from the firm's account to the workers account. This monthly pay is often called a **salary**. However they receive their pay people do not take home all the wage they earn. A person's earnings are called their **gross pay** but from this certain deductions are made (*see* previous page).

All workers are given a statement each week which itemises each deduction and addition. This is called a **wage slip** or **pay advice** (below).

Wage rate/earnings

Each job has an agreed rate of pay. This could be expressed hourly, weekly, monthly, or even as an annual figure:

Example

An annual salary of £9100, for a 35 hour week could be expressed as:

£5	per hour
£175	per week
£758.33	per month
£9100	per year

In some occupations it is possible to earn more than this basic rate for the job. This can be achieved by working for more than the agreed number of hours: **overtime**. It is usual for the hourly rate for overtime to be more than the basic hourly rate. Some firms pay a bonus on top of the basic rate if production targets are met or if difficult or dirty work has been undertaken. Bonuses are also paid for night work.

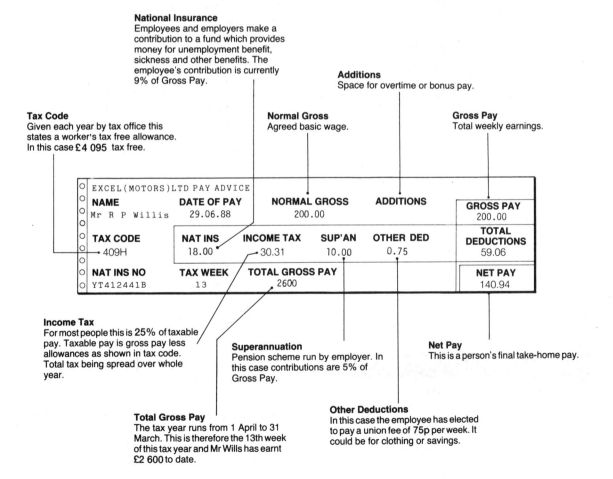

National Insurance
Employees and employers make a contribution to a fund which provides money for unemployment benefit, sickness and other benefits. The employee's contribution is currently 9% of Gross Pay.

Additions
Space for overtime or bonus pay.

Tax Code
Given each year by tax office this states a worker's tax free allowance. In this case £4 095 tax free.

Normal Gross
Agreed basic wage.

Gross Pay
Total weekly earnings.

EXCEL(MOTORS)LTD PAY ADVICE					
NAME	**DATE OF PAY**	**NORMAL GROSS**	**ADDITIONS**		**GROSS PAY**
Mr R P Willis	29.06.88	200.00			200.00
TAX CODE	**NAT INS**	**INCOME TAX**	**SUP'AN**	**OTHER DED**	**TOTAL DEDUCTIONS**
409H	18.00	30.31	10.00	0.75	59.06
NAT INS NO	**TAX WEEK**	**TOTAL GROSS PAY**			**NET PAY**
YT412441B	13	2600			140.94

Income Tax
For most people this is 25% of taxable pay. Taxable pay is gross pay less allowances as shown in tax code. Total tax being spread over whole year.

Superannuation
Pension scheme run by employer. In this case contributions are 5% of Gross Pay.

Net Pay
This is a person's final take-home pay.

Total Gross Pay
The tax year runs from 1 April to 31 March. This is therefore the 13th week of this tax year and Mr Wills has earnt £2 600 to date.

Other Deductions
In this case the employee has elected to pay a union fee of 75p per week. It could be for clothing or savings.

In some businesses profit sharing schemes operate. Here workers are given a share of the profits as part of their wage. It is therefore quite common for a person's **earnings** (what they actually earn as their **gross wage**) to be much higher than the **wage rate** (the agreed rate for the minimum number of hours worked).

Piece rate/time rate

It is possible not to pay workers by the number of hours they work: **time rate**, but instead by the amount they produce: **piece rate**. With piece rate a worker is encouraged to work faster and produce as many items as possible, to be as conscientious and to waste as little time as possible. This has obvious advantages for the owners of the factory and for those workers who can work quickly. It is, however, not always possible to pay people a piece rate. A teacher or doctor would not necessarily be more efficient if they dealt with more people. A bus driver could become very unsafe if he were to rush his job. Often jobs are collective, a group of people are involved. In these circumstances the individual's contribution to production is difficult to determine.

Exercise

1 Draw up a list of three advantages and three disadvantages of **piece rate** and **time rates** (saying clearly whether the advantage or disadvantage is to the employer or employee).
2 Which method of payment already mentioned combines many of the advantages of both piece and time rate?

Wage differences

CASE STUDY

The weekly wage ladder

Study the wages information in the diagram in Fig 12.1. It is clear from the evidence that there is considerable variation in the level of pay between different occupations. An extreme example would be

that which exists between a Chief Foreign Exchange Dealer and his hairdresser. Both work, both have a skill, but one earns considerably more than the other. This evidence shows that there are two differences in wages. The first is that which exists between different occupations, the second is that which exists between different sexes. Male nurses have an average wage of £173.4 per week but their female colleagues have an average wage of £149.7 per week. If we consider secondary school teachers again male teachers have an average wage of £248.00 but female teachers only £214.6 per week.

Exercise

Look at the information on the weekly wages ladder overleaf.

1 List the four top paid male occupations with their weekly pay as shown on the ladder.
2 List the three bottom paid male occupations with their weekly pay as shown on the ladder.
3 List two things the highest paid occupations have in common.
4 List two things the lowest paid occupations have in common.
5 Write down the average weekly pay for both male and female nurses.
6 Give one other occupations in which male workers earn on average more than female?
7 In both nursing and your answer to question 6 workers receive equal pay. Can you think why their average income is different?

This case study shows that there are two differences in pay in this country. Different occupations receive different rates of pay and different sexes on average receive different rates of pay. Twenty-two per cent of women workers are defined as being low paid while only 10 per cent of men workers are. Women in the same occupation earn on average less than men. The highest paid 10 per cent of workers share the same amount of total income as the lowest paid 50 per cent.

The reasons for this are complicated. Your answers to the questions in the case study help us to see why but there is no one satisfactory answer.

Wage differences between occupations

The case study shows that the four top male wages were all for occupations which required long

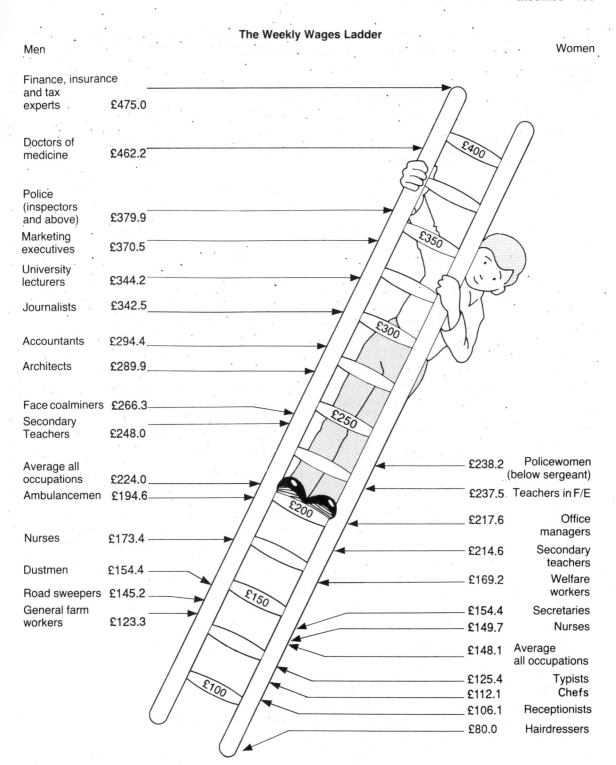

The Weekly Wages Ladder

Men

Finance, insurance and tax experts £475.0

Doctors of medicine £462.2

Police (inspectors and above) £379.9

Marketing executives £370.5

University lecturers £344.2

Journalists £342.5

Accountants £294.4

Architects £289.9

Face coalminers £266.3

Secondary Teachers £248.0

Average all occupations £224.0

Ambulancemen £194.6

Nurses £173.4

Dustmen £154.4

Road sweepers £145.2

General farm workers £123.3

Women

£238.2 Policewomen (below sergeant)

£237.5 Teachers in F/E

£217.6 Office managers

£214.6 Secondary teachers

£169.2 Welfare workers

£154.4 Secretaries

£149.7 Nurses

£148.1 Average all occupations

£125.4 Typists

£112.1 Chefs

£106.1 Receptionists

£80.0 Hairdressers

*Fig 12.1   Average gross weekly earnings for selected occupations
(Source: New Earnings Survey, 1987 HMSO)*

training, high abilities and skills. The lowest incomes were earned in occupations where the training was short and ability rather low. It is obvious that in order to attract people of high ability to certain jobs and to encourage them to train for many years they would need to be offered a higher wage.

The demand for the product the worker produces will also have an effect. Workers are not wanted by the entrepreneur for their own sake but for the particular skill they have in helping to produce a good or service. If the good or service is wanted very much by consumers who have the money to pay for it, then this might help wages to rise. For example, if a garage owner finds that he has queues of customers with cars needing servicing but has to turn them away because he has only one mechanic he would advertise for a new mechanic. If he found that no one applied for the job he might advertise again but at a higher wage.

A job might not only require a high wage because of the long training. There might also be other barriers which prevent people from taking the job unless there were high wages (*see* Fig 12.3).

People would not travel to the inhospitable North Sea to work in unpleasant surroundings, away from their families, often risking their lives, if the wages were not very high. Some professions and unions manage to keep the numbers entering the occupation low so that wages are kept high. For example, barristers and print workers. Pop stars are unique and can charge very high fees because no other person sounds quite like them and they are irreplaceable.

It is not quite so straightforward as this however, as one can find examples which do not fit our model. Nurses, for example, need dedication, work very long hours including nights, often have to undertake dirty tasks and have three years of training. One would expect them to be paid high wages, but they are not and earn much less, for example, than women police constables whose job description is very similar. This is perhaps due to the attractiveness of the job. Nurses are not very well paid, especially when compared with other countries but in spite of this being a well-known fact, nursing schools still have no shortage

TYPICAL SALARY LEVELS IN THE CITY

MANAGEMENT

Job	Sample	Salary	Total Remuneration
Chief foreign exchange dealer	119	46212	54578
Senior futures trader	26	35208	43958
Credit manager	75	29400	30436
Corporate finance executive	40	34711	38034
Asst dir portfolio management	15	50748	54772
Manager, Eurobond trading	37	50841	59819
Financial controller	53	42566	45410
Operations manager	77	27853	29440
Accountant	51	23174	24442
Manager, Systems	25	27252	28431
Adminstration manager	50	23921	25238
Head of personnel	50	33956	36572

CLERICAL & SUPERVISORY STAFF

Cashier	185	9541	9940
Junior foreign exchange clerk	341	8581	8894
Securities clerk	164	11085	11688
Eurobond settlements clerk	137	11369	12134
Foreign exchange dealer	265	26512	29279
Secretary	534	11232	11767
Executive secretary	211	14199	14982
Messenger	372	9486	9899
VDU operator	137	9229	9625
Computer operator	239	10615	10976
Graduate recruit	103	12215	12596

Survey in February 1988. Source: Wyatt Company (UK) Ltd.

Fig 12.2   (Taken from The Guardian *17.05.88)*

of applications. School leavers are attracted to nursing since they see it as a job with responsibility, variety and a sense of achievement. Perhaps such jobs do not need to offer high wages?

In some occupations the trade unions are powerful. A large percentage of the workforce are members and are united. They are prepared to take strike action to secure higher wages. In occupations where workers are spread out in small workshops, such as the clothing trade, or where there are many non-union members or even where the workers feel that they cannot strike, (such as nurses again) then wages tend to be lower. In industries where there is little or no union and owner organisation the Government establishes wages councils to set minimum wages for that occupation. These often become the normal wage and are very low.

Sex differences

Under the **Equal Pay Act, 1970**, women in the UK are entitled to equal pay with men, when undertaking work which is the same or broadly similar. The **Sex Discrimination Act, 1975**, makes it illegal to discriminate, on grounds of sex, in the recruitment, training, or promotion of staff

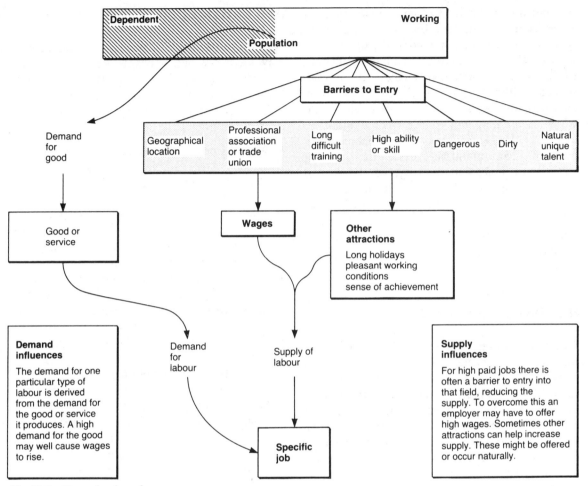

Fig 12.3 Determination of wage rates

except where there exists a genuine reason such as midwifery – reserved for women, and coal-mining – reserved for men. Advertisements might read 'attractive bar staff required' but cannot read 'attractive barmaids required'. This legislation ought to mean that in most occupations women are paid the same as their male colleagues. Our case study shows the opposite. In teaching and nursing the average wage for women is lower than that for men.

One explanation is that women do not gain posts of responsibility and therefore higher pay as often as men because they break their careers to have a family. This need not be necessarily so. **The Employment Protection Act, 1978,** gave women the right to maternity leave for 29 weeks,

with 6 weeks' pay and the right to return to their old job. This is only a right and many women choose not to exercise that right. This could be due to the lack of day-care nursery facilities in this country. If they do return to work women are often unable to work overtime since they might have to rush back home to feed and look after their family. This would explain some differences between men and women but not the very large number who are earning low wages.

Where trade unions are weak and workers spread out over many small establishments the Government has set up **wages councils** who set a legally enforceable minimum wage for those industries covered. Very often this becomes the wage and in most cases it is very low. Women are very much more likely to receive the minimum in wages council industries but most significantly about 75 per cent of wages council employees are women. Women are concentrated into occupations which are traditionally poorly paid and the wages councils, although preventing them from being exploited, tend to set the wage they will receive which is a 'minimum' figure. These industries include clothing (manufacture, i.e. machine operators in jean manufacturers), hairdressing, barworkers, hotel and catering, retail trade. In many areas such as secretarial work women are the only workers. Very few men are employed in such tasks so that the equal pay legislation made little effect and left these women in traditional 'female' employment low paid.

Non-financial rewards

Wages are often supplemented by rewarding workers with benefits in kind. Non-monetary rewards, or fringe benefits increase the total reward for a particular form of employment. They might include free or subsidised meals in a firms canteen, free clothing – a uniform or overall, subsidised hairdressers, staff discounts, company cars, non-contributory pensions, free life insurance and all sorts of other benefits. Firms offer them, in much the same way as they offer wages in order to attract and keep personnel. These benefits are not taxed in the same way as monetary income and therefore can be worth more to an employee than the money. If I receive £2.00 towards the cost of a lunch I will receive only £1.50, if a receive £2.00's worth of food I receive the whole amount. A company car, however, is taxed and there is a scale of tax charges depending upon the size and cost of the car. (1400–2000 cc costing less than 19250 is currently charged against tax at £1400). But to distinguish between those who need the car for their job like salespeople and those who receive it as a perk, the scales are halved for those who drive more than 18000 business miles in a year.

Non-monetary benefits can often work out cheaper for the business in that it is cheaper to provide them than offer wages to pay for them – for example meals.

Job satisfaction

Why do people work? The answer to this question may seem obvious – people work for financial rewards – money. The money they earn enables them to satisfy their family's needs and wants.

If we accept this model it leaves some unanswered questions:

• Why do people undertake voluntary work for no pay? For example, your teachers may run clubs and societies at lunchtime or you may belong to a youth club or voluntary organisation like the Boys' Brigade. In all of these cases the people who run them are volunteers – they receive no financial reward – very often it actually costs them money to do it.

• Why do the unemployed keep looking for jobs? The unemployed, after all, have their basic needs satisfied by the state benefits they receive (however low these may be).

• Why do people stay in certain low paid occupations when they could earn more doing something else or even nothing? During the 1982 Health Service workers dispute NUPE identified a health service gardener working in the Wigan area who would then have received £17 per week **more** if he were unemployed! Nurses could often earn more behind a bar or in a factory but they do not change their jobs.

ASSIGNMENT

Construct a questionnaire designed to show what people most like about going to work. (It might be better to have a list of 'likes' and ask people to place them in order.) When you have devised a questionnaire give it to 50 fifth year students about to leave school and 50 people who have been at work for more than one year. Chart and compare the results.

You should find that most people think money is important. But you should also discover that people work for a variety of other reasons. Most people would become bored if they had nothing to do all day. They actually enjoy working,

R B JACKSON

meeting different people at work and through their work. They enjoy the sense of achievement; in doing a job well; pleasing or helping others; developing a skill and using natural talents. They enjoy the power the job gives them over others, even if that power is limited within the confines of the job.

SUMMARY EXERCISE

1 'Workers can choose how to spend their net pay but not their gross pay.' To what extent is this true?
2 Write down two advantages of a **profit sharing scheme**; one for a worker and one for the employer.
3 Male secondary school teachers are, on average, paid more than their female colleagues. Explain why this can be so given the *Equal Pay Act, 1970*.
4 Why might a pop star earn more than a brain surgeon?
5 What might happen to the wages of car workers if people bought less cars?

6 What are **wages councils**? Why are some industries' wages covered by them and not others?
7 Why in some industries are **earnings** higher than **wage rates**?
8 Name one low paid occupation for which there is a long and difficult training and one highly paid job that most people could perform. Why does this situation exist?
9 Name three deductions which are made from **gross pay**.
10 How can trade unions influence wage rates?

ASSIGNMENTS

1 Gather as many different wages rates as you can. Either visit the local jobcentre, or look at advertisements in your local paper. Make a list in order of wage size and try to explain the differences you notice.
2 Surveys of incomes show that in the UK there exist great differences in wage rates for different occupations. For example an electricity power worker earns more than twice as much as a trained nurse. With examples explain why such differences occur, and why some people think that such differences are important.
3 After four weeks' work we are told in their advertisment on London Weekend Television that an unskilled worker at Fords Dagenham can earn £72 per week. If you were to take such a job you would take home much less. Under the following headings list what you would expect to lose and what each deduction is for:

(a) Taxes
(b) National Insurance
(c) Pension
(d) Voluntary Payments

13 Demand, Supply and the Market Clearing Price

Demand

CASE STUDY

'Popcorn'

Recently the Upper School staged performances of the hit musical GREASE.

It was a great success and played to a capacity audience (350) on each of the three nights. A small group of economics students and I offered to provide some of the refreshments. I made a deal with the local 'Pick & Pack' shop to buy their entire stock of toffee popcorn and some large bottles of Cola. (We chose these two because they fitted into the 1950's American theme). Both products were sold in plastic cups bought from the school canteen. I calculated that I had enough popcorn to fill 200 cups and that each full cup had cost about 10p. Our 'market' was the 350 people in the audience each night. We wished to sell all of the popcorn and also hoped to make a surplus for the school funds. On the Thursday night we charged 30p per cup of popcorn and sold only a disappointing 20 cups. The following night we reduced the price to 25p and sold 80 cups. I had 100 cups left and Saturday was the last performance. I reduced the price once more to 20p. I found that we ran out of popcorn before the end of the interval.

This case study illustrates a fundamental economic principle – as the price of a good falls, in general, the amount **demanded** increases. Demand is the amount of a good or service which people in a particular market are prepared to buy at a given price. It is a 'want' backed up with the ability to pay! Many children at the first performance **wanted** toffee popcorn but were unable to **buy** it because they had not brought enough money. Demand is not the same as wants. I might want a Porsche but this desire is not part of the demand

for them – as a teacher I could never afford one! At the final performance demand was higher than the supply of popcorn – people were left at the end of the queue as we ran out. Demand is not the same as **sales**.

This idea can be shown on a graph where the demand at each price is recorded – a demand schedule. The resulting line when drawn as a graph is known as the **demand curve**. (In this book shown as a straight line for simplicity)

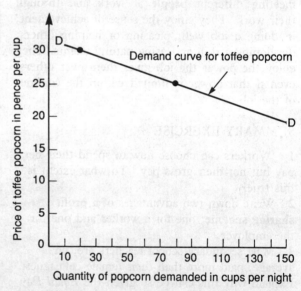

Fig 13.1

Tasks

Study the demand curve for toffee popcorn.
1 How much toffee popcorn was demanded at 25p per cup?
2 How much toffee popcorn was demanded at 20p per cup?
3 If you had this demand schedule **before** the first performance of **Grease**, what price would you recommend and why?

Shifts in the demand curve

Price is only one reason for a change in the level of demand. If more of a good or service is demanded at each price level, it is shown by a shift to the right of the demand curve. If less is demanded at each price level it is shown by a shift to the left. There are many reasons why the conditions of demand might change.

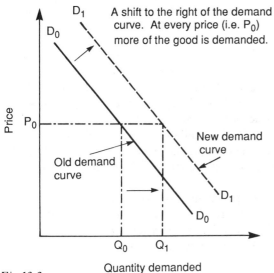

Fig 13.2

1 A change in incomes

As incomes rise, the demand for many goods will also increase. Since the war the number of private cars sold has increased. Partly because their real cost has fallen (*see* page 140) but also because real incomes have risen. The demand for meals in restaurants has also increased as incomes have risen. Some goods have experienced a reduction in demand as incomes have risen. Such goods, known as **inferior goods**, have a better, more expensive alternative. As incomes rise more people are able to afford the expensive alternative. Bread and potatoes for example are replaced by meat and cake; or a caravan holiday in Clacton is replaced by a foreign hotel! If it becomes easier to borrow money, the demand for goods may rise. A shortage of funds to finance mortgages could reduced the demand for houses for a short while.

2 A change in tastes

Fashions, tastes and habits all change or can be changed and this will cause the demand to change although the price stays the same. Clothes are very sensitive to fashion changes. Skirt lengths rise and fall, flares are in and out etc. A shop caught with clothes which are no longer 'in' is forced to lower the price to achieve higher sales. The fear of pollution from radioactive fall-out after the Chernobyl nuclear accident reduced the demand for lamb.

Taste changes can be artificially manufactured. Persuasive **advertising** aims to influence our tastes and therefore demand.

3 A change in the price of a competitive or complimentary good

We have seen above that the demand for a good or service will be influenced by the price. If the price of a similar competitive good or **substitute** changes this might alter the demand for a good. For example, beef and lamb. If the price of beef were to drop dramatically the demand for lamb might well fall as more people choose to eat beef.

Other goods are in **joint** demand – you cannot have one without the other – complimentary goods. A battery-driven toy car, for example, is useless without a battery. A shop will find that if the price of the car is lowered, perhaps during a sale, then the demand for batteries will increase, even thought their price remains the same.

4 Demographic changes

The size and structure of a population might affect demand. A growing population will have growing demands. An ageing population will have changing demands. (*See* page 58.)

Task ▰▰▰▰▰▰▰▰▰▰▰▰▰▰▰▰▰

For each of the following situations draw a demand curve shift to illustrate the change in the conditions of demand:
(*a*) The demand for video tapes – given a reduction in the price of video recorders
(*b*) The demand for a chocolate bar after a successful advertising campaign
(*c*) The demand for butter if a growing number of people believe too much animal fat to be unhealthy
(*d*) The demand for maternity wear as the birthrate falls due to an ageing population

The elasticity of demand

Elasticity is a measure of how much a change in one variable will affect another.

Price elasticity of demand is a measure of how much the demand for a good alters when its price changes. It is calculated by using the following formula:

$$\text{Price elasticity of demand} = \frac{\text{\% change in the quantity demanded}}{\text{\% change in price}}$$

Take the original popcorn example:

$$\frac{\dfrac{\text{Change in quantity}}{\text{Original quantity}}}{\dfrac{\text{Change in price}}{\text{Original price}}} \quad \frac{\dfrac{60}{20}}{\dfrac{5}{30}} = \frac{3}{\frac{1}{6}} = 18$$

If price elasticity >1 it is **elastic**
If price elasticity <1 it is **inelastic**
Was the demand for toffee popcorn elastic or inelastic?
This elasticity can be seen by the SLOPE of the demand curve:

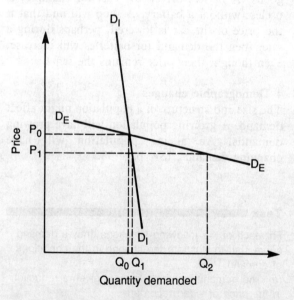

D_ID_I is 'inelastic': the reduction in price $P_0 - P_1$ produces only a small increase in quantity demanded $Q_0 - Q_1$
D_ED_E is 'elastic': the reduction in price $P_0 - P_1$ produces a large increase in the quality demanded $Q_0 - Q_2$

Fig 13.3

Task ■■■■■■■■■■■■■■■

In each of the following situations predict whether the good or service has an elastic or inelastic demand:
(a) The price of all cigarettes rises due to an increase in tax.
(b) The price of Rover Group cars rises due to higher labour costs.
(c) The price of a box of matches rises.
(d) The price of LP records rises.
(e) The price of one make of crisps rises in the school tuck shop while others remain the same.

It should be clear that goods and services for which there is a close substitute readily available (b) and (e) will tend to be price elastic. While those with no close substitute (a) and (d) will tend to be price inelastic. Goods which are very cheap (c) will also tend to be price inelastic. A 50 per cent increase in the price of a 6p box of matches will not encourage people to buy an expensive lighter!

The significance of price elasticity of demand.
A firm's **total revenue** is the value of its sales –
average price × quantity sold.
Study the following graph:

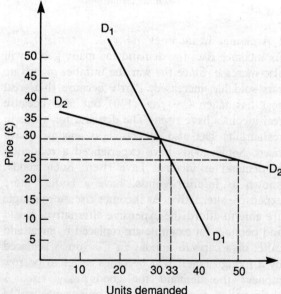

Fig 13.4

Firm 1 faces a demand schedule shown by demand curve D1D1. This is price **inelastic**. If the price **falls** from £30–£25 demand increases from 30–33.

Firm 2 faces the demand schedule shown by demand curve D2D2. This is price **elastic**. If the price falls from £30–£25 demand increase from 30–50.

Tasks

1 For each firm calculate the total revenue before and after the price reduction.
2 Which firm gained revenue due to the price fall and which firm lost revenue as a result of the falling price?
3 If a firm faced a demand schedule where the price elasticity were 1 (unit elasticity) how would price changes effect revenue?

From the task above it can be seen that when the demand for a good is price inelastic, a fall in price will decrease total revenue and a rise in price will increase total revenue. When, however, the demand for a good or service is price elastic, a fall in price will increase total revenue and a rise in price will decrease total revenue.

The demand for toffee popcorn was price elastic – when I reduced the price revenue increased.

Income elasticity of demand

Income elasticity of demand measures how much the demand for a good changes as incomes changed. It is calculated using the following formula:

$$\text{Income elasticity of demand for good X} = \frac{\text{\% change in demand for good X}}{\text{\% change in income}}$$

For most goods and services the income elasticity of demand is +ve. If incomes rise, the demand for holidays, meals in restaurants, new cars etc will also rise. Inferior goods, however, will have −ve income elasticity of demand. As incomes rise people choose a more expensive superior alternative.

Tasks

1 State which of the following goods you would expect to have +ve and which −ve income elasticities of demand.

(a) pop records
(b) foreign holidays
(c) British holidays
(d) sausages
(e) steak
2 Calculate the income elasticity of demand for the following goods:
(a) a good which shows a 30% increase in demand following a 10% increase in real incomes.
(b) a good which shows a 10% drop in demand following a 20% increase in real incomes.

Cross elasticity of demand

Cross elasticity of demand measures how much the demand for one good will change given a price change in another good. It is calculated using the following formula:

$$\text{Cross elasticity of demand} = \frac{\text{\% change in demand for good X}}{\text{\% change in the price of good Y}}$$

For goods which are complimentary, in joint demand the cross elasticity of demand will be negative. The demand for dishwasher powder will increase as the price of dishwashers fall. Whereas, goods which are in competition and are close substitutes – beef and lamb – will have positive cross elasticities of demand. As the price of one increases so the demand for the other increases.

Task

Calculate the following cross elasticities of demand:
(a) The price of toy cars falls by 10 per cent and the demand for batteries increases by 2 per cent.
(b) The price of butter increases by 30 per cent and the demand for margarine increases by 10 per cent.

Supply

Supply is the quantity of a good or service which producers are prepared to make available to a particular market at a given price.

CASE STUDY EXERCISE

Strawberry fair

Mr Higgins owns a small farm in the West Midlands. Most of his land is devoted to wheat and other cereals but over the last few years he has been experimenting with a couple of fields of strawberries. He sells these on a 'pick-your-own' basis. By displaying boards on the main road he is able to attract passing motorists. He has made a small car park and constructed a shed in which customers can weigh the strawberries they have picked and pay his son who sits and takes the money. He has calculated that to make about the same profit from a field of strawberries as a field of wheat he must sell them at about 30p per pound.

Strawberries have a very short season depending upon the weather. The first few strawberries are ready in early June but within a few weeks all the fruit is ready for picking. This year he found that when the first few strawberries were ripe by setting the price at 60p per pound only a few motorists were stopping and some fruit was being wasted by becoming over-ripe. He droped the price after a few days to 50p a pound and found that many more people stopped to pick. After one further week of very hot, sunny weather most of his field was ready for picking but not enough customers were coming. He dropped the price still further to 40p per pound and found that now most of the strawberries were being picked.

By the end of the season he found that he had made a healthy profit.

A high price in one year and good profits will encourage Mr Higgins to plant more fields with strawberries in the future. At a higher price more will be supplied. If the price fell to 25p per pound Mr Higgins would probably give up the idea and return to his wheat or try something else. At a lower price, less will be supplied. This illustrates another important economic principle. At higher prices more of a good or service is generally supplied and at low prices less of a good or service is generally supplied. This can be illustrated in graphical form and the resulting line is known as a supply curve:

Exercise

1 Why did Mr Higgins find that more people stopped to pick his strawberries as he dropped his price?

2 In a poor year, with little or no sun, less fruit would ripen. Do you think that the price charged by Mr Higgins would be higher or lower than 40p per pound?

3 Local farmers, neighbours of Mr Higgins, envious of his new car bought with the profits from his strawberries, decide to plant their own strawberries. Within a couple of years many farms along the same main road will have pick-your-own strawbery signs. How do you think this will effect the price of strawberries?

4 Mr Higgins tried to increase his custom by reducing price. What other methods might he have used?

5 If Mr Higgins found that the only way he could sell all of his crop was to lower the price to 25p per pound and in this way clear his fields what would he do next year?

6 If an authoritative report showed that strawberries were definitely a strong aphrodisiac (a substance which is supposed to increase sexual desire), what do you think would happen to the number of people wanting to pick Mr Higgins' strawberries and what do you think he would do to his price?

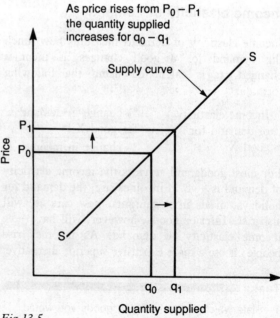

As price rises from $P_0 - P_1$ the quantity supplied increases for $q_0 - q_1$

Fig 13.5

Price elasticity of supply

This is measurement of how changes in the price of a particular good or service affect the amount firms supply. It can be calculated using this formula:

$$\text{Price elasticity of supply} = \frac{\text{\% change in the quantity supplied}}{\text{\% change in the price}}$$

For some goods and services the quantity supplied is fixed. It does not matter how high the price, rises the supply cannot increase. Recently I took my wife to see 'Phantom of the Opera' – we waited just over a year for the tickets which cost £22.50 each! The price could reach £100 and there could be no increase in the number of tickets – the theatre is sold for a year in advance. In such circumstances, economists describe the supply as totally inelastic. (0)

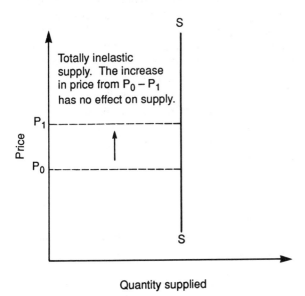

Fig 13.6

Such cases are rare and firms can usually increase supply in response to price increases – they wish to increase profits after all. Where the price elasticity of supply is >1, the supply is said to be elastic.

Elasticity and time

The way in which supply reacts to changes in price will be subject to **time-lags**. At first, the supply of most products is fixed. If people suddenly wanted more chocolate bars little could be done for a few days, economists call this the short term. The elasticity of supply being 0. After a short period, supply can be a little more responsive. Chocolate companies can ask their workers to work overtime. This is known as the medium term. The elasticity of supply is now >0. Given years new factories can be built and the supply of chocolate can expand to any level. In the long term the elasticity of supply becomes infinite.

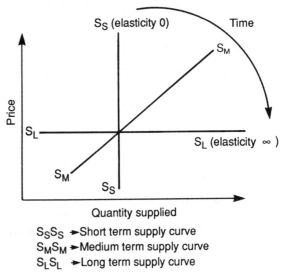

Fig 13.7

In the example above the chocolate company took time to react to changes in demand.

Tasks

1 Name one commodity for which the supply is **fixed**, i.e. unable to increase over time.
2 What would be the elasticity of supply for the product named in answer to question 1?

Shifts in the supply curve

Price is one factor which determines the level of supply for a good or service and this relationship is illustrated by the supply curve. If the conditions of supply alter more or less may be supplied at every price – there has been a shift in supply.

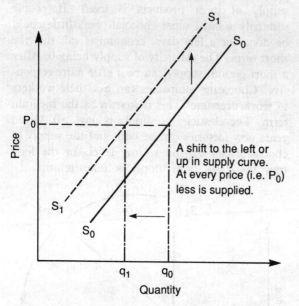

Fig 13.8

The conditions of supply can change for the following reasons:

1   Changes in the costs of production.
Technological progress will reduce the cost of production and can mean a shift to the right in the supply curve. On the other hand a rise in energy costs could shift the supply curve to the left – less supplied at each price.

2   Change in the price of other goods and services.
Some products are supplied **jointly**. When crude oil is refined into petroleum; naptha (the raw material for plastics) is also produced. If the price of petroleum falls and, as a result, a greater volume of petroleum is refined, the supply of naptha will rise which may cause a fall in its price. Other goods are in **competitive** supply. In agriculture where good land is scarce, if the price of one crop rises, farmers may switch to the cultivation of that crop to the exclusion of another. In the Sudan the increased planting of cotton has reduced the supply of wheat.

3   Natural changes
The weather has an affect on the supply of some **agricultural** products. The supply of minerals will depend upon discoveries of new deposits.

Task

For each of the following changes state whether the supply curve for strawberries will shift to the left (up) or to the right (down) or remain the same.
(*a*) A new higher yielding variety is introduced.
(*b*) The price of other soft fruits rise very quickly.
(*c*) The price of strawberries rise very quickly.
(*d*) A cold spring is followed by a very wet early summer.

The market clearing price

At any given price a certain amount will be demanded. At any given price a certain amount will be supplied.

Given the supply and demand schedules opposite at price £60 both the amount demanded and supplied equals 600. The market will be cleared: all buyers (at that price) will be able to satisfy their demands and all sellers (at that price) will exhaust their supplies. Both sides will be happy. This being the case, suppliers will tend to produce a similar amount at that price in the immediate future. This is therefore known as the equilibrium or market clearing price. If the price were much lower at £50, demand would exceed supply, a shortage would exist, queues would form, shelves would be empty. In such circumstances retailers would increase prices, in order to increase profits and suppliers would take all short-term measures possible to increase output. Prices and output would therefore rise – towards the equilibrium level.

If price levels were much higher at £70, supply exceeds demand, a surplus would exist, warehouses would be full retailers would be unable to empty shelves. In such circumstances retailers would reduce prices to clear the shelves and reduce orders, suppliers would take all short-term measures to reduce output. Prices and output would therefore fall – towards the equilibrium level.

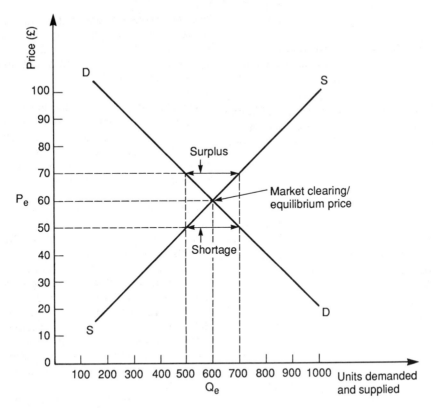

Fig 13.9   The market clearing price

Changes in the market clearing price

Changes in the market price are caused by changes in the conditions of supply, the conditions of demand or both.
Read this article:

This may at first look like a complicated sequence of events but it is not and what you have learnt above will help you analyse just what is happening.

BA Launches Price War

"British Airways is set to spark a transatlantic price war from tomorrow when it introduces a series of bargain fares to the United States.

BA is cutting the cost of summer stand-by fares to a number of US destinations. The largest cuts are on routes from Heathrow and Gatwick to Los Angeles and Heathrow-San Francisco, where the cost of a stand-by ticket will fall from £289 to £199.

While transatlantic passenger volumes have risen this year, considerable capacity has been added to routes between the US and UK, with carries such as Delta, American Continental and Piedmont all increasing routes and aircraft."

Adapted from the Observer
23.05.88

Demand

The demand for air tickets between the UK and US has risen (. . . transatlantic passenger volumes have risen . . .). This is due to rising incomes. On both sides of the Atlantic those in work are better off; they can afford better holidays and effective advertising is enticing them to try America/Europe. Both of these factors will cause the demand curve to shift to the right.

Supply

Supply has increased (. . . considerable capacity has been added to routes. . .). New airlines have begun to operate between the US and UK, presumably they have been granted route licences by the Civil Aviation Authority. This would shift the supply to the right, with more seats being offered at every price.

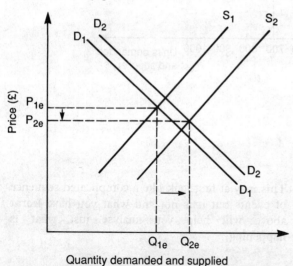

Fig 13.10   The changing market price for transatlantic airline seats

The new equilibrium price is lower because supply has increased (new airlines) but not as low as it might have been because the demand for seats has increased (higher wages/advertising).

CASE STUDY

Tea

During 1984 the price of tea reached a record £3170 a tonne. Poor harvests due to bad weather

and restrictions on exports from India (the world's biggest supplier with its 30 per cent share of the export market) combined to reduce supply and push up prices. These high prices appear to have led to falling consumption in Britain, the world's largest market.

On Christmas day 1983 the Indian Government imposed a five month ban on the export of popular varieties of tea. This was immediately followed in 1984, by the limiting of exports to 215 000 tonnes. Both these moves were aimed at conserving domestic supplies and thereby checking an advance in local prices, a politically sensitive issue.

Record harvests in 1984, of 645 000 tonnes and an expected harvest of 651 000 tonnes in 1985 were not only due to kind weather. Greater output has also been due to the increase use of fertilisers and pesticides – something that has been encouraged in most tea producing countries by the attractive prices of 1983 and 1984. This led the Indian Government to announce an export target of 220 000 tonnes and hint that it could be raised. This (combined with higher output in East Africa where there was no drought and in Sri Lanka) led to the price falling to a low of £1971 a tonne in Britain in April 1985.

Given good weather and no surprise restrictions on exports the tea market could well be over-supplied in 1985 for the first time for many years. For Britain this would be good news. Tea is still our favourite drink, with each person on average drinking four cups a day.
(*Adapted from Robin Stainer's commodities report*, The Guardian *9 April 1985.*)

Tasks

1   What reasons are given for the reduced supply of tea during 1983/4?
2   What was the effect of this reduction in supply on the price of tea in London?
3   Why might restrictions on the export of tea from India have a greater effect on price than a reduction in supplies from East Africa due to drought?
4   Copy out and complete the following diagram to explain the increased price of tea during 1983/4.

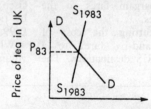

Quantity demanded/supplied in UK

5 What effect are we told the increased price of tea had on the amount consumed?

6 Would you expect the demand for tea to be elastic or inelastic? Give reasons.

7 Why did the Indian Government restrict the export of tea during 1984?

8 How were bumper crops achieved in 1985?

9 Copy out and complete the following diagram to explain the reduced price of tea in 1985:

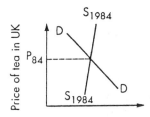

Quantity demanded/supplied in UK

10 How did high world tea prices in 1983/4 encourage the bumper crops of 1984/5?

11 Draw diagrams (as in questions **4** and **9**) and explain what effect each of the following would have on the price of tea:

(a) Rapid increase in the demand for tea in India.

(b) A report that too much tea is **bad** for your health leads to a reduction in the average daily consumption of tea in the UK from four to two cups.

(c) Civil war in East Africa and droughts lead to a very poor harvest.

(d) New varieties of tea which produce far greater crop yields are introduced in India.

12 You work for an advertising agency which has been engaged by the Indian Government. New varieties of tea which produce far greater crop yields have dramatically increased the amount of tea exported by India. This has led to a reduction in the price of tea. Your brief is to devise an effective marketing campaign aimed at raising the average daily consumption of tea from four to five cups. In groups discuss:

- The 'image' of tea. How could this be improved?
- The typical consumer. Build up a consumer profile. How could this be altered? How could tea be made attractive to the young who may prefer coffee?
- What market research would you commission?
- How could 'health and fitness' be linked to tea drinking?
- What media would you use for your campaign?
- Design the campaign itself. Can you think of a good catch phrase? (Like 'Go to work on an egg').

- Timing. When should advertising take place?
- What legal/other restrictions are there on the campaign – just what can you say?

Each member of the group ought to write a report based upon one or two aspects of your discussion for reporting back to the whole class.

Costs

CASE STUDY

The marine aquarium

Andrew, a sixth form student at West Hatch High School, has recently set up his own, small tropical fish importing business. He calls it 'The Marine Aquarium'.

Andrew had worked part-time for several years in a shop selling tropical fish. He noticed that only one business in the London area imported certain rare types of salt-water fish into the country from places like Hawaii. On holiday in America Andrew was able to contact the divers who caught these tropical fish and found that many were prepared to send fish to him. Special containers to keep the fish warm were needed and the only transport method fast enough was air freight.

Andrew made a few 'test imports' and was surprised to find that he could sell fish far cheaper than his rival and still make a profit. There were problems. He had to pay for the fish and the transport in advance – before he had sold them. This meant that he needed some cash or **working capital** and since he had very little money saved he needed to borrow. Also more tanks to keep his fish in and special equipment to filter and oxygenate the water had to be purchased. He needed a van to deliver the goods, collect them from the airport and to collect food and equipment. He found that he could insure the fish while in transit.

Faced with such problems many would have given up but Andrew went to an accountant and drew up a plan. Together they decided that he would need to borrow £10 000, but, if things went well he could expect to make a healthy profit.

One of the most important decisions Andrew had to make was what price to charge for the fish he imported. He knew that he would need to cover his **costs**. These were of two types:

Variable costs The fish had to be bought in Hawaii and transported to London. The more he imported the higher these costs would be (if he

Variable costs

The Yellow Tang – Hawaii

Cost per box – assuming 10 boxes in consignment, average weight – 35 lb per box

	$	£
Cost of fish (1 box, 30 fish)	60.00	
Freight	96.60	
Packing	7.50	
Import duty (15%)	24.61	
Total	188.71	134.80 (£1 = $1.4)
Handling charge (Heathrow) (£35 per consignment)		3.50
Transport to Barking (£15 per consignment)		1.50
*Total (28.5 fish)		139.80
Cost per fish (÷ 28.5)		4.90

*(Average 5% loss)

imported more fish he paid higher bills). Look at the example of variable costs; the cost of importing a box of Yellow Tang.

If Andrew were to charge £4.90 for each Yellow Tang he would cover these variable costs – the costs of importing the fish into the country, but, he would not cover his **overheads** or **fixed costs**.

Fixed costs   These are those costs Andrew will have to cover however many fish he manages to sell. Expenses such as interest repayments on his loan, advertising, insurance, certain of the costs of running a van (road tax and insurance) and his own wages will occur and have to be paid even if he sells no fish. Andrew was also advised to set aside some money each year in order to replace his equipment after a few years. This is called **depreciation** and would also count as a fixed cost. As can be seen in the following table this came to £13 637 in his first year. Andrew was lucky to have won a competition run by the Abbey National Building Society called 'Head Start for Business' which gave him free accommodation for a year. If he had to pay for this it would add to fixed costs. These costs had to be spread over the number of fish Andrew could sell; the price of each containing an element to cover **fixed** costs as well as the **variable** costs calculated above. The amount to be added to variable costs, in each case, to cover fixed costs would depend upon how many fish Andrew could sell. If he only sold one fish he would need to charge the variable cost *plus* £13 637. Andrew and his accountant estimated that he could expect to

Fixed costs

	£
Van	3 185
Insurance	450
Interest	1 452
Depreciation	1 550
Wages	2 600
Advertising	800
Others	3 600
Total	13 637

import 34 shipments in the first year each costing him (variable cost) £1200. If these were sold for £2000 (a 40% mark-up) a profit could be made:

The 40% mark-up means that the **final selling price** £68 000 would split 60% to cover variable costs and 40% to cover fixed and profit. (It is calculated by multiplying £40 800 by 100 and dividing by 60.)

If this 40% mark-up is applied to individual fish Andrew is able to calculate the price list.

The Yellow Tang had a variable cost of £4.90 which with a mark-up would equal:

$$\frac{£4.90 \times 100}{60} = £8.17 \text{ (Andrew charges £8 for ease)}$$

This is how it is made up:

Variable costs: Cost of fish in Hawaii	20%
Freight and duty	40%

Estimated profit (34 shipments)

	Expenses £	Income £
Sale of fish (34 shipments @ £2000)		68 000
Variable costs		
Purchase of fish (34 shipments @ £1200)	40 800	
Fixed costs	13 637	
	———	
Total costs	54 437	
	———	
Net profit (Income – total costs)		13 563
		═══

Fixed cost: Overheads (comprising van, interest, *wages, depreciation and others)	20%
Profit:	20%

Note Wages are sometimes considered to be **variable costs** since in large concerns they can alter with output. More can be produced, for example, if workers undertake overtime. Other workers will be paid the same however much is produced and are unlikely to be sacked if there is a temporary drop in production – such wages are therefore **fixed costs**. In this case Andrew expects to reward his efforts with £50 per week (£2600 per year) however many fish he imports and in this sense represents a **fixed cost**.

Exercise

1 If low orders or poor weather in Hawaii prevent Andrew from reaching his target number of shipments he will make less profit if he keeps the same mark-up. **Calculate** using the table Andrew's net profit if he only manages to import 17 shipments each costing £1200 in his first year, assuming all other costs remain unchanged.

	Expenses £	Income £
Estimated profit (17 shipments)		
Sale of fish (17 shipments @ £2000)		
Variable costs: Purchase of fish (17 shipments @ £1200)		
Fixed costs		
	———	
Total costs		
	———	
Net profit (Income – total costs)		═══

2 Using a suitable table calculate Andrew's expected profit if he manages to import only 13 shipments in his first year.

3 Using similar axes to those below complete a line graph to show profit or loss for different numbers of shipment:

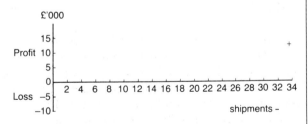

4 If Andrew found himself unable to cover his costs he would be making a loss. Since he must pay back his loan he might be tempted to increase the price of his fish. Why might this be a mistake?

5 Some large fish, for example the 'Naso Tang' have a much higher mark-up. A Naso Tang costs Andrew £10 per fish to import into the country but he can sell one for as much as £35. Give one reason for this higher mark-up.

6 In the 'Yellow Tang' example the air freight charge is $96.60 ($2.76 per pound) because Andrew imported 10 boxes at 35 lb per box – a total shipment weight of 350 lb.

Pan-Am Freight Charges Hawaii – Heathrow

Total shipment weight	Cost per lb $
100–219 lb	3.44
220–659 lb	2.76
660–1099 lb	2.10
1100 lb and over	1.69

If Andrew were to import 35 boxes (35 lb per box) of Yellow Tang in one shipment use the information above to calculate the **variable cost** of a single Yellow Tang.

	Cost per box (35 boxes average weight 35 lb)	
	$	£
Cost of fish (1 box 30 fish)	60.00	
Air freight		
Packing	7.50	
Import duty (15%)	___	___
Total	___	÷1.4 ___
Handling charge (£35 per shipment)		1.00
Transport to Barking (£15 per shipment)		.50
Total per box		___
Cost per fish (÷ 28.5)		___

7 Andrew's only competitor in the London area imports very large quantities of fish – far more than Andrew will at first. This competitor would not only pay the lower air freight charges but with a larger van and storage facilities will buy in bulk and therefore probably pay less for the fish and feed etc. It is surprising that this competitor charges similar prices to Andrew. What do you conclude about this competitor's mark-up and profit?

8 Andrew is tempted to charge lower prices than his only rival in the London area, but had heard that this rival would like to see Andrew out of business. If Andrew did lower his prices:

(*a*) What would be the likely response of Andrew's rival?
(*b*) Would this help tropical fish collectors?
(*c*) What would happen to Andrew's profit?
(*d*) What else could Andrew do with his borrowed capital?

9 If the rate of exchange of £1 to dollars were to **fall** to £1 = $1.2 what would be the effect on Andrew's **variable costs**?
10 If the rate of exchange of £1 to dollars were to **rise** to £1 = $1.6 what would be the effect on Andrew's **variable costs**?

SUMMARY

1 Andrew must charge a price which covers *all* of his costs. Fixed costs remain constant but variable costs increase as Andrew imports more. For Andrew although variable costs increase as orders increase they do so at a falling rate. The variable cost per fish *falls* as Andrew imports more fish since air freight charges are less per pound for large orders and some handling charges are fixed. Large orders result in Andrew using his capital more efficiently and enable him to make a higher profit.

2 When deciding upon a price Andrew must cover all costs but he must also be aware of his competitor's price. If Andrew charges more than this competitor he will probably sell fewer fish.

3 A rare fish can sell with a much higher mark-up. Collectors are prepared to pay these very high prices. The fish are so rare that the divers do not find them very often – or offer them to Andrew very often.

4 While his trade is small Andrew cannot afford to undercut his competitor. If Andrew were to charge a very low price for fish this competitor would do the same and both businesses would receive lower profits. The competitor with large shipments and more equipment enjoys economies of large scale operation and would be able to force Andrew out of business.

5 If Andrew is unable to make a profit he must look for an alternative use for his capital and expertise; perhaps he could specialise in importing crustacea (crabs).

6 Changes in the exchange rate of the pound to the dollar will be a major influence upon Andrew's variable costs. A fall in the exchange rate will mean that he has to pay more pounds for the same number of dollars and will therefore cause a rise in variable costs. A rise in the exchange rate will mean that he is able to buy more dollars for the number of pounds and therefore cause the variable costs to fall. The cost of the fish in Hawaii remains the same but the value of the pound has changed. This outside influence will affect *all* fish importers and not just Andrew.

Postscript

Andrew was unable to borrow the £10 000 he needed to make this business work. Although most of the banks and Government agencies he contacted all agreed that these figures were correct and that he could make a profit and perhaps in a few years have a firm which employed several people he had one problem – his age. At 17 it is very difficult to borrow money for any purpose since 18 is the legal age at which people become adults.

Andrew did not give up and has, through various contacts, managed to arrange an overdraft facility for £5000 at the National Westminster Bank. He has been promised a further £1000 from a charitable trust. This has meant a reduction in plans. He has not got the cash to order large shipments from abroad to sell and he is short of working capital. But he still trades as this recent advertisement in a specialist magazine shows.

The advertisement mentions 'consolidation'. This means acting as an importing agent for a number of customers – in this case shops. Each shop does not require a full order or have the expertise to arrange a shipment. Andrew will undertake the paperwork required for a number of shops adding their small orders together to make one large worthwhile shipment. The shops pay him in advance for the cost of the fish they require plus a commission to cover Andrew's costs and provide him with a profit. This is not what Andrew wants and the profits are much less but he does not need so much working capital and it suits him until he is 18 and can start importing on a large scale.

SUMMARY EXERCISE

1 What is the difference between a want and a demand?

2 Name one good for which the demand might fall if the price fell.

3 Give **three** examples of complimentary goods and competitive goods.

4 How might a falling birth rate affect (a) Mothercare? (b) a County Council?

5 Draw demand curves which illustrate the results of a successful advertising campaign for Ariel Automatic.

6 Name one good you would expect to have income inelastic demand.

7 Draw supply curves for wheat which illustrate the 1988 American drought. What happened to the world price of wheat?

8 Is the supply of anything fixed in the long run?

9 How could you illustrate the Government-imposed expenditure tax on petrol using a supply curve?

10 How does the shift in the supply curve, illustrated in your answer to **9**, affect the equilibrium price?

11 Give one example of a fixed cost faced by an entrepreneur and one example of a variable cost.

12 As output increases do fixed costs represent an increasing or decreasing proportion of total costs?

14 Distribution

Transporting finished products to the customer from the producer is an important part of satisfying wants. It is therefore a part of the production process. People 'want' goods and services close to their homes, not 200 miles away in a factory. This last element of production is known as **distribution**.

Traditionally distribution is split into two steps:

1 Manufacturers deliver large loads of their one product to a **wholesaler**.
2 The wholesaler delivers consignments of many types of goods from many different manufacturers to the shops or **retailers**.

Wholesaling

The **wholesaler** is sometimes called the middleman – he stands between the producer and retailer. At first it would seem possible and even desirable to do away with the wholesaler since as businesses in their own right they must make a profit and therefore charge more for the goods they sell to the retailer than that they pay the producer. When we consider what they do it becomes clear that the wholesaler performs a number of useful services.

The functions of the wholesaler

1 Breaking bulk By taking large loads from the producer and dividing them into smaller consignments we say that the wholesaler is **breaking bulk**. This provides a service for both the producer and retailer. The producer does not want the trouble of selling many small loads and the retailer does not want the bother of contacting many producers so as to provide a choice for his customers. It also saves money since having a middleman is more efficient.

2 Warehousing Retailers have little room for storing goods – they require maximum space for selling. Producers do not wish to fill their factories with finished goods as they will take up the space needed for production. The wholesaler allows the retailer space to sell and the producer room to produce by storing goods in bulk. In doing so they take a risk. If the goods they hold go out of fashion retailers will not buy them and the wholesaler will make a loss.

3 Finance The wholesaler will often give the retailer time to pay or credit. This is particularly useful for small businesses that might need time to sell goods before paying for them. The producer needs payment immediately, however, in order to be able to pay wages and buy raw materials. The wholesaler will pay for the goods soon after delivery.

4 Specialist services Wholesalers employ expert buyers and can give expert advice. They also package items often putting them on to cards which hang in the retailer's shop. Wine wholesalers bottle and blend.

Some wholesalers like Nerdin and Peacock offer **cash and carry** services to the small retailer or caterer. They look like huge supermarkets and customers, either retailers or caterers, buy items for sale or bulk catering packs for use. They pay by **cash** and then **carry** their purchases away in their own vans. This reduces the cost since they do not have to pay delivery charges. It also gives them choice since it presents them with a range of products on show.

Large supermarket chains such as Sainsbury or the Coop and voluntary groups like Londis must still have a wholesaling operation but they undertake this themselves thus keeping the profits within one firm or organisation. It would be incorrect to think that the wholesaling function had been removed. Such organisations will still have central depots or warehouses to which bulk orders are delivered and from where smaller multi-product deliveries are made to branches. The wholesaler as a separate business unit may well have been removed but not the function.

Retailing

Retailers or shops provide a valuable service to the customer. They are the last link in the chain of production and provide a range of goods locally thus saving the customer time and trouble as well as providing a choice of products, specialist help and advice and after sales service. Think of a consumer who wants a video recorder. By going to one shop he can look at many models, some produced in other countries. He can try them and ask an expert about the qualities of each. He can have the machine he purchases serviced and repaired at the same shop and be given advice on how best to look after it. The shop will sell him blank tapes and even sell or rent him pre-recorded ones.

CASE STUDY

'Open all hours'

Study the following two shop profiles and then answer the questions.

Profile 1 **Universal Stores**

OPENING HOURS
Mon	8.00–20.00
Tue	8.00–20.00
Wed	8.00–20.00
Thur	8.00–20.00
Fri	8.00–20.30
Sat	8.00–18.00
Sun	9.30–12.00

Ownership Sole proprietor – one family, Mr Reynolds, aged 40, and his wife aged 38.

Location Main road in suburban area. Opposite factory and close to railway station. A bus stop is quite close and the shop is surrounded by terraced and semi-detached housing. A new housing estate is being built opposite, next to the factory.

Fig 14.1

Type of Shop Converted front room of terraced house. Counter service but limited range of groceries, cigarettes and frozen food only. Will serve any amount of unwrapped food – even one slice of bacon.

Car parking Difficult – main road but side – streets quite close.

Staff Mr Reynolds and his wife only. Very friendly, always a laugh and joke, especially with regulars.

Prices Expensive compared with supermarkets:

Five Price Survey

1 pt Homogenised milk	28 p
50 g Nescafé coffee	81 p
1 kg Granulated sugar	60 p
540 ml Fairy washing-up liquid	54 p
Johnson Glade Air Machine	61 p
Total	£2.84

Profile 2 **Starbuy Supermarket Ltd**

OPENING HOURS
Mon	9.00–18.00
Tue	8.30–20.00
Wed	8.30–20.00
Thur	8.30–20.00
Fri	8.30–20.00
Sat	8.30–17.00
Sun	CLOSED

Ownership Public joint stock company – thousands of shareholders, many of whom are customers or employees. The majority of shares, however, are owned by institutions like pension funds or banks.

Fig 14.2

Location   Centre of large town shopping precinct purpose built by council and Starbuy Supermarkets Ltd seven years ago. All bus routes from neighbouring villages run to the centre. It would cost 30 p each way from the bus stop outside Universal Stores.

Types of shop   Modern supermarket selling all lines from groceries, fresh fruit and vegetables, toiletries, household goods, some clothes, beer, wines and spirits, cigarettes. It has a delicatessen, hot bread shop, fresh meat and wet fish counters. All self-service with trollies and baskets.

Car parking   The centre has two multi-storey car parks with lifts to all shops. Cost 35 p flat rate. (Open-air car parks surround the centre with pay and display at 25 p but they are a good half mile from the shops.)

Staff   Starbuy employs nearly 100 staff throughout the week – many working flexi-time. Specialist managers run the major departments – all have been trained.

Prices   Much cheaper than Universal. Many 'own brand' items cheaper still. In our Five Item Survey we compared the same brands. It must be remembered that a cheaper 'own brand' often existed which we did not buy.

Five Price Survey

1 pt Homogenised milk	22 p
50 g Nescafé coffee	75 p
1 kg Granulated sugar	54 p
540 ml Fairy washing-up liquid	45 p
Johnson Glade Air Machine	54 p
Total	**£2.50**

Exercise

1   Universal Stores are at least 10 per cent more expensive than Starbuy on all items. If a shopper lived close to Universal, approximately how much would they need to spend to make it worthwhile travelling into the town centre if:
(*a*) they had a car and
(*b*) they did not have a car?
2   Why might a young couple, with a car, prefer to shop in Starbuy even if they plan only to spend a few pounds?

3 Why might an old age pensioner prefer to do her weekly shop at Universal.

4 What would be the likely effect on Universal's trade if the Council reduced bus fares and car parking charges?

5 Give three advantages Starbuy has for the customer over Universal other than price and location.

6 Give three advantages Universal has for the customer over Starbuy.

7 Write two sentences describing the typical customer at Universal.

8 Write two sentences describing the typical customer at Starbuy.

9 Give two reasons which might explain why Universal prices are higher than Starbuy.

Types of shop

Independent, single outlet retailer Universal is an example of an independently owned shop. The owners, in this case Mr and Mrs Reynolds, only have one shop from which to sell goods. Such small establishments like Universal in our case study are to be found in residential areas where they survive by providing a service because they are convenient and open unusual hours. They can be found in villages again proving far more convenient than a long trip into town. Some small shops offer a specialist service selling unusual products and giving expert advice.

Multiple retailers Public companies like Tesco and J Sainsbury have opened hundreds of similar outlets all over the country. They have a chain of stores and are therefore often called **chain stores**. They can buy large quantities of the goods they wish to sell at lower prices. As we saw in the Tesco case study it became worthwhile for Tesco to produce its own brands – indeed Tesco Tea was the product which started Jack Cohen on the road to success.

Customers become familiar with these chain stores and stay loyal to them even when they move.

Retail cooperatives also fall into the above category (*see* Chapter 4).

Supermarkets Most chain stores are organised as supermarkets. This means that goods are laid out

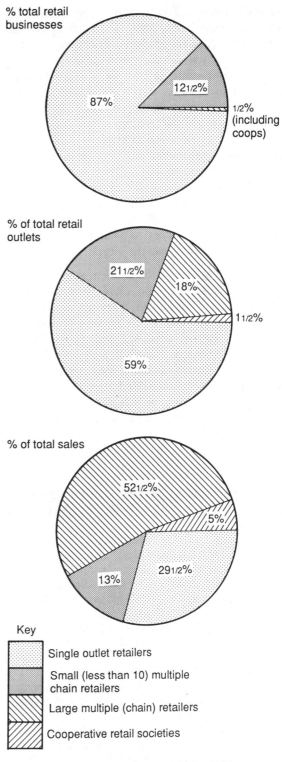

Fig 14.3 *Retail trade in Great Britain, 1984*
            Annual Abstract of Statistics, 1988 HMSO

on shelves and the customers serve themselves. They are very large (2000 → 10 000 sq ft) and carry many different products. Prices are kept low because they sell so much to so many customers that they can afford to make a little profit from each customer. Fewer staff are required since the customer does much of the work and, as we have seen, they are able to undertake their own wholesaling cutting out the middleman's profit. They also produce their own products cutting out the manufacturer's profit.

As we can see from the chart on page 175, although single outlet retailers represent a very large percentage of all businesses involved in retailing when it comes to total sales the larger chain stores have by far the largest share.

Department stores   A department store is a large shop (25 000 sq ft + on more than one floor) which can cater for all of a shopper's needs under one roof. The store is really several specialist shops in one. It is organised into many different departments such as electrical goods, food, mens clothing etc. Each will offer a wide range of goods and trained staff to advise and assist the customer. Within the building, which is often extremely luxurious, many services are offered. Such stores often rent out sales space to well-known chain stores, for example the Sketchley Dry Cleaning Centre in Selfridges.

CASE STUDY

Selfridges

The Selfridges department store, perhaps one of the most well-known and largest stores in London, was opened in 1909 by Mr Harry Gordon Selfridge, a 52 year old American. Gordon Selfridge had worked his way up to the top in a Chicago department store called Marshall Field. He left as a junior partner feeling that many of his best ideas had been rejected and it was on a subsequent tour of Europe that he decided to build his London store.

Selfridges were different to most shops in London. There were very few department stores and goods were not displayed with the flare that Gordon Selfridge had used in America. Conditions for the customer were better than in most shops in London at that time. The new store had 130 departments

and was carpeted throughout. Mr Selfridge brought a specialist from his old American store to help with display work – it was the first time that a shop had a display department. At that time it was usual to pile as many goods as possible into the windows. Selfridges introduced such ideas as an annual sale and the bargain basement.

In order to generate custom Selfridges staged 'events' such as the exhibition of Bleriot's aeroplane; the first to fly the Channel. By the time he died at the age of 90 Gordon Selfridge had seen his Oxford Street shop more than double in size.

Today it is a landmark and institution with numerous departments and services for the customer. Some of these services includes men's and ladies' hairdressers; Lloyds Bank cashpoint and foreign exchange counter, ear-piercing, electric shaver service centre, 24-hour film service, a fur store, Interflora, jewellery and watch repair, picture framing, opticians, photographer, six restaurants, safe deposit facilities, photocopying, key cutting, heel bar, theatre ticket booking service, formal dress hire and even an underground garage with a 'valet service'. Selfridges is now part of Sears Holdings but is run as a separate unit with its own board of directors.

Buying without shops

It is possible to buy goods and services without going to a shop.

Mail order   About nine per cent of all non-food retail sales is made through mail order. One family in two will buy something from a mail order catalogue this year. Perhaps your family has such a catalogue. People are able to choose in the comfort of their own home from a wide range of goods and order them on a special form. Goods are sent direct from a warehouse by post to the customer who can keep them and pay or return them. Often credit is available so that the customer can pay so much per week. With some firms the person who keeps the catalogue is known as the **agent** and is given a small percentage of the value of all goods sold, as a commission. With other firms there is no agent and any shopper can have the catalogue.

Door-to-door selling   Some products are traditionally brought to the door by the salesman. Most milk is delivered in this way, also papers and even bread. In country areas **mobile shops**, often converted vans or coaches, travel around from village to village taking the shop to the customers. The range of goods is limited and prices high but this is a valuable service to the old and handicapped who cannot get out.

Street markets   In many areas traditional street markets are held on certain days of the week. Traders rent the space from the local council by paying a small fee. This space is known as **a pitch**. Most councils will only grant a limited number of pitches in order to control the number of traders. The only other cost to the trader is the price of a cheap stall and somewhere to store his goods. Overheads – that is all of the traders' costs – are much lower for the stall holder than small shopkeeper. For this reason prices are lower in a market. Many people enjoy the hustle and bustle of a market and the fact that they can pick and choose from many stalls. It is usually difficult to try clothes on or take goods back but markets flourish in most towns.

The structure of retail trade has been changing with a movement towards more supermarkets and chain stores and away from the traditional corner shop, independently run.

As the population has become better off spending patterns have changed. More families now have cars and can travel to large shops in town centres. More women work and only have time for one visit to a large shop where they can stock up on all the families needs. Many families now have a deep-freeze which enables bulk purchases of perishables. In the future we may all visit one huge shop (50 000 + sq ft) called a **hypermarket**. This is a shop much larger than a supermarket selling not only food and clothes but furniture and household goods all in one building along self-service lines. These are very popular in America and Europe but not so much in the UK. They are usually situated outside the town centre where land is not so expensive.

Mail order has been expanding again due to the lack of shopping time. Soon it will be possible to view goods on our own television screen and order using a small computer terminal. Perhaps this will bring about a decline in shops as we know them.

Voluntary Groups

The small independent retailer faces several problems. Being unable to buy large quantities of goods he is forced to pay much higher prices than the large supermarket chains. He must therefore charge higher prices. Being small he will have less customers and need to make more profit on each item sold. The shopper does not recognise his shop since he cannot afford to advertise on television or in the national papers.

CASE STUDY

The Londis Group

Peter White bought a small shop (500 sq ft) in the Midlands about five years ago. The shop had a low turnover (value of goods sold) about £350 per week and faced stiff opposition from nearby supermarkets selling goods at lower prices.

He heard of a group of independent grocers who in the 1960s had joined together to buy goods in bulk. They now owned their own wholesaling operation. They all called their shops **Londis** so that they could advertise together although they still owned their own shops. Today they own four warehouses to which goods are delivered in bulk. Members receive a price list of items in stock every week and order from the closest depot. Goods are delivered within 48 hours and the member then has seven days to credit his account at the head office. Fresh goods, like bread, are delivered straight to the member from the producer but charged through the Londis head office so that the member is charged cheaper bulk rates.

Each fortnight 20 popular brands are cut in price and bright posters sent to members. The company also organises advertising campaigns, competitions etc to encourage shoppers to use a Londis store. Each store has the same distinctive façade which members rent. The group also produces 150 own brands which are cheaper still.

The company is run by a board elected by members the majority of whom are retailers, although experts are also employed. A member can always receive help and advice.

Peter decided to join. He had to pay a fee and sign a membership agreement but within five years his turnover had increased to £9000 a week and he had been able to increase the size of his shop.

Fig 14.4

Being a member of a voluntary group gave him the independence he needed to make his own decisions coupled with the lower prices of bulk buying, brand loyalty and back-up usually only found in a large chain store.

Other voluntary groups such as VG and Spar operate on slightly different lines as the group is run by the wholesaler which is not owned by members. Other than this, however, the services they offer their members are similar to Londis.

Exercise

1 Why are prices higher in a shop than a market stall?

2 Give one reason why a person might prefer a department store to a market stall.

3 Name three services any shop performs for its customers.

4 Give two disadvantages of using a small independent store for the customer.

5 If small independent stores have the disadvantages stated before, give two reasons that help explain their survival.

ASSIGNMENT

Undertake your own shopping survey. Choose about 10 common products and visit a number of different types of shop in the same week recording the prices. Construct a graph to show the differences and then write an explanation of these differences. (*See* page 243.)

Advertising

Most goods are advertised in one or more of a variety of ways. The aim of advertising is to both inform potential customers that a certain product is available and to persuade them to buy it. Advertising is not cheap – in 1986 it cost industry – £5117 million (or 1.6 per cent of total output). A producer spends money on advertising to increase sales of his product and to make larger profits for the company.

Some advertisements are purely **informative** – they present only the basic facts about a product that is for sale and do not attempt to encourage people to buy it. In your local paper, for example, you may find a *Small Ads* section where people inform others that they have items for sale.

Most advertisements are tempting people into trying a product. We call this **persuasive advertising**. This can be done in many ways.

Scientific advertisements Some advertisements concentrate upon the scientific advances made by the product, such as motor car manufacturers who might stress the petrol consumption figures or margarine makers who might stress market research findings.

Sexy advertisements Many advertisements either feature physically attractive men and women or show a person who uses a certain product being attractive to the opposite sex.

Worrying advertisements Some advertisements ask worrying questions. Do my feet smell? Are my clothes as clean as they could be? By playing on our fears they cause us to change our buying habits.

Funny advertisements Radio and television advertisements are today often very humourous – you probably have your favourite. We remember the name of the product because we enjoy the advertisement.

Life-style advertisements Many advertisements show the product being used in a perfect setting. The implication is that the model modern home is not complete without that product.

Dream-world advertisements These present a fantasy world, perhaps of pink clouds or knights in shining armour well removed from reality.

Now try the assignment below.

Advertising costs

In 1986 the Advertising Association estimated that £5117 m was spent on advertising.
This was divided as follows:

Press	61.3%
Television	32.7%
Poster and transport	3.8%
Radio	1.8%
Cinema	0.4%

ASSIGNMENT

Collect advertisements from magazines which illustrate each of these methods of persuading consumers to buy. For each state which type it is and why you think it is or is not a good advertisement. When next you are watching commercial television or listening to commercial radio list all of the advertisements in one hour and for each say which type it is and why you think that it is or is not a good advertisement.

Fig 14.5

Which form of advertising is used here?

The costs of different methods of advertising differ widely. The costs for an average television commercial are shown in Fig 14.6.

Advertising on radio is considerably cheaper as you can see:

LBC News Radio (Rates from 2 May 1988)

Time	Cost of 30 sec
Monday–Friday	
05.30–06.00	£100
06.00–10.00	£700
10.00–17.00	£250
17.00–24.00	£150
24.00–5.30	£ 20

(Discount for early and volume bookings etc)

National newspapers also prove expensive, yet do reach a very wide market:

	Costs for unspecified whole page Spring 1988	Circulation (millions) 1988
Daily Mail	£20 664	1.7
Daily Mirror	£26 000	3.0

There are many different methods of advertising. The most popular methods are newspapers, magazines and of course the television.

Exercise

1 List four further ways goods are commonly promoted.
2 Why is it cheaper to advertise on television on ITV at 11.00 hrs than at 20.00 hrs?
3 Why is it cheaper to advertise on Channel 4 than ITV at the same time?
4 Why is it cheaper to advertise on commercial radio during the evening when it becomes more expensive to advertise on commercial television? What could change this?
5 Why is a full page advertisement more expensive in the Daily Mail than the Daily Mirror when the size and cost of printing would be the same?

ANGLIA TELEVISION LIMITED
ITV
Rates effective from 4th January 1988

SEGMENTS – MONDAY TO SUNDAY

Peak	*17.26-23.00*
Prime Peak	*17.26-23.00*
Off Peak	*09.25-17.25*
	23.01-26.00
Through the Night	*24.00-29.59*

BASE RATES

	10 sec £	20 sec £	30 sec £
PEAK	350	700	1050
OFF PEAK	117	233	350

THROUGH THE NIGHT – PACKAGES

24.00 – 29.59 Mon – Sun	10 sec £	20 sec £	30 sec £
10 SPOT PACKAGE:	250	500	750

Normally at least 5 spots transmitted before 0300.

Normally at least 2 spots transmitted 2400 – close across Friday, Saturday and Sunday.

CHANNEL 4 SPOT RATES

	10 sec £	20 sec £	30 sec £
Starting from:	100	160	200

Fig 14.6 (Courtesy: Anglia Television Limited)

The advertising campaign

Most companies do not undertake their own advertising. They employ the specialist services of an advertising agency. These agencies, for a fee, will put together an advertising campaign for a customer. The agency may well undertake market research to discover what customers attitudes are to a product and help to design an effective campaign. They will decide upon which types of advertisements to use and produce TV commercials, magazine advertisements etc. A company can either leave the whole exercise in the hands of the experts or retain some control.

ASSIGNMENT

You work for an advertising agency. One of your clients manufactures high quality fountain pens but their sales have been falling steadily over the years.

Your own market research shows that most people find fountain pens a bother to keep filling up and more likely to make a mess *but* readily concede that their own handwriting is better when they use a proper pen. The firm has limited funds but is prepared to make one last attempt to increase sales through an advertising campaign.

Your task is to:

(*a*) Think of a new name for the pens which retail for £15.

(*b*) Devise an original theme for an advertising campaign.

(*c*) Design posters and TV commercials deciding what type of advertising you will use.

(*d*) Decide which age group to sell to and when and where you will advertise.

Control of advertising

Advertising is controlled in two ways in this country. First, there are a number of laws which prevent certain tyes of advertising. It is, for example illegal under the **1968 Trade Description Act** for false claims to be made in an advertisement. This same act made it an offence for a trader to put false price reductions on items. If a price has been crossed out and a lower one written over it the original higher price must have been charged for that good in that shop for at least 28 consecutive days in the previous six months.

The advertising industry also enforces its own **Code of Practice** through two watch-dog organisations: **The Advertising Standards Authority** (ASA) which looks at all non-broadcast advertising (press, posters etc) and the **Independent Broadcasting Authority** (IBA) which watches television and radio advertising.

The ASA has a Council whose chairperson (and at least half of its members) has nothing to do with the advertising industry. This body tries to ensure that all advertisements are in line with the industry's own agreed codes of practice: **The British Code of Advertising Practice** and the **British Code of Sales and Promotion Practice**. These codes state that advertisements should be legal, decent, honest and truthful. They have specific rules about the running of competitions, the use of children and the advertising of medicinal and health products for example. If members of the public complain to the ASA they will investigate the complaint and publish their findings in a monthly case reports or even stop the advertisement from being published.

If an advertisement is wrong we're here to put it right.

If you see an advertisement in the press, in print, on posters or in the cinema which you find unacceptable, write to us at the address below.

The Advertising Standards Authority.

ASA Ltd, Dept 3 Brook House, Torrington Place, London WC1E 7HN

The IBA enforces the IBA **Code of Advertising Standards and Practice**. This states that all television and radio advertisements should be accurate and not misleading. It also has many other specific regulations. All advertisements are studied before they can appear on television. Members of the public are invited to write and complain if they find advertisements misleading or offensive. You may have seen their advertisements in *TV Times*.

CASE STUDY

'I see no ships'

Kevin saw advertised a holiday break at an hotel in the South West. The advertisement said the hotel was five minutes from the sea and that you could see the sea from the bedrooms. Having two small children he thought this looked fine and booked up for a week.

When he arrived he was disappointed to discover that the hotel was in fact five miles from the sea and although you could just about see the sea from the bedroom it took a good half hour to walk to the beach – and much longer to walk back as it was all up hill! He complained to the Manager of the hotel who said that it must have been a misprint and that they meant five miles not five minutes.

When he returned home Kevin wrote to the Advertising Standards Authority who investigated the complaint. They wrote to the agency who had been responsible for the advertisement and gave them a reasonable time to investigate. The agency replied that the advertisement was not misleading since the hotel was only five minutes from the beach – if you used a car or the local bus.

Exercise

1 Do you think that Kevin was misled by the advertisement?
2 Do you think that Kevin should be compensated and if so by whom?
3 How should the ASA deal with the agency?

In 1981 the ASA had a budget of £8000 000 and 38 staff. Some people were not happy with their findings. Three nurses objected to an advertisement which appeared in the *Nursing Mirror* which showed a nurse being seduced under the heading 'Are you willing to be seduced?'. The nurses felt

it showed women in a degrading light. The ASA found:

'Although the advertisement was not considered likely to cause grave or widespread offence, the Authority none the less deprecated the copy approach which they considered to be in bad taste and demeaning to the nursing profession.'

The ASA did not call for the withdrawal of the advertisement. It is much easier to prove that an advertisement is inaccurate than degrading to women. For this reason some people feel that the rules should be altered.

Advantages and disadvantages of advertising

Advantages

Informs public about the range of products on sale Without it how would consumers know what was available or good value?

Helps consumers make rational choices By providing information about products the consumer knows what is a good buy for them.

Advertising money helps to finance newspapers, radio and television ITV and Channel 4, commercial radio, local and national newspapers all depend upon advertising revenue. Without advertising there would not be the range of entertainment and news media.

Supports sporting events Most sporting events are sponsored by firms who want the advertising this gives them. Football players wear slogans on their shirts and the cups and trophies bear the names of their sponsors – Milk Cup, Canon League. Without advertising many sports would not take place at all.

Advertising increases sales This might keep firms in business and therefore keep jobs for the workers. Advertising also helps to increase profits. If increased sales mean companies can enjoy economies of scale it might even reduce prices.

Disadvantages

Could cause people to buy things they do not really want Weak-minded people and children might find they are tempted into purchasing an item they did not want.

Advertising can spoil the environment Large posters can offend people who would rather look at the countryside.

Expensive and puts up prices In some industries millions of pounds are spent by a few firms competing for the same market.

Can cause dissatisfaction Advertising paints a perfect picture of the world; people begin to believe that this is how real life ought to be and become dissatisfied with their life.

Advertising creates 'media stereotypes' which could influence attitudes Many people complain that women are usually shown merely as sex objects in advertising. This builds up a stereotype image of women which could affect the way the next generation thinks of them.

Consumer protection

In this country the consumer is protected by a number of laws which prevent the retailer taking

Law	Goods/rights covered	Example	Enforcement
Sale of Goods Act 1893 and 1979	Trader must ensure: • goods of merchantable quality – fit for normal purpose • goods fit for any purpose made known to trader • goods must be as described	Handle should not fall off new kettle If you ask 'does this glue stick plastic' and are told yes then it should A sheet described as double should fit a 4'6'' bed	If goods are returned to seller then they must be replaced or money refunded. Consumer has rights under civil law therefore and would have to take trader to court if not satisfied
Consumer Safety Act 1978	Enables Secretary of State to require that certain goods are labelled with warnings, or to ban very dangerous goods	A child's toy that proves to be dangerous can be banned	It is a criminal offence to sell goods which do not comply with regulations
Food and Drug Act 1955	Food must be fit for human consumption and sold under hygienic conditions. Many specific regulations	Shop assistants must be able to wash their hands when serving fresh food	It is a criminal offence to sell goods which do not comply with regulations
Trade Descriptions Acts 1968/1972	Must not describe goods falsely	Turn back a clock on a car and say it has a low mileage	This is a criminal offence
Unsolicited Goods Act 1972	Trader cannot ask for payment for goods delivered but not ordered	Carbon paper sent to firms and then an invoice	This is a criminal offence. If goods are not collected within six months they become the property of the recipient – a gift
Weights and Measures Act 1963/1979	It is an offence not to mark weight or quantity on packaged groceries	Unmarked box of sweets	This is a criminal offence

advantage of him or selling faulty or dangerous goods.

The laws are divided into two types. The **civil laws** which give the customer the right to take a trader to court if he has an individual grievance against the trader and the **criminal laws** which protect the general public from unsafe goods. The table on page 183 shows the main consumer laws.

Perhaps the most quoted is **The Sale of Goods Act** which gives the consumer far reaching rights when buying goods from a shop. In most cases if a good is not 'of merchantable quality' or fit for the purpose described or as described the trader will exchange the faulty good or give the customer back his money. If he does not the consumer would have to take him to court since he has not broken a criminal law and the customer has only civil law rights. Taking a trader to court has, however, become very much easier. For large amounts (over £5000) it would still be necessary to seek the advice of a solicitor which may be very expensive (although there is a system of legal aid). For small amounts the case would be dealt with by the **Small Claims Court**, which is a division of the Country Court. For amounts of less than £500 this is usually done by **arbitration**, that is an informal discussion between customer and trader in front of an arbitrator appointed by the court. Costs are very low. Although cases involving larger amounts might be heard in a full court session the proceedings are explained to the consumer and they would not need a solicitor.

The other laws – those which affect the health and safety of us all – are criminal laws and are enforced for us by the local authority. **The Trading Standards Office** (in some local authorities known as the **Consumer Protection** or **Weights and Measures Department**) will make sure that retailers in a local area are not breaking **Trade Descriptions** and **Weights and Measures Acts**. This will involve regular inspections and following-up complaints. They are also responsible for enforcing some of the food laws such as correct labelling. Some local authorities have **Consumer Advice Centres** either as part of the town hall or even in high street shopping centres. Here consumers can receive help and advice on a whole range of shopping matters in some areas. The local authority may even run a mobile advice centre from a converted van. **The Environmental Health Department** will be responsible for all health aspects of food sales as well as the cleanliness of such places as hairdressing salons.

Consumers not lucky enough to have an advice centre can use the **Citizens Advice Bureaux**. These are independent advice centres and there are some 900 throughout the country. They will give advice on far more than just consumer affairs.

Many manufacturers and retailers belong to **Employers' Associations** as we saw in Chapter 6. Some of these have their own Codes of Practice. For example, Association of British Travel Agents (ABTA) have codes of practice covering overbooking, cancellations and package holidays. They operate a fund into which all members contribute so that if a company which is a member fails then the customer is compensated. Remember also that in Chapter 3 (public services) **consumer consultative councils** were also mentioned.

Buying goods under special circumstances

Most shops will refund money if they sell faulty goods, but what about secondhand goods and auctions? Here is a summary of your rights:

Secondhand goods   Sale of Goods Act rights still apply but the right to compensation will depend upon the price paid and its description. You cannot expect a secondhand car to be perfect, but if it is sold as in good condition the purchaser would not expect the engine to drop out after two miles.

Auctions   Unlike other traders an auctioneer can disclaim Sale of Goods Act responsibilities if there is a notice in the catalogue or in the sale room. A court might think that this is unreasonable but also might not. Most auctions have a preview and it is best to examine goods carefully.

Buying privately   The Sale of Goods Act covers only traders not private individuals. A private person cannot lie to a potential buyer however, the item must be as described. If it is not then the purchaser could sue the seller for misrepresentation. For this reason when buying large items, like a motorbike, it is best to take a friend who can act as a witness.

Sales Goods bought in Sales must conform to the rules laid down in the Sale of Goods Act. A notice saying 'No refund on sale goods' is illegal.

Public bodies which help protect the consumer

1 Office of Fair Trading (OFT)

Under the 1973 Fair Trading Act the OFT was established with a Director General, a paid staff and a voluntary Consumer Protection Advisory Committee. The Director General's tasks are:

(*a*) to review and put together information about commercial activities from the consumer's point of view, e.g. selling techniques;

(*b*) to look, in particular, into activites which seem to 'adversely affect consumer interests' e.g. hire-purchase of houses;

(*c*) to study monopoly situations which may not be in consumers' best interests;

(*d*) publish information on consumer matters.

2 Ministry of Agriculture, Fisheries and Food

This government department aims to work on consumers' behalf by:

(*a*) initiating legislation aimed at protecting food standards, e.g. date marking and labelling Acts;

(*b*) maintaining a close watch on what goes into foods e.g. additives and also measures levels of heavey metals in foods;

(*c*) lists permitted pesticides.

3 Home Office

The government department is concerned mainly with product safety under the 1961, 1971 and 1978 Consumer Protection/Safety Acts.

4 Local authorities

County Councils have responsibility for enforcing the law of central government, through Trading Standards Departments and Environmental Health Offices.

5 EC and consumer protection

In an attempt to achieve higher standards of living and a better quality of life, the European Community has laid down a consumer policy which aims to:

(*a*) provide better protection for EC consumers against health and safety risks and also a fairer deal in relation to goods and services (i.e. pricing, quality, service);

(*b*) provide more complete, accurate and objective information about goods and services (i.e. pricing, quality, service);

(*c*) provide more details about the policies and measures of the EC in matters relating to consumer interests, i.e. consultation, representation, participation.

Independent bodies which help protect the consumer

There are several organisations established with one main purpose; to serve the interests of consumers:

1 National Consumer Council

Established in 1975, financed by the government, yet independent enough to:

- persuade the government to introduce consumer protection policies
- pressure businesses to meet the needs of consumers more effectively through codes of practice and safety standards
- pressure public services, like nationalised industries and civil service departments, to be more responsive to consumer needs and give value for money.

This pressure is applied through research, reports and the publishing of leaflets.

2 The Association for Consumer Research (ACRE)

Formally known as the Consumers' Association this has recently changed its name and structure.

ACRE as a charity now conducts all the research and testing activity of consumer products and services (cars, washing machines and insurance). It has a wholly-owned trading subsidiary which publishes the Charity's research and represents the consumer interests to government, to the EC and so on.

The wholly-owned subsidiary is called the Consumers' Association Ltd, (CA). It campaigns, publishes *Which?* (the consumer watchdog magazine) and organises subscriptions.

The gaining of charitable status for research activities means that more of CA's money can be used for constructive consumer research. Furthermore, the gaining of charitable status is a mark of CA's standing as a serious research organisation that makes a contribution to the public good.

It was the Consumer's Association which pressured for the appointment in 1972 of the first British Consumer Affairs Minister and later encouraged the high street consumer advcice centre to spring up all over Britain. In 1973 the CA helped set up the European Office of Consumer Organisations (BEUC).

Only four per cent of the CA's work is campaigning, yet it has won many important battles likc the breaking in 1985 of the solicitor's conveyancing monopoly, and in Europe, through BEUC and the International Organisation of Consumers Unions (IOCU) it has made importing cars easier and promoted product safety thorugh the Consumer Interpol.

1987 saw the 30th anniversary of the CA; in that time its membership has grown to over 900 000 and it can claim to have filled more pages of the statute book than any other pressure group this century.

3 The British Standards Institute (BSI)

The BSI draws up and issues 'standards' for all kinds of good produced by industry, in terms of safety and efficiency. It is non-political, non-profit making and yet supported by both government and industry.

It awards a KITE mark to products which have been tested by the BSI and passed stringent technical requirements of a product or process in terms of: dimensions, quality and performance, test methods, terms and symbols, codes of practice.

Other organisations or pressure groups which aim to protect consumers, apart from those mentioned above, include:

- Housewife Trust – watchdog organisation to help housewives with daily shopping problems
- National Federation of Consumer Groups
- Consumer Consultative Councils for public services (*see* Chapter 3).

Exercise

Your neighbour uses a glue to stick a broken handle back on to a china cup. The glue has been recommended by the owner of a do-it-yourself shop as being perfect for this job. The first time that this cup is used after the handle has been stuck on it falls off again.

1 What are your neighbour's 'rights' under the **Sale of Goods Act**?

2 What additional rights does this act give her? For each give an example of where it would apply.

3 Your neighbour, acting on your advice, returns the glue to the shop and demands her money back. The owner of the shop refuses to give her back the money because she has opened the glue. Where could she go for additional advice and how could the law help her get back the money?

What would be your rights if you bought goods which were faulty:

(*a*) at an auction
(*b*) secondhand from a shop
(*c*) in a sale
(*d*) from a friend?

SUMMARY EXERCISE

1 Wholesalers buy goods from producers at a lower price than they charge the retailers they sell them to. Give four services provided by wholesalers in return for these higher prices.

2 Give two industries where there are no wholesalers. (In other words the producer has a distribution network and supplies retail outlets.)

3 Think of a country where there would be little or no advertising and explain why this is true.

4 Name two ways in which the consumer benefits-form advertising.

5 Name two ways in which the consumer suffers from advertising.

6 In what ways does an organisation like the Consumers' Association help to protect the consumer?

7 What advantage is there for a tourist to book a holiday through a travel agency which is a member of ABTA?

ASSIGNMENTS

1 (*a*) Show the difference with examples, between *informative* and *persuasive* advertising.

  (*b*) Why do firms advertise?

  (*c*) Describe in detail two advantages and two disadvantages of advertising.

2 Some people argue that a wholesaler only serves to increase prices. Explain the services undertaken by the wholesaler and their importance to the small shopkeeper.

3 In a supermarket the shopper undertakes much of the work including weighing and packing fresh vegetables, pushing and unloading the trolley and reaching up to the high shelves. Given the truth of the statement above explain why supermarkets are growing in popularity. Are there some types of good which will never be sold in supermarkets? If so, give examples and explain why this is so.

The Individual and Money

Saving

CASE STUDY

Who saves most?

Profile 1

George and Hilary aged 30 – one child. George is the only wage earner. He is a civil servant.

Monthly Budget	
Income:	£
Take-home pay	982
Child benefit	29
Interest (savings)	29
Total	1 040
Expenses:	£
Mortgage	180
Standing orders at bank (rates, insurance)	350
Cash payments (food, petrol)	250
Cheques (electricity, phone)	160
Total	940

Profile 2

Susan aged 20 lives at home, is unmarried and a hairdresser.

Weekly Budget	
Income:	£
Take-home pay	81
Expenses:	£
Rent to mum	18
Entertainment	20
Clothes	17
Food (mid-day)	10
Total	65

In each of these profiles the income is in excess of the expenditure. This means that both George and Hilary and Susan can save part of their incomes.

Exercise

1 How much can George and Hilary save per month?

2 What percentage of their total income would this saving represent for George and Hilary

3 How much can Susan save per week?

4 What percentage of her total weekly income would this saving represent for Susan.

5 List four things George and Hilary might be saving up for.

6 Can you think of any other reason George and Hilary might have for saving?

7 List four things that Susan might be saving up for.

8 Can you think of any other reason Susan might have for saving?

9 If Hilary were to take a part-time job what might happen to her family's savings and expenses?

10 Susan decides that her life is dull and decides to take up horse riding. This costs £9 per week. How might an economist describe the opportunity cost of Susan saving £9 per week.

Reasons for saving

Saving is therefore that part of current income which is not spent on consumption. Individuals and companies (both in the private and public sectors) can and do save. In order to save, people or firms must give up some spending.

People save for many different reasons.

Luxury items Families save up for those expensive items which they cannot buy out of their normal wage. For example, people save in order to buy a new car or take a foreign holiday.

Emergency funds Most families like to have a sum of money available in case of an unexpected

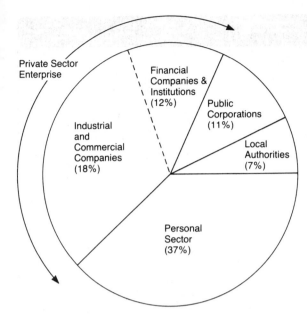

Fig 15.1 Saving in the UK 1983
Financial Statistics March 1983 HMSO

financial problem. For example, their car might suddenly develop trouble needing major repair work. The wage earner might lose his or her job or, on a happier note, an elder daugher might decide to get married. Some financial experts feel that the average family ought to have about £5000–6000 in such a fund which for most families would mean all of their savings.

Saving by mistake   A family with a high income might simply not spend all of their income. Saving does not take place intentionally but funds tend to build up. This could happen with a middle-aged couple, both in paid employment, whose children have grown up and left home. It would be a good opportunity to save for old age when income inevitably falls.

Companies save by not distributing all of their profits to the shareholders. This retained profit is a form of saving and can be used to finance large capital expenditure, such as a new plant, or to pay tax liabilities in the future or even to pay for the unexpected (contingency reserves).

People with high income will be able to save more than those with low incomes. A company making a high profit in any one year will be able to retain or save a larger amount than a company

making a small profit. The size of income is therefore one of the most important factors in determining the level of saving in the society.

In Chapter 1 it was shown that income flows in a circle between producers and consumers, business and households. Wealth, created by business is paid to households as wages – the reward to human resources, rent – the reward to natural resources and profit – the reward to enterprise. Most of this income is spent by households on goods and services but as we know not all of it since some is **saved**. Much of this saving takes place in financial institutions like banks. These financial institutions lend this saved part of national income to both households and businesses who need extra income for consumption or investment.

Government too is able to borrow from financial institutions and directly from households and spends such borrowed funds on the provision of public and merit goods. People who do not want to spend all of their share of income at the present time are able to have this spending power rerouted, via the financial institutions, to those who do want to use this spending power now. Of course, those who save can be paid for giving up this present consumption. They can receive **interest** – an agreed percentage of the sum saved every year is added to this amount saved if it takes place with an institution in a special type of account. Those who borrow must pay interest for the privilege of using someone else's spending power.

If unwanted cash were to be saved under the bed then the owner would not receive interest. Most people who save, however, do put the money in a financial institution and receive interest.

Where to save

The **rate of interest** was mentioned earlier as the reward for saving. The rate of interest is not the same for all institutions or for all forms of saving. It varies considerably even on the same day. A person could receive between 4.75 per cent and 8.5 per cent on the same day in the same institution for different forms of saving. (*See* Fig 15.2.)

	ORDINARY SHARES	MONEYWISE CHEQUE BOOK, CHEQUE GUARANTEE/VISA CARD, LINK MONEY MACHINE CARD				SUPERSHARES Immediate withdrawal*		SUPER 60 60 Days' Notice of withdrawal			2 YEAR SUPER TERM SHARES
The tables show the wide choice of competitive terms available for all your savings and investment needs	For easy money management with a good rate of interest	An ideal payment account with your own cheque book. Cheque Guarantee/VISA card. Moneywise LINK Cash Machine card and a full account record of a normal passbook savings account. Moneywise interest rates rise with the size of balance you maintain				Supershares for a high rate of interest on money for immediate call*		Super 60 for a high rate of interest on money at 60 days' notice			Super Term Shares for longer term investment with capital growth or a regular income but still with access to your money
Minimum investment	£1	£1	£2,500	£10,000	£25,000	£500	£10,000	£500	£10,000	£25,000	£500
End of Day Balance		£1-£2,499	£2,500-£9,999	£10,000-£24,999	£25,000-£200,000	£500 - £9,999	£10,000 - £200,000	£500-£9,999	£10,000-£24,999	£25,000-£200,000	£500 - £200,000
Net interest rate paid per annum	4.75%	4.75%	6.75%	7.25%	7.75%	7.25%	7.75%	Annual Interest 8.0%	8.25%	8.5%	8.25%
Gross equivalent † (see income tax note overleaf)	6.33%	6.33%	9.0%	9.67%	10.33%	9.67%	10.33%	10.67%	11.0%	11.33%	11.0%
Interest rate for other payment options	As above	None				None		Interest paid 7.75%= half yearly 10.33%†	8.0%= 10.67%†	8.25%= 11.0%†	Interest paid monthly 8.0%=10.67%†
								Interest paid 7.50%= monthly 10.0%†	7.75% 10.33%†	8.0% 10.67%†	
Interest	Variable rate. Interest paid half yearly on 30 June and 31 December	Variable rate. Interest paid annually on 30 June				Variable rate. Interest paid annually on 30 June		Variable net interest rate paid is 0.25% less if interest is paid half yearly and 0.5% less if paid monthly. Interest paid annually on 30 June or half yearly on 30 June and 31 December			Guaranteed extra interest at least 3.5% over Variable Ordinary Share Rate. Interest paid annually on 30 June
Monthly income	No	No				No		Yes			Yes. Interest rate 0.25% less for monthly income
Minimum investment for Monthly income	—	—				—		£1,000			£1,000
Withdrawals. Terms also apply to transfers between accounts. Up to £250 per day in cash or up to £25,000 per day by cheque at any branch (some overleaf for larger amounts) by cheque and withdrawal from District Agents.	Immediate withdrawal* no penalty	Immediate no penalty withdrawals by writing your own cheques. Up to £250 in cash per day can be obtained by presenting your passbook at any Town & Country branch or using your Moneywise LINK Cash Machine Card anywhere you see the LINK sign.				Immediate withdrawal* no penalty		60 days' notice for no penalty withdrawal or immediate withdrawal* with loss of 60 days' interest at current rate on the amount withdrawn. Immediate no penalty withdrawal* provided a minimum balance of £5,000 remains in the account after any withdrawal is made			90 days' notice for no penalty withdrawal or immediate withdrawal* with loss of 90 days' interest at current rate on the amount withdrawn
Future additions to account	Yes	Yes				Yes, provided issue is still open		Yes, provided issue is still open			No, but further investment possible in a new Super Term Share on the terms then prevailing
Other features		Cheque Book - Cheque Guarantee/VISA Card - Moneywise LINK Cash Machine Card - Up to 5 Standing Orders - Unlimited Direct Debits. There are no charges for withdrawals, cheques, standing orders and direct debits providing your account stays in credit with a minimum cleared balance of £1. You can pay your VISA account, either in full or the minimum amount, every month automatically from your Moneywise account.				If balance falls and remains below £500 interest will be paid at the variable Ordinary Share rate		If balance falls and remains below £500 interest will be paid at the Ordinary Share rate			If balance falls and remains below £500 interest will be paid at the variable Ordinary Share rate

Town & Country offer you the best choice of top terms. Many investors find a combination of Town & Country accounts is ideal. For example, long	term investment in a Super Term Share, some funds in a Supershare account, with immediate withdrawals available*; or in a Super 60 account	with 60 days' notice; and a Moneywise account to handle day to day transactions and the receipt of interest transferred automatically from other	investments. The maximum total investment usually accepted by the Society is £200,000.

Fig 15.2 (Courtesy: Town and Country Building Society)

If a person wants to take out their savings from the institutions (make a **withdrawal**) whenever they choose they will receive a lower rate of interest than if they are prepared to leave their savings for up to two years. This is because the institution wishes to lend these savings to another person or business. Savings which are not likely to be withdrawn can be lent, but where a person might draw on their savings enough must be kept ready for such withdrawals.

As can be seen from the example in Fig 15.2, the opportunity cost of wanting to be able to withdraw savings on demand (whenever one wants) is lost interest.

There are other factors at work however. The highest rate of interest offered at the Town and Country Building Society is only available for a saver who is not only prepared to leave savings alone for at least 60 days, but also has £25 000 in the account. This is true in general. The more the saver has to deposit in an institution the higher the rate of interest.

With some forms of National Savings (money lent to Government) there is a slight tax incentive. The interest or part of it is tax free. Some institutions are more convenient than others with a greater number of outlets or longer opening hours – the post office for example. Others such as the

banks and building societies may promise a mortgage to savers who have had an account for a minimum period.

There are, therefore, many places to save your money. The following paragraphs highlight these places.

The Post Office Many of you may have a **Post Office National Savings Account**. The ordinary account pays 5% and investment account 8.5% but the former allows up to £100 to be withdrawn on demand whereas the latter takes one month. These are both very popular probably because of the convenience of using the Post Office. There are 20 000 post offices all over the country. Nearly every village has one and they open on a Saturday and have longer hours than a bank. It is also possible to purchase **National Savings Certificates** at a post office. These are loans to the Government for 1–5 years. With the **non-index-linked National Savings Certificates** the purchaser pays for them in units of £10 (up to a maximum of £1500). No interest is paid but after one year the holder can sell them back to the Post Office and receive the original purchase price plus 7.5% per year. They may be held for up to 7 years. **Index-Linked National Savings Certificates** were introduced in 1975 originally for the retired. Now everyone can buy them. They are essentially the same as ordinary saving certificates but carry no specific rate of interest. The purchase price is repaid and the amount of measured inflation (Retail Price Index) is added in addition to a bonus of 0.2% per month. **Premium Bonds** can also be purchased at the post office. These are similar to saving certificates but they can be held for ever. Bought in units of £5 up to a maximum of £19 000 they can be sold back to the Post Office at any time (taking eight working days to gain repayment). The difference is that no interest is paid. Instead all of the interest which would have been paid to all of the small bond holders is added up and given to a few lucky bond holders each month in the form of a prize. The numbers of the prize winners are selected electronically and are designed to be completely fair with everybody having an equal chance of winning. **Save as you earn schemes** (SAYE) are also run. A person can save between £4 and £20 per month either by paying cash into a post office, by having the amount transferred from their bank account or some employers will take it directly from the workers pay packet. As with Index-Linked Savings Certificates this SAYE service offers the RPI plus 0.2% bonus monthly.

All Saving Certificate Interest is tax free as is the first £70 interest paid each year on National Savings Accounts.

Saving at a bank. Banks normally offer **deposit accounts** and **savings accounts**. However, the difference lies in the fact that the deposit account is for irregular deposits of £1 or more whereas the saving account is for regular additions to the account of £10 or more. People with large sums, such as £2000 or more, can place the amount in an account for an agreed length of time (in excess of three months) and receive a higher rate of interest. Those banks which offer a mortgage guarantee account as previously described (*see* Chapter 11) have obvious attractions for the young married couple.

All bank interest is subject to income tax.

Saving at a building society Building societies have become far more like banks. Most now offer their account holders cheque book facilities on some accounts, and a variety of banking type services as well as accounts which offer higher interest the longer funds are left untouched. They are excellent places for young people to save since they often give priority to account holders when granting mortgages.

Most accounts pay tax for the saver at 25 p in the pound. If you are someone who does not pay tax, then this is lost and means lower interest than say the National Savings Bank Investment Account.

Life assurance Looked at in detail later in this chapter.

Exercise

> For each of the following suggest where they might best save giving reasons for each. Why might the institution offering the highest rate of interest not necessarily be the best place to save?
>
> 1 An elderly, retired couple who have recently sold a valuable house and bought a much smaller flat. They have a net gain of £25 000 but other than this have only a pension to live on.
> 2 A young school leaver who only takes home £40 after tax from a junior cherk's job. He pays his mother £10 a week for keep and spends most of the remainder on entertainment and clothes. He can save up to £10 per week.
> 3 A middle-aged couple, both at work, children grown up, find they can save up to £100 a month with little trouble. They wish to save for their old age.
> 4 A new-born baby has many rich relatives who keep giving money to the baby for 'when he is older'. Where should his parents save this money until he wants it?

ASSIGNMENT

Conduct your own detailed savings survey. Either:

(*a*) ask a large number of students within your school how much they have saved and where it is kept. Construct a graph to show the most popular way of saving and the average amount saved. See whether there is any difference between age groups and sex and if you think these savings patterns would be different if all students learnt about the alternatives they have.

or

(*b*) visit all of the institutions where people in your nearest town or shopping centre can save and find out about the saving schemes offered. Construct your own chart or table to show the different schemes which exist between different types of institutions and similar institutions that are different companies. (*See* page 243.)

Insurance

Insurance is a simple idea which developed towards the end of the 15th century to help traders reduce the risk of importing valuable cargoes from America and India. In those days ships were much more likely to be lost at sea and when this happened the merchant who owned the ship lost everything. On the other hand if the ship survived he stood to make a healthy profit. The merchants soon realised that bad luck could hit any of them but not all of them. If they put a percentage of the value of the ship into a common pool then those who were unlucky and lost a ship, could draw out their loss from the common fund. In this way all of the merchants were able to prosper. The idea was adapted to cover fire after the Great Fire of London in 1666 with the first fire insurance company founded in 1680.

The principle was the same. Those houses wishing to be insured against the risk of fire would pay a small sum known as the **premium** to people known as **underwriters**. This was put with all other premiums into a common fund. Those unlucky few whose house was burnt would be able to make a **claim** and receive the value of their house or repair from the common fund.

Life Assurance operates on the same lines but here people do not insure against dying since everyone dies. They are able to ensure against dying before a certain date. This became popular during the 18th Century, although it was used before then. People are able to insure their own lives (or those of their wife or husband) but not anyone else's. Again a premium is paid each year calculated upon the age and health of the insured person. It is interesting that smokers have to pay higher premiums than non-smokers. If the insured person dies before the policy matures (agreed final date) their family benefit from a lump sum benefit or pension. Other policies called **endowment policies** are a way of saving as well as insuring a life. Here is the policy holder dies before a certain date their family receive a benefit but if they reach that date they receive a tax-free lump sum.

The end of the 18th century saw the development of far more machines. Machines for moving people, railway engines, and for making goods more efficiently in factories. This increased the risk of accident. Special companies were established in 1850 to insure rail travellers. By 1889 it was possible to insure against burglary and soon after loss of valuables. In 1865 motor cars were beginning to be seen. They became very popular after World War I and in 1930 the Government made it a requirment of law for all motorists to have enough insurance to compensate any third party they might injure or kill on the roads. This is still a legal requirement. During this same period air travel was developing and in 1919 aviation insurance began.

Today it is possible to insure against most things where the likelihood of an event happening can be worked out. It is possible to insure against it raining on a holiday, at a wedding or fête, or for shopkeepers to insure their plate glass windows.

Some risks remain **uninsurable**. A shopkeeper cannot insure against a change of fashion which may make some of his stock difficult to sell.

Taking out insurance

CASE STUDY

John's Car

John is 21 and has been driving his father's car for two years. He has now bought his own small English car for £790. He know that he must take out insurance. How can he do this? This is the procedure he should follow.

1 Obtain prospectus Any insurance company of broker will send a prospectus which lays down the details of the policies they offer. John discovers that he has three policies (exact cover given) to choose from:

(*a*) *Third Party* This would cover his legal costs and any compensation he would have to pay if he were to have an accident and injure or kill someone else.

(*b*) *Third Party, Fire and Theft* As above but would cover the cost of replacing his car if it were to be stolen or catch fire.

(*c*) *Comprehensive* As (*b*) above, but protects car against accidental damage, medical expenses of occupants if car involved in a crash and the contents of the car against theft.

Obviously (*a*) is cheaper than (*b*) which is cheaper than (*c*).

2 Proposal form filled in John would now fill in a form called the **proposal form**. This is often part of the prospectus and is sent back to the broker or company asking them to calculate the cost of insurance.

3 Cover note John has decided on a company and is sent a **cover note** which gives him temporary insurance cover while the details are worked out.

4 The premium John is told how much it will cost for his chosen policy (third party, fire and theft). The premium will depend upon the type of policy, type of car, age of driver, region of the country it is to be driven in and type of use it is to be given. For John, driving in London, for pleasure only will cost £200 per year. John decides to pay this over three months.

5 The policy After a few weeks John receives a full **Certificate of Insurance** and a detailed policy which sets out exactly what is covered.

This is how John insured his car. The procedure is the same for a motorbike. John would have to pay the first £50 of any claim as he is under 25. As he grows older the premium will fall and if he does not claim he will be given a discount over the next few years.

Exercise

> Which of the following would be more expensive to insure to drive and why:
>
> (*a*) A mini or a sports car?
> (*b*) A man aged 21 or a man aged 31?
> (*c*) A car in London or a car in the Isle of Wight?
> (*d*) A male driver or female driver?

Insurance terms

Someone requiring insurance cover can approach either an insurance company or use an agent (might be a garage owner or bank manager) who put people in touch with the insurance companies (*see* Fig 15.3 overleaf). **Friendly Societies** offer life and sickness insurance often operating through local agents who might collect the premium on a weekly door-to-door basis. A broker is a full-time insurance salesman, he does not work for any company or underwriter but is paid a commission for placing insurance work with a company or underwriter. He is able to give advice to the customer.

One well-known group of underwriters is Lloyds of London. You've probably heard of them. It dates back to, and takes its name from, a 17th century coffee house where insurance was undertaken. Lloyds is not a company and has no shareholders. It is simply a society of underwriters or individuals who accept insurance risks in return for a premium. The public are not allowed to approach these 19 000 underwriters directly but do so through several hundred Lloyds brokers who can be found all over the country. Today the constitution of Lloyds is governed by Acts of Parliament and they have their own modern building.

Summary of insurance cover

There is a variety of insurance cover available. These include:

Household Can insure 'contents' or 'buildings' against loss or damage caused by such things as theft, flood, fire and even aircraft hitting it!

Motorist **The Road Traffic Act 1972** makes it illegal not to have third party cover.

Businesses Not only is it possible for a business to be covered against loss or damage due to theft, fire, flood etc, but they can also have special policies to cover plate glass windows, company vehicles etc. They can also insure themselves against **employers liability**; if an employer is careless and one of his workers hurts themselves it is the employer's fault (or liability) and businesses can insure against any compensation they might

Insurance Terms

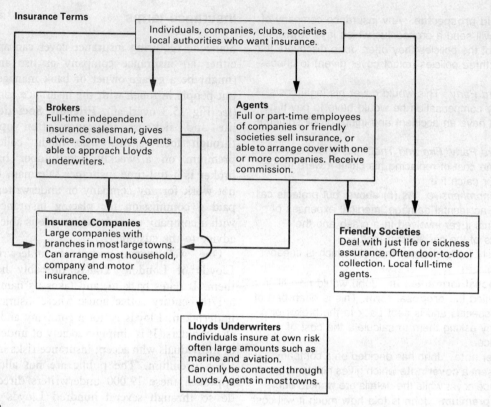

Fig 15.3

need to pay. They can also insure against any claim from the general public who may be hurt due to the carelessness of the business.

Apart from these the **holidaymaker** can insure against loss or theft of baggage, cancellation of the holiday or medical expenses abroad. **Cyclists** can insure against theft, damage in an accident or third party liability. **Sportsmen** can insure against loss or damage to expensive equipment and against the compensation they might need to pay if they hurt someone. An **individual** can insure against any compensation they may have to pay due to their carelessness. This is called **personal liability insurance**.

Insurance companies and investment

Insurance companies take vast sums of money every year in the form of premiums. Much of this is not paid out at once. A small percentage (11 per cent) is kept for paying claims and the rest is invested. The approximate distribution of insurance company funds looks something like this:

Stocks and shares in companies	34%
Mortgages and loans	29%
British Government (local and central) borrowing	26%
Money kept in reserve for claims	11%

Exercise

1 It is impossible to insure against a change in fashion. Why do you think this is so?
2 When 'fire insurance' was first offered, policy holders were given a special plate or 'fire mark' to attach to the outside of their house. Each insurance company ran its own fire brigade which would extinguish a fire in one of their insured homes. In 1833 a single brigade was formed in London which eventually passed into the control of the London Country Council (now London Boroughs).

(a) Why do you think the early fire insurance companies ran their own fire brigades?

(b) Why do you think they formed one brigade in London in 1833?

(c) Why do we now consider a fire service a merit good and provide it through taxes to all householders?

3 Why does the law make motorists take out third party cover?

4 Why do some car insurance policies cost more than others?

5 Why does a life insurance policy cost more for a smoker than a non-smoker?

Housing

Housing needs our special attention since it represents the largest single item in the expenditure of most families (16 per cent in 1981) and is surely one good that we all need. In 1980 the Department of the Environment accepted that 64 000 people were homeless in England and Shelter, the national campaign for the homeless, estimate that this figure was closer to 70 000 for England and Wales in 1981. Clearly some needs are not being satisfied.

For those who have somewhere to live there are three main methods of acquiring a home:

- buy with the help of a loan (owner-occupied housing – the occupier owns or is buying the house)
- rent from the local council (public rented housing)
- rent from a private landlord (private rented)

Tenure of housing [UK]	%	
	1971	1985
Owner Occupied	49	61
Local Authority rented	31	28
Private rented:		
furnished	3	2
unfurnished	17	9
	100	
		100

(Source: *Social Trends 1988*)

Over half of all homes are owner occupied, the majority of these bought with the aid of a loan. Only 11 per cent of homes are rented from private landlords and the figure is falling. In city centres this figure is far higher due to the higher concentration of young single people. **The 1980 Housing Act** gave those who rent from the local authorities certain rights which included the right to purchase the property they rented at a discount if they had lived there for more than three years. This will obviously affect the number of publicly rented homes.

Most people who buy a home do so with the aid of a loan. This is because the price of a house usually represents a very high proportion of their expected working life's income.

Table 15.1

House Price Earnings Ratios by Region; Great Britain 1987 Q.2

Region	1987 Q2		House Price/Earnings Ratio	
	Average Price All Houses £	Average Earnings £	1987 Q2	1986 Q2
Northern	28 507	10 712	2.66	2.51
Yorks & Humber	27 704	10 754	2.58	2.57
East Midlands	32 862	10 618	3.09	2.90
East Anglia	41 543	10 863	3.82	3.49
Greater London	65 801	14 586	4.51	4.11
South East	57 532	11 986	4.80	4.31
South West	44 097	10 884	4.05	3.80
West Midlands	33 425	10 748	3.11	2.81
North West	29 875	11 050	2.70	2.64
Wales	30 243	10 624	2.85	2.86
Scotland	33 414	11 159	2.99	2.73
Great Britian	41 243	11 648	3.54	3.35

Notes: 1. Average house prices are at the completion stage for the second quarter 1986. Figures exclude properties purchased by local authority sitting tenants.

2. Average earnings are based upon the **New Earnings Survey 1987 Part E**. Analyses by region and age group. Figures refer to weekly earnings in April 1987 for those employees whose pay was not affected by absence.

Building society loan

In the second quarter of 1988 for Great Britain we see that the average house price was £43 587 but average earnings were only £14 530. To save up such a figure would take a life-time and where would a family live while this saving was taking place? About 80 per cent of these loans come from special institutions called **building societies**.

Building societies developed in 1775 and were just what the name suggests. Working people would gather together to save up to build houses. As money accumulated land was purchased and houses constructed. When all of the members of a society had a home the society was closed having achieved its aim. In 1845 the first permanent building society was established where people could save any extra cash they had and receive a rate of interest and others could borrow in order to buy property. This is their role today. They were non-profit-making organisations controlled by various Acts of Parliament (for example the **Building Societies Act 1962**), supervised by the Chief Registrar of Friendly Societies, which attract savings on the one hand and lend money to home buyers on the other.

There are approximately 42 million accounts in some 137 building societies in the UK which save a total of £150 billions. These accounts earn interest at a rate of roughly nine per cent. Borrowers, roughly 3.2 million of them, borrow, £130 billion and repay the amount borrowed at an interest rate of roughly 13 per cent From 1 January 1987 Building Societies were able to offer banking services similar to those of the High Street Banks, many changing from Friendly Societies to public limited companies.

The six mortgage steps

There are six steps in taking a building society loan to buy a house.

Step 1 Agree size of loan with building society Building societies exist to help people buy homes. It would be foolish for them to lend so much to a person who could never afford to repay the loan plus interest. For this reason they apply a simple rule of thumb usually lending up to $2\frac{1}{2}$ times a person's income. Someone on £10 000 a year could expect to borrow up to £25 000. A couple can often borrow more – $2\frac{1}{2}$

Table 15.2 Building society loans: regional figures: 1st Quarter 1988

Region	1 Number of Loans (000's)	2 Percentage of U.K. Total	3 Percentage of Loans to First-Time Buyers	4 Percentage of loans on New Houses	5 Average House Price £	6 Average Advance £	7 Average Percentage Advance	8 Average Income of Borrowers £
Northern	15	6	43	9	28 699	21 845	76	12 592
Yorks & Humber	29	11	49	10	29 091	21 587	74	11 797
East Midlands	23	9	47	11	35 269	24 749	70	12 589
East Anglia	10	4	43	18	48 961	32 247	66	14 829
Greater London	21	8	64	5	69 289	49 070	71	21 066
South East (excl. GLC)	55	21	43	10	64 933	41 087	63	18 108
South West	26	10	45	12	50 146	32 785	65	14 400
West Midlands	27	10	50	8	34 884	25 240	72	12 556
North West	29	11	51	7	30 685	22 882	75	12 357
Wales	10	4	53	10	29 358	22 287	76	11 563
Scotland	16	6	59	8	26 808	21 575	80	13 163
Northern Ireland	5	2	69	30	28 951	22 624	78	12 488
United Kingdom	267	100	49	10	43 587	30 112	69	14 530

Source: The Building Societies Association and Department of the Environment: Five per cent, sample survey of building society mortgage completions.

times the larger income plus once times the lower. The potential borrower could then add this to his savings, deduct the cost of buying (legal costs etc) and decide upon the price of house he was looking for. Once the loan is agreed in principle, a house must now be found. The average is under double the income but this includes second mortgages of older people.

Step 2 Find a house Finding a suitable house can be made very easy by using an **estate agent**. These companies specialise in putting potential buyers in touch with potential sellers. They charge a commission but only to the seller. They will provide list of suitable houses and arrange visits. Once having found a suitable house the buyer informs the building society.

Step 3 Survey/valuation The building society will have the house checked by a surveyor. This involves a valuation, that is an independent assessment of the value of the property. Although the purchases pays for this (average cost about £50, he does not see it and it is not a full structural survey. He might be well advised to ask for a full structural survey from a proper surveyor. This will cost a further £150.

Step 4 Offer of loan If all is in order the building society will offer a loan. Building societies do not give mortgages – the **mortgage** is a legal contract between the purchaser and the building society which the purchaser signs and gives to the building society. As a legal contract, once signed, it puts certain requirements upon the borrower (he must make the agreed repayments and insure the property etc). It does not state the rate of interest since with a building society loan this can vary. The loan can last for many years, the most usual being 25 years and over this time a person will repay the sum borrowed and the interest. (The interest on the first £30 000 of a loan qualifies for income tax relief and is calculated by the building society and never charged.)

Step 5 Legalities Although it is possible to undertake the legal paperwork oneself most people use a solicitor. The solicitors fees are about one per cent of the cost of the house. For this the solicitor will check with the local authority on development which might affect the house, make sure there are no people renting the property, draw up the contract and check the mortgage deed, as well as many more important jobs.

Step 6 Exchange of contracts/completion At this stage both the buyer and seller sign a contract to sell. Once signed neither side can back out. The purchaser is asked to pay a deposit of 10 per cent to be handed over to the seller's solicitor. Usually one month later the mortgage money is paid and the house becomes the purchaser's property – or at least he can move in and start repaying his loan!

All in all it is a very expensive business. Further costs also include **stamp duty**, a tax of half a per cent which is paid to the Government on house purchases over the value of £25 000, **land registry fees** and **moving fees** (removal charges or self-hire van).

SUMMARY EXERCISE

1 Give one reason why companies save part of their net profit (retained profits) and state why the shareholders might be pleased for this to happen even though it means lower dividends.

2 If an old age pensioner saved £10 per week in a box under her bed what would be the opportunity cost to her of such a method of saving and why might she be happy to accept this?

3 What might be the results to the economy if most people saved in the manner described in question 2?

4 Financial institutions act like huge sponges. They soak up spare cash in one part of the economy and squeeze it out where it is needed. Name three such institutions about which you have learnt in this chapter.

5 What type of insurance could be considered a form of saving and why?

6 In what circumstances would **index-linked national savings certificates** prove a better form of saving than **ordinary national savings certificates**?

7 Since no interest is paid on **premium saving bonds** and the odds against winning are very

high explain their popularity amongst small savers.

8 Some people feel that cyclists should be compelled by law to have third party insurance. Why do people think like this and what would premiums for such a policy be like – high or low?

9 Give an example of two types of people who would find it very difficult to borrow from a building society.

10 A man lives in a flat which is worth £50 000. He rents it at a monthly cost of £200 (just under five per cent per annum of the capital value of the flat). He inherits £50 000 and is offered the flat to buy but refuses to do so claiming he is better off financially not buying the property. Do you agree with him? Explain your answer.

ASSIGNMENTS

1 People like to save some of their income. You may well save already. They like to save up for things or just 'for a rainy day'.

(*a*) List four different institutions where you could save and receive interest.

(*b*) For each institution you have listed give one advantage and one disadvantage of saving there.

(*c*) For each institution give an example of a group of people for whom you would suggest it would be a good place to save giving your reasons.

2 Suppose your father owned a small engineering firm on a local industrial estate. Explain fully five important forms of insurance you would expect him to have to protect his business interest.

3 You are thinking of getting married. How would you go about securing a mortgage to buy your first home? Be sure to mention *all* of the steps that would be needed including the calculations of how much you could borrow.

4 Insurance is expensive and with any luck you may never need it. Write a letter to a small shop owner, as if you were an insurance agent trying to sell him adequate

insurance. Be sure to point out all the advantages he will gain from proper insurance.

5 'Principles of Insurance – What can you insure?'

'You can insure against losses which can be calculated and predicted but you cannot insure against things which are not measurable by past experience.

You must also have what is called an 'insurable interest', which means that you can only insure against something causing you or your dependents financial loss.'

Source BIA Insurance Series Pamphlet 8

(*a*) Give two losses, other than motor accidents, which you can insure against.

(*b*) Give an example of things you cannot insure against because the 'risks' cannot be calculated.

(*c*) In motor insurance what is understood by:

third party cover, and fully comprehensive cover

(*d*) We are told you must have 'an insurable interest' to ensure something. With examples explain why you think this is so.

16 Government Income and Spending

Chapter 1 considered certain types of goods and services and concluded that two special types of goods and services, **public goods** and **merit goods**, would have to be provided by the state.

Public goods, merit goods and transfer payments

Public goods These were goods and services which when provided for *one* consumer actually satisfied the wants of *other* consumers. If defence is provided for one person it is also provided for most others. Such a service is almost impossible to sell in a normal way for who would be silly enough to pay for it? For this reason no entrepreneur could provide such a service as they would lose money.

Merit goods Other goods society considers so important and essential that people should have them when they need or deserve them – not only if they can afford to buy them. Services like the health service fall into this category. The state therefore provides a minimum level of health care for those who need it. This does not prevent entrepreneurs offering private sector health care and people who can afford it from buying it.

To this list we can now add a third – **transfer payments**.

Transfer payments In most developed countries people are not allowed to starve if their income falls below a level necessary to provide basic needs. People who cannot work because they are disabled, have small children or simply cannot find work are likely to fall into this position of not being able to provide basic needs. The Government therefore takes part of the income from those who can provide for their families needs and gives or transfers it to those who cannot. These payments are called **social security payments**.

Chapter 3 showed how, for various reasons, the Government becomes an entrepreneur taking over and running certain industries. The Government needs to have, therefore, an income and will obviously be undertaking a great deal of spending.

The Budget

Each year the Government must plan how much it requires to take from the circular flow of income either by taxation or borrowing to meet its spending plans. Since a Government must seek the permission of Parliament and since the financial year runs from April to March these plans are usually presented to Parliament at the end of March in what is called **the Budget**. Here is a summary of the 1988 budget proposals:

1988 Budget Proposals

Government Income:

Expenditure taxes	
Income Tax	
Nat Insurance	184.9 bn
Other	

Government Spending:

Defence	
Health	
Social Security	182.9 bn
Other	

Government Borrowing:

Total	1.2 bn
Budget Surplus	£3.2 bn

The Government plans to spend less than it will take out of the circular flow in taxation. The difference, £3.2 billion, is called a budget surplus.

Government spending

The chief items of Government expenditure (local and central) are social security benefits, defence, health and education. Social Security has grown as a percentage of government spending from $16\frac{1}{2}$ per cent in 1973/4 to 27 per cent 1988/9, largely due to increased unemployment.

Table 16.1

Public money 1988–89			
Pence in every £1[1]			
Receipts		**Expenditure**	
Income tax	23	DHSS: social security	27
National insurance contributions	17	DHSS: health and personal social services	11
Value added tax	14		
Local authority rates	10	Defence	11
Road fuel, alcohol and tobacco duties	10	Education and science	10
Corporation tax[2]	9	Scotland, Wales and Northern Ireland	9
Capital taxes	3	Other departments	18
Interest, dividends	3	Interest payments	10
North Sea taxation	2	Other	5
Other	9		
Total	100		100

[1] Rounded to the nearest penny.
[2] Excluding North Sea.

Source: The Treasury March 1988.

The Welfare State

During the 20th Century Government has provided more goods and services for the population. These, we have seen, are called **merit goods** and are provided for people who need them. The National Health Service (1946) is a good example. State Education also comes under this heading. Alongside the provision of these goods and services has been the development of a comprehensive system of **transfer payments** or

benefits which are paid to people at different times in their lives.

National Insurance is a direct tax paid by all people in paid employment and by their employers. This is a percentage of income (between a lower and upper limit) and is currently nine per cent for the employee. This money is paid into the National Insurance Fund and people who have made sufficient contributions qualify for the following sorts of transfer payments when and if the need arises:

Retirement pensions Payable to women over 60 and men over 65. It is possible for an employer to provide own pension and contract out of state scheme thus paying lower contributions.

Sickness and invalidity benefit Sickness benefit lasts for 28 weeks after which an invalidity pension is paid.

Unemployment benefit Same rates as sickness benefits payable for one year of unemployment.

Widow's benefit Payable for first 26 weeks of widowhood, with additions for children. Then a widowed mother's allowance followed by widow's pension for women over 40. All would cease if the women remarried or reached 60.

Maternity allowance Paid for 11 weeks prior to expected date of birth and for six weeks afterwards. A non-contributory £25 maternity grant is also paid.

Death grant A small sum of £30 is paid to a contributor's relatives to help with funeral arrangements.

Industrial injuries benefit Non-contributory but paid from the National Insurance Fund.

These are non-means tested, that is they are not dependent upon the size of a person's gross income. They are, with the exception of a maternity grant and industrial injuries benefit, paid to those who have satisfied the correct criteria with regard to National Insurance Contributions and are of course in need (i.e. to claim maternity allowance a woman has to be pregnant).

A number of non-contributory, means tested benefits also exist as a safety net for the welfare state. Families whose gross income falls below a prescribed level, 'the poverty line', are able to claim certain benefits:

Income Support

Income Support is a means-tested Social Security Benefit designed to help people who do not have sufficient money income according to their individual situation. It can be claimed by those who are:

- unemployed (or work less than 24 hours per week)
- over 60
- single parent families
- sick or disabled
- looking after the sick or disabled

Anyone in one or more of the categories above may qualify as long as they have less than £6000 personal savings and are not financially supported by a partner. The amount they can claim will depend upon their income (from other Social Security Benefits, part-time work etc.) and their circumstances – their need. This is calculated using a series of 'Allowances' for which they qualify, i.e. for each child in the family etc., and 'Premiums' for people with special needs. A person receives all the allowances for which they qualify but normally only the highest premium for which they qualify in addition to family premium, disabled child's premium and severe disability premiums where appropriate.

Examples of 1988/9 Allowances and Premiums

allowances

Single people

16–17	£19.40
18–24	£26.05
25 and over	£33.40
Couples	
both under 18	£38.80
at least one 18+	£51.45
For each child	
under 11	£10.75
11–15	£16.10
16–17	£19.40
18+	£26.05

Premiums

Family	£ 6.15
Disabled child's	£ 6.15
Loan Parent	£ 3.70

Disability	(single)	£13.05
	(couple)	£18.60
Pensioner	(single)	£10.65
	(couple)	£16.25

Housing Benefit

Housing Benefit is a government scheme to help people with low incomes pay for their housing costs (rent and community charge). Anyone on a low income can claim Housing Benefit and their income (earnings, social security benefits (not including mobility and attendance allowance), savings income (from savings between £3000 and £6000)) is calculated. If a person's net income is less than their total allowances and premiums (*see* above) they are entitled to full Housing Benefit. (*Note*: Since Income Support raises a person's net income to this level, anyone, in general, on Income Support will receive full Housing Benefit). People on slightly 'higher' low income will receive reduced Housing Benefit. Full Housing Benefit currently pays *all* rent and 80 per cent of a person's community charge. If the claimant rents from the Council the rent is simply reduced but if they rent from a private landlord they will receive a cheque or cash.

Family Credit

Family Credit is a Social Security Benefit to help working people who have at least one child. A family is entitled to Family Credit if their total net income (not including child benefit and/or one-parent benefit) is less than an amount determined by the government. Currently the weekly amount is:

Couple	(single parent)	£96.50
Children	(for each)	
	under 11	£ 8.50
	11–15	£16.00
	16–17	£21.00
	18	£30.50

A couple with one child aged 4 and one aged 6 with a total net income of £90.00 per week would be entitled to £17.00 per week Family Credit.

Health and education benefits

People claiming Income Support or Family Credit may also be able to claim free prescriptions, and free dental treatment on the National Health Service, vouchers to help with the cost of glasses, help with the cost of travelling to hospital for NHS treatment, free milk and vitamins for pregnant women and children under five and free school meals. (*Note*: dental treatment and prescriptions are free to pregnant women and all children until they leave full-time education).

Social fund

Low income families in need of a large item – perhaps new shoes for children can make a claim for a loan from the social fund from their local Department of Social Security office. Each office has a limit on the amount of these loans it can give per month: once this limit has been reached no more loans can be made. If refused a loan for what ever reason, a claimant cannot resubmit their request for six months. The Social Security Officer cannot give loans unless the claimant is able to pay it back and if charitable sources of finance might be available.

Other benefits include a non-contributory **Child Benefit** which is given to each family per child. Currently standing at £7.25 per child per week it is paid monthly through the Post Office.

The administration of all these benefits is undertaken by the Department of Social Security.

Problems with transfer payments:

(*a*) *The poverty trap*
Means-tested transfer payments like Family Credit are paid to people whose net income has fallen below the poverty line. If their income rises above this level, it, for example, they are offered more hours at work or promotion, then it could result in a **loss** of benefit which could be nearly as great as the increase in net income. By working harder or being promoted they could end up no better off. This is known as the **poverty trap**. For example, claimants in receipt of Family Credit and Housing Benefit could lose up to 96p in benefit for every extra £1 earned. This leads to a disincentive to

work. Someone in the position above is unlikely to work overtime for an extra £10 if they will lose £9.60 in benefit ending up with a mere 40 p!

(*b*) *Take-up*
Take-up refers to the percentage of those who are entitled to a particular benefit who actually apply for it. The system outlined above replaced a more complicated system in April 1988 which had an annual estimated £750 million not claimed! The old Family Income Supplement (replaced by Family Credit) had only a 50 per cent take-up. It is too soon, to tell whether there has been a significant improvement in take-up. The new system has been simplified and links the process of claiming Social Security Benefits and Housing Benefit.

The forms are, however, because of the detailed information required, extremely long and complicated. The Income Support form having 20 pages and 154 different questions. Some people believe complicated forms and ignorance can cause a lack of take-up. The worst areas of take-up are in areas such as free milk and vitamins for unemployed pregnant women where currently only four per cent of those entitled to claim actually do. In areas such as this, education and information will help.

ASSIGNMENT

Find out the levels of as many of the transfer payments listed above as you can. (There should be at least one claimed on you!)

Central government taxation

While governments can borrow and sell services to the country (i.e. electricity) the major source of income for a government to finance a programme of spending lies in **taxation**. National Insurance is a form of tax already considered. We will look in detail at the other major central government taxes.

There are two Government bodies responsible for collecting taxes. Taxes charged directly upon

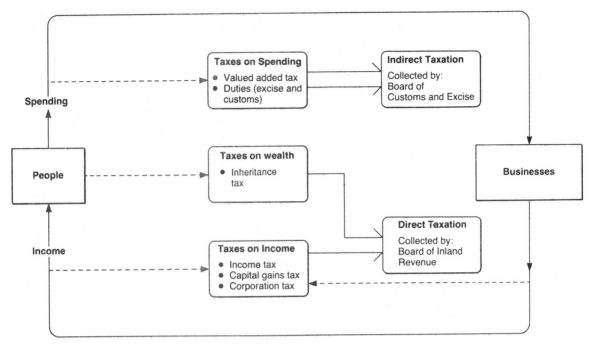

Fig 16.1 Central government taxes in the UK

the country are collected by the **Board of Inland Revenue**. These include income tax, corporation tax and capital gains tax which are taxes on income and capital transfer tax which is a tax on wealth. Some taxes are charged indirectly, that is people pay the tax as they purchase goods and services. These indirect taxes are collected by the **Board of Customs and Excise** and include value added tax, customs and excise duties.

Direct taxes

Income tax This is the most important tax levied. It accounts for about one quarter of all tax revenue. For most people it is charged at 25 pence in the pound but everyone is allowed a certain amount of income, tax free. This is their allowance and it is deducted from their gross income to calculate their taxable income. The allowances are, for most people:

£4095 Higher Allowance (married man)
£2605 Lower Allowance (single person or wife's earned income relief)

To this is added expenses incurred in earning the income (other than the cost of travelling to work) and allowances for a housekeeper and other expenses. The total is deducted from gross earnings to give taxable income. (These allowances minus the last figure are a person's tax code. The letter H or L is put at the end to signify the higher or lower allowance.)

Taxable income is then taxed as follows:

1988/89 Taxable Income Bands
£1 → £19 300 – 25%
£19 301 → and over – 40%

Taking into account the tax-free allowances Fig 16.2 shows how the average amount of gross income paid in tax increases as gross income increases. In this example a married man with only the higher tax free allowance of £4095 has to earn over £45 000 per year to be losing 30% of his income in income tax.

People in full-time regular employment usually pay their tax as they earn it – PAYE. Under this system the tax a person is due to pay throughout

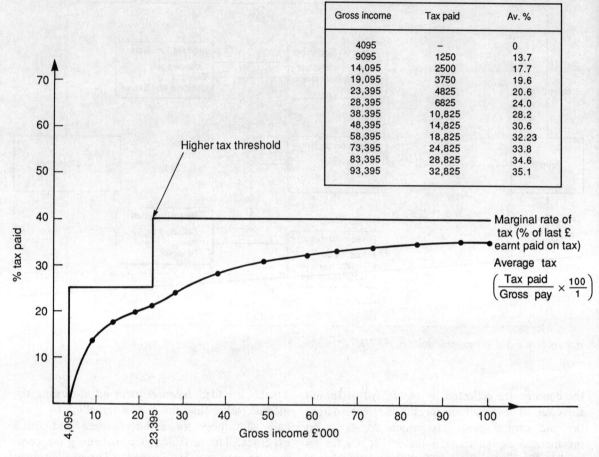

Gross income	Tax paid	Av. %
4095	–	0
9095	1250	13.7
14,095	2500	17.7
19,095	3750	19.6
23,395	4825	20.6
28,395	6825	24.0
38.395	10,825	28.2
48,395	14,825	30.6
58,395	18,825	32.23
73,395	24,825	33.8
83,395	28,825	34.6
93,395	32,825	35.1

Fig 16.2   Income tax liability of persons on higher earned income allowance £4095 1988/9 rates

the year is divided by 12 if they are paid monthly or 52 if they are paid weekly and simply deducted by the employer from their pay who then pays the Inland Revenue. In this way the tax payer does not face a large bill at the end of the financial year and the Government receives a steady income throughout the year.

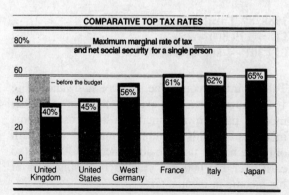

Fig 16.3   Since the 1988 budget the UK has one of the lowest maximum marginal rates of tax

Corporation Tax Companies much like individuals are taxed upon their income or profits and this tax is called **corporation tax**. The rate charged is 35 per cent. Small businesses whose taxable profits do not exceed £100 000 pay the reduced rate of 25 per cent.

Companies do not have tax free allowances like individuals but can deduct expenses incurred in earning those profits and sums set aside to replace the capital of the firm (depreciation allowances).

There are also allowances for increases in stock and for investment in the assisted areas.

Capital Gains Tax   In Chapter 2 it was demonstrated how through clever anticipation a person or company could buy and sell stocks and shares and make a **capital gain**. Such gains, using 1982 as a base year, are taxed at the same rates as income tax. Individuals have a tax free allowance of £5000. A capital loss can offset a gain.

Inheritance Tax   This is a tax on wealth, or rather the accumulated wealth of a family. Originally such taxes were only imposed when a person died. Since it was possible for people to give away their wealth before they died only a few who died young ever paid it. It became known as the 'unfortunate tax' rather than the proper title – **estate duty**. In 1974/75 **capital transfer tax** was introduced. This taxed a person on their lifetime gifts. In 1986 it was replaced by **Inheritance Tax**. Now, lifetime gifts are exempt from tax up to 7 years before death but, on death the value of an estate is taxed as follows:

Value of Estate	Tax Rate
£'000	%
0–110	nil
over 110	40

Gifts in the years before death are subject to the following taper:

Years between gift and death	% of full charge at death rates
0–3	100
3–4	80
4–5	60
5–6	40
6–7	20
over 7	nil

There is no tax when an estate is left to a husband or wife.

Indirect taxes

Value Added Tax   This is a tax on spending and is levied on most goods and services at a standard rate of 15 per cent. You might well have received a bill in a restaurant for £10 and seen 'plus 15 per cent VAT £11.50'. That extra £1.50 is a tax and goes to the Government. VAT is an important source of revenue. A few items such as basic food, children's clothing and educational services are exempt.

The name comes from the manner in which it is collected. At each stage of production value is added. A carpenter might buy wood costing £50 and produce furniture which sells at £250. He has added £200 to the value. He would have to pay £30 VAT (15 per cent of £200). He can pass this on to the furniture retailer by charging £280. He can also claim back that part of the £50 he paid for the wood which was VAT. The retailer might add a further £100 to the value and thus pay £15 VAT but would charge £395. In this way the full tax is passed on to the consumer.

Customs Duties   As members of the EEC it was explained in Chapter 9 that goods imported into this country face the **common external tariff**. The importer will add all or part of this to the price he charges. Such taxes are not imposed to raise revenue but to prevent or discourage imported goods from non-EEC countries.

Excise Duties   Certain goods, whether they are imported or manufactured in this country, face an additional tax to VAT. These goods include beer, wine, spirits, tobacco, petrol and others. They are known as excise duties. Typical examples for 1988/9 are shown in Fig 16.4.

In addition there are special specific expenditure taxes in the form of licences. For example, television and road fund licences (for cars) are annual and raise a good deal of revenue. Legal documents often have a stamp duty in particular when selling a house of over £25 000 value.

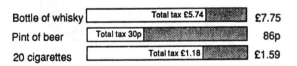

Fig 16.4 Excise duties

Exercise

Assume 1988/89 tax rates throughout.

1 Calculate the total income tax for a single person with a gross annual income of £12 205.
2 In the above example how much would this person pay per month under PAYE.
3 If a speculator on the Stock Exchange made a £10 000 capital gain on one deal but a £3400 capital loss on a second, what would be his capital gains tax liability if these were the only two deals he undertook in a year?
4 Income tax increases as a proportion of gross income, as gross income increases. That is to say, the more a person earns, the greater proportion of income is lost in tax. Is the same true of VAT? Explain your answer.
5 Petrol, beer and cigarettes all have high revenue excise duties on them. (A large % tax designed to raise money for the Government.) Why do you think the Government chose to tax the drinker, smoker and motorist so heavily?

The burden of taxation

Income tax takes a larger proportion of a person's income the higher that income is.

Exercise

Look at Fig. 16.2. What % of gross income would be taken in income tax if the man earned:

(*a*) 10 000
(*b*) 30 000
(*c*) 50 000
(*d*) 70 000
(*e*) 100 000 per annum?

Such a tax is called a **progressive tax**. It ensures that high income earners contribute more to the provision of Government goods and services than low income earners. With the system of tax free allowances some income earners pay no income tax at all.

The opposite is a **regressive tax**. Look at the following example:

Two men are drinking in a pub. Both buy a pint of beer. Suppose that the excise duty is 50p. One of the men is a pop star who earns £20 000 a week. The second is unemployed and is given £25 a week. Both pay the same tax on the beer. For the pop star this represents a mere 1/40 000th of his weekly income but for the unemployed lad the tax represents 1/50th of his weekly income.

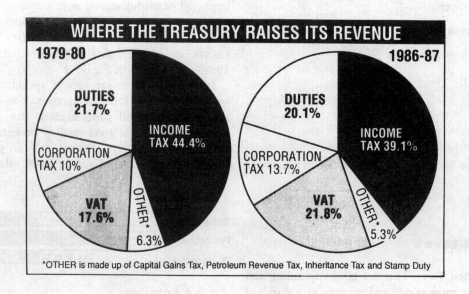

Fig 16.5

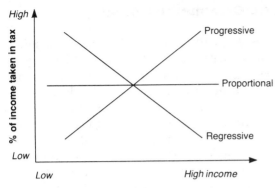

Fig 16.6

Excise duties are regressive. They take a larger proportion of a low wage earner's income than a high wage earner's income.

It would be possible to devise a tax which took the same proportion of everyone's income. Income tax, with no tax free allowances, set at a constant 25 per cent for example would do this. Such a tax would be known as a **proportional tax**. This can be shown diagramatically (*see* Fig. 16.6).

Local government spending

Local governments are responsible for providing many services for the local community. Central government often requires through law that local governments provide minimum services for their residents.

Education is the largest single item of expenditure. **Social services** is another and includes the provision of social workers and residential care facilities for children and the elderly. **Environmental services** deal with refuse collection, parks and housing. **Roads**, minor roads not trunk roads and motorways need to be maintained. The **police** are also on the spending list. **Local** authorities can also give **subsidies** to organisations, clubs and societies as well as local industry. **Grants** are given to students and **rebates** to housing tenants on low incomes. Local authorities **borrow** to build large projects like shopping centres and housing estates and have to pay back the interest on funds thus borrowed. To organise all of this they have to employ many officials and have offices. All the **administration** involved also needs to be paid for.

Table 16.2

Public Expenditure Planning Total by Spending Authority and Programme 1987/8

£ million

	Local authorities[a]
Defence	—
Overseas aid and other overseas services	—
Agriculture, fisheries, food and forestry	180
Industry, energy, trade and employment	202
Arts and libraries	469
Transport	2 719
Housing	1 801
Other environmental services	3 324
Law, order and protective services	4 515
Education and science	13 956
Health and personal social services	2 928
Social security	3 634
Other public services	—
Common services	—
Scotland[b]	4 193
Wales[b]	1 598
Northern Ireland[b]	700
Local authority expenditure not allocated to programmes (England) Admin. Misc	
Totals	40 220

Source: *The Government's Expenditure Plans 1985–86 to 1987–88* (the public expenditure White Paper).
a Including finance for public corporations.
b Expenditure on these programmes includes provision for services such as education.
Differences between totals and the sums of their component parts are due to rounding.
Note: Expenditures on certain services (such as educational) are made under the programmes for Scotland, Wales and Northern Ireland in addition to other departmental programmes.

We have a two-tier system of local government in this country, that is the major services are provided by a County Council and more local needs satisfied by a District Council. In some areas even smaller Parish Councils look after services such as bus shelters and allotments.

In the major cities where people are much more concentrated a smaller area will contain enough people to make such services as education worth providing. In this case the Metropolitan County provides mainly overall planning functions, police and fire services leaving education, libraries etc to smaller Metropolitan Districts.

County Councils	Education
	Large-scale planning
	Roads
	Police
	Fire services
	Libraries
	Museums and art galleries
	Social services
	Consumer protection
	Waste disposal
	Pollution control
	Old people's welfare
	Youth employment
District Councils	Planning applications
	Housing
	Refuse collections
	Parks, sports and leisure facilities
	Local museums
Parish Councils	Parish halls
	Bus shelters
	Playing fields
	Footpaths and allotments

Local authority income

Local authorities have three main sources of finance:

Central government grants Since much of the work of local authorities is as a result of central government legislation it seems only fair that some of the money comes from central government taxation.

Fees and charges Many of the services provided by local government, although subsidised, have a fee or charge which is paid by the local citizens. Car parking, swimming pool entrance, rent of property (school lettings etc) and of course council house rent.

The Community Charge

From April 1990 (1989 in Scotland) local authorities will collect a new form of tax known as the **Community Charge**. Under the new system everyone over the age of 18 will be eligible to pay the local authority in which they live a flat rate tax. (Because people become eligible to vote at 18 the Community Charge has been called a poll tax.)

Each local authority will keep a Register of those eligible to pay the Community Charge and it will be constantly kept up-to-date. The Register will be compiled by sending out forms to each known address where a responsible person will fill in the names of all those who live at the address with their date of birth if under 18. Fines of £50–£200 can be made on those who do not fill in the form. Those who do not appear on the register will not pay the charge. To prevent widespread omissions the local authority has the power to compare the Community Charge register with the electoral role and other records such as state schools. If a person has more than one home they will pay one charge on the main residence (decided by the community charge registration officer).

This new system is thought to be fairer than the old **rates** system it replaces. Under the old system a property tax, called the rates was placed upon each dwelling in a local authority. Each house had a **rateable value**, which was roughly in line with size. Each year the local authority decided upon a **rate poundage**, the amount by which a properties rateable value was multiplied in order to determine the rates. Many people felt that such a system was unfair for two main reasons:

1 It takes no account of ability to pay. My retired neighbour pays the same rates as me although he has a very much lower income.
2 It takes no account of the number of people living in one property. A single person living nextdoor to a middle-aged couple and three sons all of whom work would pay the same rates.

The weaknesses of the rates are well known. In 1963 the Allen Committee found that the rates system benefitted the better-off at the expense of the poor which led the Labour Government of

1964–69 to introduce rate rebates. In 1974 the Layfield Committee suggested a local income tax, once the Inland Revenue became computerised. The Conservative Government for the 1979 election promised to reform rates but could not find parliamentary time until their third term where it became an important change. Supporters of the new system point out that under the Community Charge 37 million people will be required to contribute fully towards local authority spending as opposed to only 16 million who pay rates.

There are exceptions. Students, old people in old peoples' homes convicted prisoners, American forces stationed in the UK, muns and monks and the Queen and the Prince of Wales will all not have to pay the charge. The poorest people who receive full Housing Benefit will qualify for an 80 per cent rebate but as their income rises above the poverty line they will lose 15p in rebate for each additional £1 earnt. Critics argue that the tax is regressive. The lower paid who are just above the social security net will pay the same as the very rich.

The predicted national average annual community charge is £250 (double in inner London) and it is expected that, like the rates, it will be possible to pay monthly by direct debit from a bank account.

Exercise

You will require a calculator for this exercise. Study the three family profiles of the neighbours illustrated below. If the rate poundage is set at £1.50 in April 1989, and the Community Charge is set at £350 in April 1990:

1 What was the rate bill for each family in 1989?
2 What percentage of their total income did this represent? (rates/total gross family income × 100)
3 What will be the total community charge on each family in 1990?
4 Assuming their incomes do not change, what percentage of their total incomes did this represent?
5 Which family has gained from the change? Which family has lost due to the change?

CASE STUDY

Local authority spending

In 1988/9 Northamptonshire estimated that it needed to spend £344.6 million in order to provide

UNEQUAL NEIGHBOURS

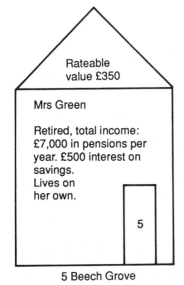

Rateable value £350

Mrs Green

Retired, total income: £7,000 in pensions per year. £500 interest on savings. Lives on her own.

5

5 Beech Grove

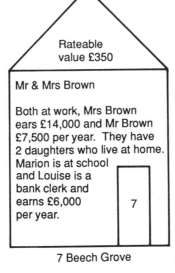

Rateable value £350

Mr & Mrs Brown

Both at work, Mrs Brown ears £14,000 and Mr Brown £7,500 per year. They have 2 daughters who live at home. Marion is at school and Louise is a bank clerk and earns £6,000 per year.

7

7 Beech Grove

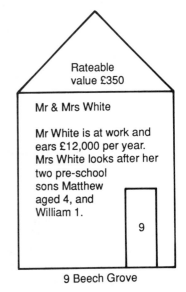

Rateable value £350

Mr & Mrs White

Mr White is at work and ears £12,000 per year. Mrs White looks after her two pre-school sons Matthew aged 4, and William 1.

9

9 Beech Grove

services for the County. The money came from the following sources:

Ratepayers 55%
Grants from central government
Rate support grant 22%
Specific grants 7%
Charges for services 11%
Government reimbursements 3%
Reserves 2%

As can be seen, only a little over half of this County's spending is financed from the collection of rates – or will be by the collection of a community charge. The item government reimbursements is money given back from central government to the local authority to cover payments made by the local authority on behalf of central government. For example, giving student grants, maintaining motorways etc.

The money was spent as follows:

Education 58%
Highways 8%
Social services 11%
Police 10%
Fire & rescue 2%
Libraries 1%
Waste disposal 1%
Other services 5%
*Inflation 4%

* 4% or £14.8m was set aside to cover the expected increase in prices during the year.

Education is by far the largest item of expenditure. The County has 94 700 pupils in schools and 23 200 in further education colleges. It employs 16 716 people of whom 10 765 are involved in education (the majority teachers). The County also maintains a police force of 1553 and a fire service of 474.

Control of local authority spending

Local authorities are not free to raise as much as they wish from rates (or community charges). The government has two controls over local authority spending. Each year the Central Government sets prescribed spending targets for each local authority. If an authority spends more than the target the Government will reduce the block grants given

to that authority by more than the overspending. To prevent the authority asking for higher rates the government passed legislation in 1983 which enabled it to put a legal ceiling upon a authorities ratepoundage – 'ratecapping'.

Where an authority will not set a legal rate the Councillors can be prosecuted and removed from office.

SUMMARY EXERCISES

1 In 1377 the King introduced a poll tax. This simply meant that everybody over the age of 14 had to pay four old pence ($1\frac{1}{2}$p) to help fight the war against France. Is a poll tax regressive or progressive?

2 In 1837 a horse tax was still in existence. A person was allowed one tax free horse if it was necessary for their job but after that the tax was:

1 horse: £18 shillings 9d
10 horses: £33 shillings 6d
20 horses: £36 shillings 0d.

Is this a progressive or regressive tax? To which modern expenditure tax is the horse tax equivalent?

3 Name one group of people who might prefer the Community Charge to rates as a system of financing local authority expenditure.

4 Name three regressive taxes other than the Community Charge. What have they in common?

5 The UK now has one of the lowest maximum marginal rates of income tax. How might this help to reduce unemployment?

6 Inheritance tax raises very little revenue since it costs so much to collect and can be avoided. Why was it first introduced?

7 Child benefit replaced tax free allowances. The benefit is paid through the Post Office to mothers – the tax free allowance did increase the take home pay of fathers who paid tax. Give two reasons that might have been given for the change.

8 Some people believe that the levels of Social Security Benefit ought to be reduced to make people less dependent upon the State and more responsible. Explain why you consider this suggestion would or would not work.

9 If the national insurance scheme, the national health service and state education were to be abolished and replaced by private insurance, private health schemes and private education; name one group of people who would be financially better off.

10 Name one group of people who would suffer in the situation described in question **9**.

ASSIGNMENTS

1 (*a*) The Government often produces goods and services for the public. Give detailed examples of four such Government produced goods and services. In each case explain the type of business organisation and suggest two reasons as to why the Government produces it.

(*b*) Why do some goods, public goods, have to be produced by the Government?

2 (*a*) What do you understand by the term **the national insurance scheme**?

(*b*) How would you, if in paid employment, make contributions to the national insurance scheme?

(*c*) Give two examples of benefits to which you might at some stage in your life be able to claim from the national insurance scheme – and describe fully in what circumstances you would have to be, how you would claim and how you would expect to be paid.

3 If you were to become unemployed after working for about 10 years:

(*a*) What benefits would you be entitled to and how would you claim them?

(*b*) What help would you expect to be given and from whom in finding a new job?

17 Government Management of the Economy

Economic goals

All governments, of whatever political party have four principal economic goals or targets which are:

- full employment
- increased prosperity or economic growth
- minimal price increases – control of inflation
- current account balance

The government would like to see all of those who wish to have a job secure one. They would also wish the standard of living for all the population to be increasing, or at least not falling. Inflation presents several problems for an economy and governments would like to have stable prices. Finally, a country cannot indefinitely import more than it exports and a government would wish to stimulate exports and reduce imports. To this list we could add further goals: a government might wish to see greater equality in the **distribution of income and wealth**, and in addition, better use of the environment and less pollution. Some might argue that these last two are not strictly economic, but they do have implications for the economy.

Before considering these six aims in detail it is important to remember two key facts:

1 The United Kingdom is a mixed economy. The government has no direct control over the private sector, and no magic wand can be waved to reduce imports. Students often write that a government can import less and export more. This may be true but government imports and exports account for a tiny proportion of the total of international trade. Our government can create an economic environment where private sector businesses will be able to export more or where private individuals will wish to purchase fewer foreign goods but it cannot make that happen. The meas-

ures which can be taken by the government are limited and often take time to have any effect. Events over which the government has no control often have far greater influence – for example the OPEC oil price rises.

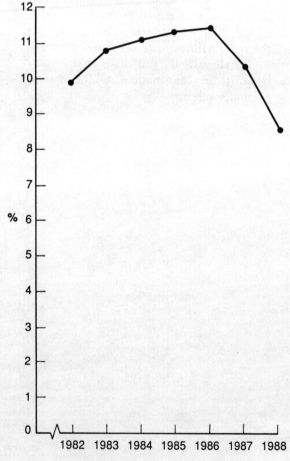

Fig 17.1   Unemployed claimants (excluding school leavers) in UK as percentage of working population

Gross Domestic Product (at 1980) % increase on 1/4 of previous year		Gross Domestic product (at 1980 prices); factor cost
1983	1 3.2	1978 – 99.7
	2 2.3	1979 – 102.4
	3 3.8	1980 – 100
	4 3.7	1981 – 99.1
1984	1 2.9	1982 – 100.7
	2 2.3	1983 – 104.0
	3 2.0	1984 – 106.5
	4 2.4	1985 – 110.4
1985	1 3.2	1986 – 113.6
	2 4.9	1987 – 116.7
	3 3.8	
	4 2.7	
1986	1 2.7	
	2 2.0	
	3 2.6	
	4 4.2	
1987	1 3.7	
	2 3.6	
	3 5.2	
	4 4.4	
1988	1 4.0	
Source: Trends July 1988 HMSO		

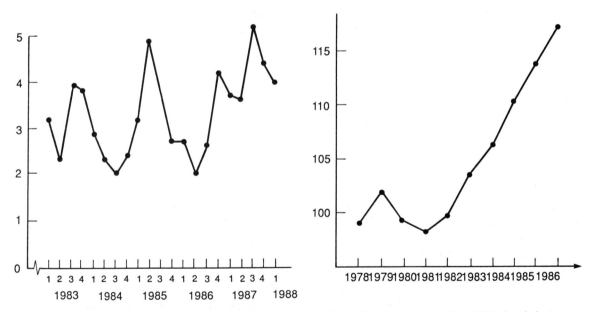

Gross Domestic Product (at 1980 prices), factor cost (an est.)
Percent increase on 1/4 of previous year.

Gross Domestic Product (at 1980 prices), factor cost.

Source: *Economic Trends July 1988 HMSO*

Fig 17.2   Economic growth

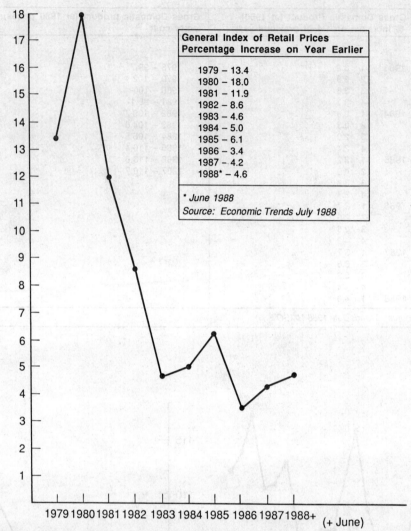

General Index of Retail Prices
Percentage Increase on Year Earlier

1979 – 13.4
1980 – 18.0
1981 – 11.9
1982 – 8.6
1983 – 4.6
1984 – 5.0
1985 – 6.1
1986 – 3.4
1987 – 4.2
1988* – 4.6

* June 1988
Source: Economic Trends July 1988

*Fig 17.3   Inflation in the UK
(Source: Economic Trends July 1988 HMSO)*

2 The policies taken by the government to achieve one economic goal may well worsen the position of another target: for example, lower interest rates and more credit may well increase output and reduce unemployment. At the same time, it could stimulate imports and lead to price increases – there are no simple answers.

The UK economy has been through a period of very high inflation followed by high levels of unemployment. Unemployment, although still high by post war standards, is falling and inflation rates appear to be under control. At the time of

writing, growth rates are high by UK standards but the balance of trade is heading for a record deficit!

Exercise

Study the four sets of data above and then answer these questions:

1 During which of the years shown has the unemployment rate fallen?
2 With a working population of 27 million how many people are unable to find paid

Current Account Balance of Payments £million – seasonally adjusted			
	Visible balance +	Invisible balance =	Current balance
1977	−2284	+2172	−112
1978	−1542	+2504	+965
1979	−3449	+2845	−604
1980	+1353	+1682	+3035
1981	+3350	+3394	+6744
1982	+2324	+2157	+4481
1983	−863	+4606	+3743
1984	−4396	+6385	+1989
1985	−2190	+5463	+3273
1986	−8463	+8579	+116
1987	−9625	+8065	−1560

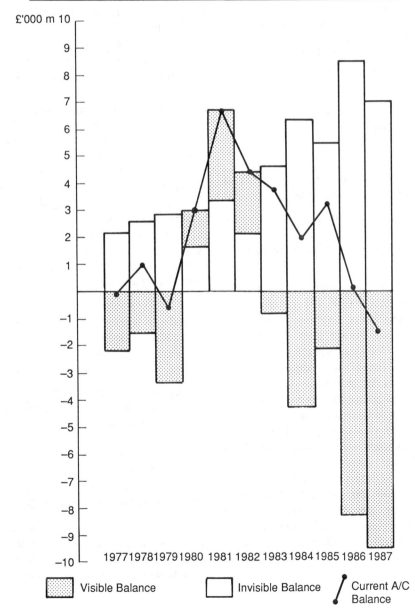

*Fig 17.4   Current account balance of payments UK 1977–87
(Source: Economic Trends July 1988 HMSO)*

employment if the country has 10 per cent unemployed.

3 In which year was Gross Domestic Product higher 1978, 1979, 1980, 1981 or 1982?

4 Did output rise or fall between 1979 and 1981?

5 What happened to output between 1982 and 1987?

6 During which year shown was the annual rate of inflation highest?

7 During which year shown was the annual rate of inflation lowest?

8 During which of the years shown was the visible trade balance positive?

9 During which of the years shown was the invisible trade balance lowest?

10 During which of the years shown is the current account balance positive?

Full employment

(*Look back at Chapter 5*)

As we have seen, unemployment presents a government with two economic costs:

1 The cost of providing unemployment/social security benefits

2 The cost of lost output and therefore national income.

The government of an economy with a large number of unemployed people will therefore face higher spending and lower taxation receipts. To this must be added the human costs. People who remain unemployed for long periods of time face a lower standard of living and a sense of failure. For both these reasons, governments put great emphasis upon maintaining full employment.

Unemployment is measured as those who claim benefit. Since a large number of people (estimated at 190 000), are unemployed and unable to claim benefit (married women wishing to return to work for example), this method does not produce very reliable figures. In addition, young people on YTS schemes and older people on the Training Agency's various schemes are also not counted. As long as the figures are collected in the same way over time, however, the overall trends can be analysed.

Unemployment grew rapidly during the early 1980s and reached a peak of over 13 per cent adult unemployment. During the latter part of 1987 and through 1988 there has been a gradual but sustained reduction in the number of unemployed so that by August 1988 the number stood at 2 313 900 or 8.2 per cent. Full employment – that is, no registered unemployed is a very unrealistic aim. There will always be some people just changing jobs who are claiming benefit for a very short period. This is known as **frictional** unemployment and is quite healthy. New businesses need workers and old dying industries must close down. There will also always be those few who are unemployable and those who do not wish to work. The numbers are very small and it is perhaps a small price to pay for living in a free society.

Causes of unemployment

1   Changes in the pattern of demand

If the product a person produces is no longer required because new technology has made it obsolete or if a foreign country can produce a better product more cheaply then that person may become unemployed. Mechanical calculators or the valves which used to glow in televisions are examples of this. Skilled workers made these items. This type of unemployment is called **structural** unemployment.

Possible Government response   Measure to increase the industrial and occupational mobility of labour. Re-training schemes (*see* pages 72–3). Measures to encourage enterprise. Redundant workers starting their own businesses.

2   Regional unemployment

Where structural unemployment hits an industry which is highly localised it can cause higher than average levels on unemployment in certain regions. This we have seen in chapter 7. It has been made worse by the rapid growth of new industries in the south of the country and led to the so called North-South divide in the UK.

Possible Government response   Measures to increase geographical mobility of labour and financial support for firms which move to the areas of highest unemployment (*see* pages 103–4).

3 Technological unemployment

Look at these figures that refer to the Ford Motor Company:

	Passenger cars produced	Total no. hourly paid workers
1981	342 176	51 938
1986	346 265	32 152

The introduction of new technology into such manufacturing process as car production throughout the last decade has produced unemployment. Firms such as Ford and Rover rarely sack workers. The reduction in workforce is achieved, through negotiation with the unions, by offering workers close to retirement an early retirement package and by reducing the numbers recruited into the firm. This will have a particular effect on young people.

Possible Government response Measure to increase occupational mobility and to encourage enterprise (*see* pages 72–3).

4 Youth unemployment

For a number of reasons the UK has experienced high levels of youth unemployment in certain regions.

As explained above firms have not always needed to recruit replacements for those retiring; increasingly large numbers of women are remaining economically active, young people now expect higher rates of pay and are not the cheap alternative they once were; during a recession firms do not wish to lose experienced workers – so cut down on recruitment rather than sack trained personnel.

Possible Government response Youth training scheme (*see* page 71–2).

5 General unemployment

A situation known as a slump can affect an economy where consumption of goods and services falls and leaves producers with excess stocks. If, as is common, this affects a number of different countries at the same time, no foreign market exists in which to sell this surplus. The only alternative is to reduce the output and therefore workforce. The unemployed having lower incomes will reduce their consumption and so deepen the depression.

Possible Government response In the past, governments would protect home industry by imposing a high tariff barrier. Today the likely response is to encourage consumer spending by lower taxes and low interest rates. Perhaps subsidies to exporting industries and increased government spending.

Economic growth

(*Look back at Chapter 1*)

Most governments, reflecting the wishes of the population, would wish for the general standard of living to rise. Most people want to become better off as the years go by. This can be measured by looking at the value of goods and services produced within a country during one year. A measure known as the Gross Domestic Product (GDP). This, as we saw in Chapter one, is measured each year. Inflation will increase the value of output but not necessarily mean that the country produces more, for this reason GDP is normally measured at constant prices (in the Fig 17.2 above those of 1980) and any increase is known as a real increase. A real increase in the level of GDP is known as economic growth. As can be seen between 1983 and 1987 the real rate of increase has fluctuated between two and five per cent with a 16.7 per cent increase between 1980 and 1987. This meant that the country produced 16.7 per cent more – it does not mean that everyone earned 16.7 per cent more. Individuals will benefit according to the distribution of income and according to what has been produced. It is, however, more likely that the majority of people can achieve higher living standards during a period of rapid growth. It is possible to redistribute income but if one took a person with £1 000 000 and distributed it evenly to 1 000 000 poor people it would leave 1 000 001 poor people!

Economic growth could also be due to increased military production. This will not materially improve the standard of living. In some countries population may grow faster than output, again leaving the mass of people no better off.

Economic growth is therefore only a crude measure of living standards other measures can help. Consider these figures:

% of households having use of:

	1966	1986
Car	44.0	62.4
Television	82.9	97.1
Telephone	24.9	80.9
Central heating	13.0	70.1
Refrigerator	45.3	96.9
Washing machine	61.6	82.9

The information above clearly indicates that living standards are rising. Economic growth will occur if businesses wish to produce more. Entrepreneurs will invest in new plant if they believe demand is rising or will rise.

Possible Government response A government will wish to encourage business investment. This can be achieved by stimulating demand by lower income or expenditure taxes or increasing government spending. Or it can be achieved by increasing the rewards to entrepreneurs by reducing company taxation and keeping low interest rates.

Problems The measures outlined above might stimulate growth but they could also increase imports and contribute to inflation. (Many people blame the large tax reductions in the 1988 budget for the record trade deficit of 1988.)

Inflation

(Look back at Chapter 11)
Inflation can be defined as a sustained increase in the general level of prices. In 1976 41 pence bought the same as £1 in 1986 during the same period however, average wages rose from £64.40 per week to £184.70 in GB. It might be argued that there is no harm done, but during rapid periods of inflation there are a number of concerns:

* People on fixed incomes have less spending power
* Saving is discouraged
* British goods become uncompetitive with those of foreign countries.

There are many possible causes of inflation and economists and governments are not in complete agreement. Some believe that inflation is due to increasing costs such as wages and raw materials, others excess demand – too much spending power driving up prices still others feel that inflation is always caused by too much money within an economy.

Possible Government responses High interest rates and other controls on the growth of money, reductions in government spending, higher taxes, restrictions on wage and price increases.

Problems Some of the measures above might reduce inflation but they may also reduce economic growth and increase the level of unemployment.

Current account balance

(Look back at Chapter 9)
If a country has a large current account deficit on the balance of payments it will have several implications. Since imports exceed exports the demand for the country's currency might be lower than its supply. If the country has a fixed exchange rate this will mean government support which involves the central bank buying the currency to prevent the value falling too low. The central bank will use reserves or be forced to borrow from international organisations such as the International Monetary Fund (IMF). This happened to the UK in many of the post war years.

A country with a floating exchange rate such as the UK today might experience an automatic currency depreciation due to the lower demand for the currency and this, since it will reduce the price of exports abroad could help solve the problem. It might also increase the rate of inflation since the price of foreign raw materials will increase. If there is a flow of money into the country on the capital account, however, it is quite possible for a country to sustain a balance of payments current account deficit with no apparent problems – since there is plenty of demand for country's currency. This can lead to a problem: if confidence in the economy were to fall, foreign investors might all withdraw their deposits at the same time leading to a panic selling of the currency – the so called 'hot money' phenomenon.

It can be argued that high levels of imports of goods which could be produced within the home market is rather like importing unemployment.

For these reasons governments try to avoid current account deficits in the long run.

Possible Government responses As seen in Chapter 9:

- deflation – the government increases taxes and the cost of borrowing. This reduces spending on **all** goods and services and therefore imports.
- trade barriers – artificial barriers to foreign trade. Membership of GATT and EEC rule this out but it would lead to retaliation and reduced world trade from which the UK as a trading nation is likely to suffer.
- currency depreciation – a fall in the value of the pound against other currencies will reduce the cost of British goods abroad but increase the cost of foreign goods at home. In theory, since the UK in common with many other countries, has a 'floating' exchange rate a currency depreciation should be the automatic response to a trade deficit, but this is to ignore capital movements.

Problems

1 Deflation, if it works, reduces all demand and therefore has an adverse effect on home employment. High interest rates seem to have little effect upon consumer demand but encourage foreign investment and reduce the likelihood of currency depreciation.
2 Trade barriers are thought not to work in the long-run and are against international agreements.
3 Currency deflation will increase the cost of raw materials and could increase inflation. The extent to which it will work will depend upon the price elasticity of demand for the country's exports.

CASE STUDY

'The Chancellor's dilemma'

When in the summer of 1988 large monthly current account trade deficits were announced, base interest rates were increased (in several stages) from 9 per cent to 12 per cent. The aim was to reduce home demand (deflation). This maintained demand for the pound, however, and therefore exchange rates as foreign governments, companies and individuals still wished to deposit funds (save) in the UK. Higher interest rates affected home investment and the resulting high foreign exchange rate reduced exports still further:

Example

In August 1988 Jaguar announced the following disappointing half-year profits:

1st half 1987 – £45.7 m
1st half 1988 – £22.5 m

The company blamed the high value of the pound which they maintain in the US (Jaguar's largest market taking 50 per cent of cars manufactured) had pushed up the price of their cars just when the market for luxury cars was falling and led to a nine per cent drop in sales over the half-year.

Cost of Jaguar in US Autumn 1987 .... $40 500
Cost of Jaguar in US Summer 1988 .... $43 500

In response, Jaguar aim to increase the productivity of their workers from 4.6 to 6 cars per worker each year. This will mean cutting 1200 of the existing 12 700 jobs by natural wastage between 1988 and 1991.

Exercise

1 By what percentage have Jaguar cars increased in the US due to currency appreciation?
2 By what percentage have sales fallen in the US?
3 Is the demand for Jaguar cars in the US elastic or inelastic?
4 By increasing productivity what do Jaguar hope to achieve?
5 What **disadvantages** would there be to Jaguar if the value of the pound were to depreciate by 10 per cent?

Income and wealth distribution

Income

The distribution of income in the UK is extremely uneven and is becoming more uneven.

Table 17.1

Distribution of original, disposable, and final household income (UK)

	Bottom fifth %	Next fifth %	Middle fifth %	Next fifth %	Top fifth %	Total
		Quintile groups of households				
Original income[1]						
1976	0.8	9.4	18.8	26.6	44.4	100.0
1981	0.6	8.1	18.0	26.9	46.4	100.0
1983	0.3	6.7	17.7	27.2	48.0	100.0
1984	0.3	6.1	17.5	27.5	48.6	100.0
1985	0.3	6.0	17.2	27.3	49.2	100.0
Disposable income[2]						
1976	7.0	12.6	18.2	24.1	38.1	100.0
1981	6.7	12.1	17.7	24.1	39.4	100.0
1983	6.9	11.9	17.6	24.0	39.6	100.0
1984	6.7	11.7	17.5	24.4	39.7	100.0
1985	6.5	11.3	17.3	24.3	40.6	100.0
Final income[3]						
1976	7.4	12.7	18.0	24.0	37.9	100.0
1981	7.1	12.4	17.9	24.0	38.6	100.0
1983	6.9	12.2	17.6	24.0	39.3	100.0
1984	7.1	12.1	17.5	24.3	39.0	100.0
1985	6.7	11.8	17.4	24.0	40.2	100.0

1 Households ranked by original income.
2 Households ranked by disposable income.
3 Households ranked by final income.
Source: Central Statistical Office, from Family Expenditure Survey

Between 1976 and 1985 the percentage of original income earned by the bottom 20 per cent of households fell from 0.8 to 0.3 while during the same period the percentage of original income earned by the top 20 per cent rose from 44.4 to 49.2.

When final income is looked at the bottom 20 per cent fare much better. The effects of social security benefits and progressive taxation increase their share to 7.4 per cent in 1976 but this has again fallen to 6.7 per cent in 1985. While the top 20 per cent rise from 37.9 per cent to 40.2 per cent. The existence of the welfare state and the effect of non-contributory benefits and progressive taxation prevents the bottom 20 per cent from falling too far below the 'poverty line' – which is why these were introduced. Without this safety net of benefits society's casualties; the unemployed, the ill, the homeless etc, would end up

existing upon charity or dying. It makes sound economic sense for a civilised society to educate, feed and house the entire population. To pay for this taxation reflects the same pattern with 'the broadest backs bearing the greatest burden' – that is those who can afford it most paying the highest taxes with the lowest paid not paying any income tax. The table does show however that taxes have become less progressive and, in relative terms, the poorest have become poorer.

Wealth

Wealth is even more unevenly distributed within the UK and is, of course, linked to income. The highest paid can 'save' part of their incomes in the form of shares and property which grow in value and generate an income.

% population	total share of wealth			
	1971	1976	1981	1985
top 1.0	31	24	21	20
top 5.0	52	45	40	40
top 10.0	65	60	54	54
top 25.0	86	84	77	76
top 50.0	97	95	94	93
bottom 50.00	3	5	6	7

Source: *Social Trends '88.* HMSO

Although there has been a very slight redistribution between 1971 and 1985 at the end of the period shown the richest half of the population share 93 per cent of the country's wealth leaving only seven per cent for the poorest half.

The taxation system does little to alter this uneven distribution. The major wealth tax being the inheritance tax. As was seen in Chapter 16, however, the tax can be avoided by the passing on of inheritances seven years before death. Capital gains, unearned income – profits, interest, dividends etc are treated as earned income and taxed in the same way.

Many European countries have an annual progressive 'wealth tax'. In 1988/9 Capital taxes accounted for just three per cent of total government income in the UK and have, therefore, little effect upon wealth. In 1986 by far the largest component of personal wealth was dwellings which accounted for 31.6 per cent of wealth, shares representing just 9.3 per cent. These two account for the slight shift in the distribution of wealth. The 1980 Housing Act which gave tenants in Council housing the right to buy – at a discount the home they had been renting – has certainly increased the level of home ownership, which now stands at 61 per cent of households as opposed to 49 per cent in 1971. A second change has been the privatisation of public corporations which has widened the level of share ownership. In 1987 an NOP survey for the Treasury found that 20 per cent of the adult population of the UK now owns shares (15 per cent in privatised businesses).

Possible Government response If the government wished to make income and wealth more evenly distributed it could increase taxation and make it more steeply progressive and introduce a wealth tax. While increasing the level of non-contributory benefits.

Problems Higher taxes could act as a disincentive to initiative and enterprise and encourage the movement of highly qualified people and businesses to foreign countries with lower taxation.

The environment

During the latter part of this century people have become far more aware of the damage being done to the environment by our life styles and the industrial base needed to support it. Some economists believe that the developed world must stop all economic growth otherwise a combination of lack of resources and global pollution will lead to a sudden rapid decline in living standards. Others maintain that through economic growth new technology and ecologically sound processes can be developed which will allow development to continue.

The UK government has passed laws which set minimum standards of pollution.

- *Noise and vibration* Part 3 of the Control of Pollution Act 1974 states that any noise or vibration caused by new industry moving into an area must not exceed levels already set as acceptable for that area. This aims to protect noise sensitive development such as housing.
- *Emissions to the atmosphere* Two main laws: Clean Air Acts 1956, 1968 and Public Health Act 1936 enforced by the local Environmental Health Department. The clean air act deals with the emissions of grit, dust, smoke and fumes which must be below an approved level. The Public Health Acts requires 'offensive trades' – those likely to cause an odour problem to register with the local authority.

Many feel however that the laws we have need tightening up. Read the following article carefully:

£600m plan to reduce acid rain emissions by Hugh Clayton

The Government is to spend £600m in the next ten years on controls that will curb British emissions of acid rain. The measure may push up electricity prices by 1.5 per cent.

A £200m chemical works is to be built next to three of Britain's coal fired power stations so that sulphur dioxide emissions can be neutralised.

The Central Electricity Generating Board said that the new control works might create more than 2000 jobs, but that the increase in electricity prices might lead to job losses elsewhere in industry.

The controls which will cut Britain's emissions of acid rain by 14 per cent will not meet complaints from environmental campaigners at home and scientists abroad about the impact of power station smoke on forests and fisheries.

Gasses from coal-burning and other factory processes are trapped in airborne moisture and fall as acid rain. Two-thirds of such gases in Britain come from power stations.

(Adapted from *The Times* 12.09.86)
© Times Newspapers Ltd 1986

Fig 17.5 Air pollution

Exercise

1   What is acid rain?
2   What is the chief cause of acid rain in the UK?
3   Why might cleaning up coal burning power stations put up the price of electricity by 1.5 per cent?
4   Why might 'the increase in electricity prices lead to job losses elsewhere in industry'?
5   Electricity is about to be privatised. Will a privately run electricity industry be more or less likely to clean up power stations?

Pollution is a 'cost' or negative, unwanted by-product from most production processes. Private industry is unlikely to reduce pollution if it increases their costs and leads to lower profits. For this reason it is unlikely that pollution of the environment will be halted without government intervention for it is only the government which can take fully into account **all** costs and benefits.

Cost benefit analysis

When the government is deciding whether to make a particular investment it is possible to use cost benefit analysis. Here a value is put upon all benefits and these are compared with the value of all costs. If benefits exceed costs then the project should go ahead and not otherwise. Costs not only include 'enterprise or private costs' such as the costs a equipment but also 'social or external costs' such as pollution. Benefits include enterprise benefits such as profit and social benefits such as better roads etc.

Only a government can take all social costs and benefits into account. Many people believe that businesses will not put a price on the environment unless they are legally made so to do.

SUMMARY EXERCISE

1 Why might lower interest rates and easily available credit lead to a trade deficit?

2 Name the two 'costs' faced by a country experiencing very high levels of unemployment?

3 Why would it be impossible for a country to achieve zero unemployment?

4 How does the Government's Employment Training Scheme help to increase occupational mobility?

5 Name two ways of measuring a country's standard of living.

6 Why might government policies which are aimed at encouraging growth lead to inflation?

7 How can higher expenditure taxes **reduce** inflation?

8 Given that the UK has a floating exchange rate how was it possible to achieve a £1560 m trade deficit in 1987?

9 Has the distribution of wealth become more or less even during the last 15 years? How do you account for this?

10 Give an example of a 'social cost' which occurs as a result of a 1st division football match.

Worked Example of GCSE Examination Questions

Mock examination

The following paper is a compilation of GCSE examination questions from a variety of examination boards and sylabuses.

Section A.

1 *Oil price collapse cost 20 000 jobs*
A shock announcement by the government showed 20 000 job losses in the oil industry in 1986. The fall in oil prices was blamed.

The actual number of job losses may be greater because these figures only include workers in the oil industry and those other companies wholly involved in North Sea oil activities. It is not known how many more workers have lost jobs in firms which are only partly dependent on North Sea oil but which also have seen order books empty.

In 1985 300 000 people had found work in the North Sea oil industry. Unless the price of oil recovers significantly tens of thousands more jobs are likely to go.

There was a marked rise in oil prices in 1987. But they were still one third lower than the price in 1985 before OPEC stopped restricting supplies.

The government offered little hope, moreover, that the budget would make sweeping changes in taxation to encourage further development of the North Sea oil fields.

(a) How many people were employed in 1985 in the North Sea oil industry? [1]
(b) What percentage of jobs were lost in 1986? [1]
(c) Explain why this unemployment was not confined to the oil industry. [4]
(d) What was the cause of this unemployment? [1]
(e) The article says that the controlling organisation stopped restricting supplies. What does restricting supply mean? [3]
(f) What does the article say is necessary to prevent a further decline in employment? [1]
(g) (i) The supply of oil is fixed or perfectly inelastic. What does this mean? [2]
(ii) Look at the following supply curves. Which of the above diagrams represents OPEC's fixed supply of oil? [1]

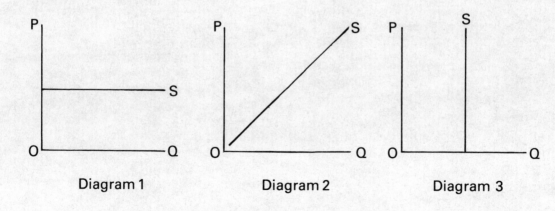

Diagram 1   Diagram 2   Diagram 3

(iii) Re-draw the diagram you have chosen and add a downward sloping demand curve. Show the equilibrium price and label it P_1.   [2]

(iv) What would happen to the equilibrium price if the supply was decreased? Show this change on a diagram and label the new equilibrium price P_2.   [2]

(v) Explain what would happen to P_2 if demand became more elastic when the supply was decreased.   [5]

(h) Aberdeen is a city which expanded in the 1970s because of the discovery of North Sea oil. Many houses were built to accommodate oil workers.

(i) Draw a diagram showing a demand curve and a supply curve for houses in Aberdeen before 1970. Label the curves D and S.   [2]

(ii) Show what happened to the demand and the supply for houses during the 1970s.   [4]

(i) (i) How will a fall in oil prices affect the income of many who work in Aberdeen?   [1]

(ii) Explain how this change in income will affect the demand for houses in Aberdeen. Draw a diagram to illustrate this change.   [4]

(j) The article refers to 'further development of the North Sea' in the last paragraph.

(i) If further oil was discovered in the North Sea what would be likely to happen to the price of oil?

(ii) If this occurred how would it help the employment situation in Aberdeen?   [2]

(iii) Explain how far you think this situation would benefit workers in Aberdeen who are not connected with the oil industry.   [3]

(Reproduced by permission of the Midland Examining Group)

Section B

2 The fastest selling item in any supermarket in the UK is said to be Whiskas cat food. Thousands of pounds are spent each year on advertising this product.

> **Whiskas supermeat.**
> **In tests, 8 out of 10 owners**
> **who expressed a preference**
> **said their cats preferred it.**

(a) What effect does advertising Whiskas pet food have on

(i)   the magazine publisher?   [3]

(ii) the makers of a rival cat food?   [3]

(iii) the management of a supermarket?   [3]

(b) The above advertisement appeared in a national magazine. State two other methods of advertising a product like Whiskas.   [2]

(c) Where does the money come from to pay for these advertisements?   [3]

(d) (i) How does a buyer, for example of cat food, benefit from advertising?   [3]

(ii) How does a seller, for example of cat food, benefit from advertising?   [3]

(Reproduced by permission, of the Midland Examining Group)

3 In a local market the demand for ready picked strawberries on one day was as follows.

Price (pence)	Quantity demanded (punnets)
35	800
40	700
45	600
50	500
55	400
60	300

(a) (i) Draw and label a demand curve for strawberries on that day.   [2]

(ii) The supply of strawberries on that day was fixed at 500 punnets. What, in theory, was the equilibrium market price?   [1]

(iii) In theory, what effects would a fall in supply to 400 punnets per day have on the local market?   [4]

(iv) What factors might affect the supply of strawberries onto the local market   [4]

(b) On 20th July a farm in the area had the following strawberry sales:

Self picked: 600 punnets at 30 pence per punnet

Ready picked: 50 punnets at 60 pence per punnet

(i)   Calculate the farm's total revenue on 20th July.
     Show your working   [2]

(ii) Suggest **two** reasons why more self picked strawberries than ready picked were bought.   [2]

(c)   Strawberries are sold at the Wimbledon tennis tournament in late June for £2.00 per punnet.

Self picked strawberries can be bought in late July for 30 pence per punnet.

What **economic** reasons do you think explain these price differences?   [6]

(Reproduced by permission of the Northern Examining Association)

4   The diagram below shows unemployment rates in the eleven regions of the United Kingdom, and in the United Kingdom as a whole, over the years 1982 to 1987.

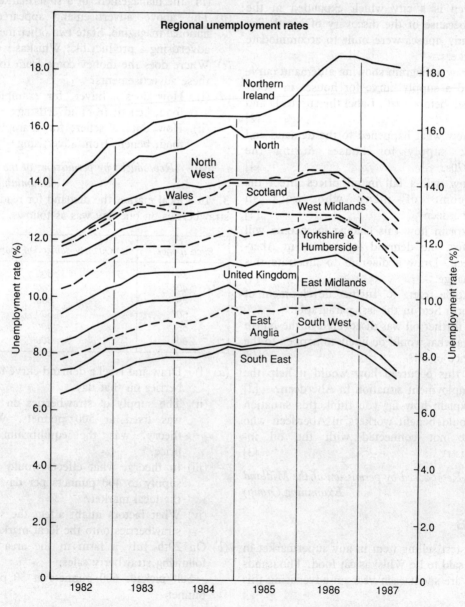

Source: Central Statistical Office, *Economic Trends No. 410*, December 1987.

(*a*) From the data opposite:
   (i)   Which region had the highest percentage rate of unemployment in 1985?   [1]
   (ii) Which region had the lowest percentage rate of unemployment in 1985?   [1]
   (iii) What was the percentage rate of unemployment in the United Kingdom as a whole at the end of 1986? Give your answer to the nearest whole number. [1]
(*b*) Use the data shown in the diagram opposite to compare unemployment in different regions between 1982 and 1987.   [6]
(*c*) Why do some regions have higher rates of unemployment than others?   [8]
(*d*) What policies do you think the government should follow to reduce the differences in regional unemployment rates? Explain your answer.   [8]

(Reproduced by permission of the Northern Examining Association)

5 (*a*) What is meant by a 'trade barrier'?   [6]
  (*b*) Explain whether you think the United Kingdom would be better off or worse off if it imposed high trade barriers on Japanese goods coming into the UK.   [24]

(Reproduced by courtesy of the Northern Examining Association)

6 Examine the diagram below and answer the questions which follow.
(*a*) Why do the records of *all* consumer durables not begin in 1972?   [3]
(*b*) Which consumer durable is found in most homes?   [2]
(*c*) In how many homes per hundred would you expect to have found a dishwasher in 1985?   [2]
(*d*) (i) What do you understand by the term 'standard of living?'   [2]
     (ii) How is it usually measured?   [2]
(*e*) Did the standard of living improve between 1972 and 1985? Give reasons for your answer.   [6]

(Reproduced by permission of the Northern Ireland Schools Examination Council)

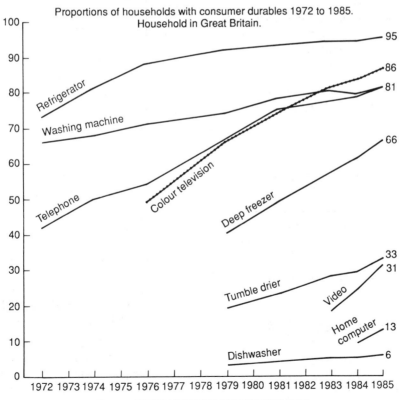

Proportions of households with consumer durables 1972 to 1985. Household in Great Britain.

Source: OPCS MONITOR SEPTEMBER 1986

7 (a) Distinguish between:
  (i) gross pay and net pay: [3]
  (ii) wage rates and earnings.   [3]
  (b) What is meant by 'bonus'?   [3]
  (c) Explain why it would be easier to pay carpenters and bricklayers by piece-rates than it would be to pay managing directors in this way.   [6]
  (d) Why do carpenters and bricklayers usually earn more than labourers?   [8]
  (e) Explain, with examples, why the Government operates schemes for people who wish to retrain in another skill.   [10]

  (*Reproduced by courtesy of the London and East Anglian Group*)

8 (a) (i) Describe briefly **one** *internal* economy of scale, and **one** *external* economy of scale.
     (ii) Explain **briefly** why firms seek *economies of scale*.   [4]
  (b) Explain the main features of a *limited company* using the following headings:
     (i) ownership;
     (ii) providing finance.   [6]
  (c) Assess the advantages of company mergers, using the following headings:
     (i) horizontal integration;
     (ii) vertical integration.   [6]

  (*Reproduced by permission, of the Welsh Joint Education Committee*)

Authors suggested answers

> **NOTE:** The following answers are included by the author for the general guidance of students, and in no way do they carry the authority of the Examining Boards.

Suggested answers to Section A

1 [Revise chapter 13]
(a) 300 000
(b) 6.666% (20 000/300 000 × 100)

(c) Additional workers have lost jobs in firms which are partly dependent upon the oil industry. This will include those who provide services for the rigs, for example helicopter services, shipping and catering. It will also include those whose work on shore is dependent upon oil workers – house building, banks, insurance etc.
(d) The fall in the price of oil.
(e) For several years before 1985 OPEC (the Organisation of Petroleum Exporting Countries) had controlled the amount of crude oil produced by member countries by giving each member country a quota – or fixed level of production – this reduced the supply and increased prices.

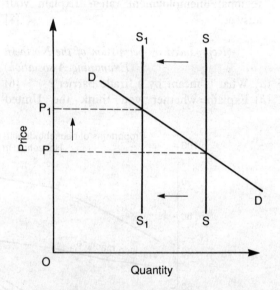

S = Supply before quotas
S_1 = Supply after quotas

(f) A significant increase in the price of oil.
(g) (i) Elasticity of supply is a measure of how responsive the supply of a product is to changes in its price. It is measured by:

$$\frac{\% \text{ change in quantity supplied}}{\% \text{ change in price}}$$

The supply of oil being fixed means that the same amount is supplied what ever happens to price. Being perfectly inelastic would mean an elasticity of 0.

(ii) 3
(iii)

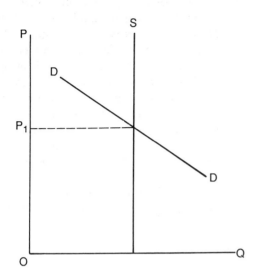

(iv) The equilibrium price would increase.

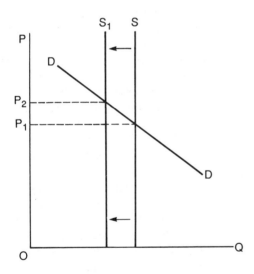

(v) If the demand were to become more elastic it would mean that the demand had become more responsive to changes in price. The reduction in supply would initially cause prices to rise. If consumers could now find alternatives to oil then demand would fall and the new equilibrium price (P3) would be lower than if the demand remains inelastic.

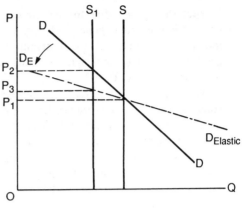

(h) (i)

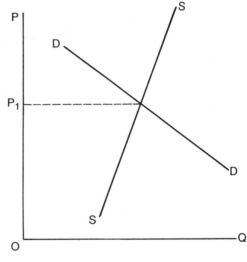

(ii)

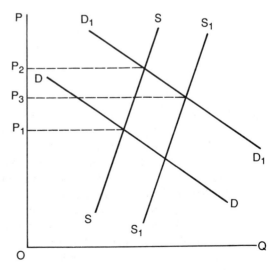

During the 1970s, due to the increased level of employment generated by the oil industry, the demand for housing was greater (shifted to the right) causing an increase in prices (P1-P2).

Although this may have encouraged some locals to sell and move, the supply would have been inelastic in the short run. Property developers would then built new housing increasing the supply and causing the booming house prices to fall a little, or at least steady (P2–P3).

(*i*) (i) For those who are made unemployed and/or whose incomes are dependent upon oil workers their incomes will fall.

(ii) For those who are made unemployed it may well result in them switching from expensive to cheaper housing since they can no longer afford high mortgage repayments. In the longer term since new workers are not required in the oil industry there will be a shift in demand to the left – demand will be less.

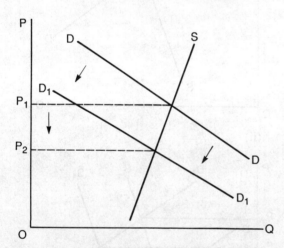

(*j*) (i) If further oil was discovered, it would increase supply and perhaps cause a further drop in the price of oil.

(ii) This would depend upon unknown factors. If the price of oil were to fall further it could mean an increase in demand for oil and therefore an expansion in the North Sea oil industry and increased employment. If however, the fall in the price of oil made the new discoveries uneconomic to exploit at this

time the oil companies may decide to leave them and this would therefore leave the employment position unaltered.

(iii) Given that further development of the North Sea increases employment, then other workers in Aberdeen will benefit. The new workers will spend their income in shops, on housing and will need recreation and entertainment. From building houses for the new workers to selling newspapers to them the local people will benefit from increased demand. Some would say that the influx of new workers will cause congestion and a strain on local services which might be seen, by some, not to be of benefit to existing workers in Aberdeen.

(*Revision Chapter 13 – pages 158–171*)

Suggested answers to Section B

2 (*a*) (i) The magazine 'sells' advertising space to companies such as Whiskas. Advertising proves to be a valuable source of revenue and can help to keep the price of magazines down and sales high. The higher the circulation the higher the price for advertising space. Taken to the extreme, many local newspapers are distributed free, with the production costs being met entirely from advertising revenue.

(ii) A successful advertising campaign for Whiskas will cause the demand for a rival cat food producer's product to fall. This will cause a fall in revenue. The response may well be to mount its own advertising campaign.

(iii) The management of a supermarket will have to respond to changes in demand brought about by such a campaign. This may mean increasing orders and stocks of Whiskas. It is unlikely that such a campaign will result in higher cat food consumption – since it will not make cats hungry, only influence which food the owners buy. If more Whiskas is consumed it will mean less of other brands – which could include the supermarket's own brand. The management may well need to consider pricing or shelf layout to counter such adverse trends.

(b) Commercial Television and Radio
Roadside hoardings

(c) Advertising is part of a company's variable costs and will be covered by revenue. In that sense consumers pay for advertising since it will form part of the price. When a new product is launched, advertising may be paid for using the profits from other products produced by the company or even borrowing.

(d) (i) Through advertising the buyer is able to compare different brands and be better informed about the choice available. The consumer is therefore able to make more informed choices. In addition, if an advertising campaign is successful it will increase sales and this can result in lower prices, as the firm gains economies of scale.

(ii) Assuming the advertising to be successful, the producer of cat food will gain from increased sales, and market share and therefore revenue. It will lead to increased brand loyalty which will form a barrier to potential competition and might reduce the strength of competitors.

(*Revision – Chapter 14 pages 178–183*)

3 (Revise Chapter 13)
(a) (i)

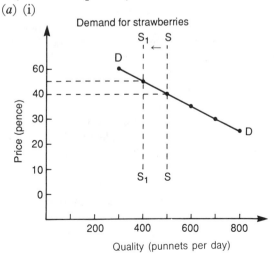

(ii) 50p

(iii) If the supply fell to 400 punnets on that day and the price remained at the old equilibrium price, demand would exceed supply. This could mean that retailers would sell out of strawberries before the close of business or sellers might increase price by a maximum of 5p per punnet.

(iv) The supply of strawberries onto the local market could be affected by a number of factors. Weather plays a major role in determining the supply of locally grown strawberries – a frost-free spring and many hours of sunshine in the early summer will increase the supply of locally grown strawberries. Technology also plays a role. New, faster methods of transport have meant strawberries grown from places like South Africa have been available in some English shops. The controversial irradiation of soft fruit prolongs shelf-life and therefore increases supply.

The price of farm land and its use for alternative – more profitable ventures could also reduce supply.

(b) (i) Total revenue $= 600 \times 30 + 50 \times 60$
$= £210.00$

(ii) Self-picked are cheaper
People enjoy picking and can choose only the best, ripe strawberries.

(c) There are a number of economic reasons which explain the price differences for strawberries at Wimbledon and self-picked. The products being compared are not the same: at Wimbledon, the strawberries are the very best selected, and are washed and served to the customer with cream. The self picker must drive to the farm and provide much of the labour themselves. Thus the **costs** are far greater for the Wimbledon strawberries and must be covered. The customer at Wimbledon has no **choice**. The Wimbledon authorities have a local **monopoly** they are therefore able to make a much greater profit. Pick-your-own farms are often situated close to alternative farms so **competition** will keep prices low.

The consumption of strawberries has become part of the 'custom' at Wimbledon – it is the 'done thing' and most ticket holders go only once. They might not buy strawberries at home for £2.00 but at Wimbledon they are prepared to – this keeps **demand** artificially high.

4 (Revise Chapters 5, 8 and 17)
(a) (i) Northern Ireland
(ii) The South East
(iii) 11 per cent
(b) The data shows that between 1982 and 1986, in general, unemployment rose throughout the UK and that from mid-1986 the unemployment levels began to fall. Of the eleven regions shown seven have unemployment rates significantly above the national average. These are Northern Ireland, the North and North West of England, Wales and Scotland, the West Midlands and Yorkshire & Humberside. The other four regions East Midlands, South West, East Anglia and the South East have an unemployment rate significantly below the national average. It is interesting to note that these regions are all grouped in the south eastern corner of the UK. The **highest** level of unemployment recorded in any of these four regions is 10 per cent, just less than the **lowest** recorded in the other seven regions. The trend in unemployment rates is similar in many of the regions with a gradual increase until late 1984 then a sharp but short drop, a period of steady unemployment followed by a slight increase in mid-1986 followed by a sharp and prolonged drop. This is not true for Northern Ireland where there is a sharp increase in late 1985 and where the fall has been less marked since 1986 leaving a rate just above 18 per cent. Scotland has experienced a greater than average increase since 1985, overtaking Wales and the North West to become the third worst region.
(c) Regional unemployment is not a new problem. One major reason for higher levels of regional unemployment is regional specialisation and industrial concentration. Some industries tend to be concentrated because the factors which influence their choice of location occur in a limited number of geographical areas. Many of the so called 'staple' industries, upon which much of British prosperity was formerly based, tended to be located in only a few

regions. These were textiles, iron and steel, ship building and coal mining. All of these industries have been in decline since before the Second World War due to foreign competition and changing patterns of demand. This has led to higher than average levels of unemployment in those regions which specialised in their production – for example, Newcastle and shipbuilding, Lancashire and textiles, Corby and steel. Unfortunately, many of the new industries which have taken their place, such as electronics and chemicals, have tended to locate in the South so as to be close to the ferry ports for quick and easy exports to Europe which is now our largest export market.
(d) If the Government is to reduce the differences in the regional rates of unemployment it is clear that it must influence the location of firms. It would not make economic sense to help unemployed people move since it would leave under-utilised social capital. Giving grants to firms which create jobs in the regions of highest unemployment is one such method. Currently the Government offers **regional selective assistance** in areas of extreme unemployment known as the assisted areas, which could mean for small firms setting-up up to £40 000 in government grants. In areas of acute unemployment the Government has also introduced **enterprise zones** where businesses are encouraged by a combination of reduced taxes and the speeding up of planning controls. Within these regions of high unemployment the Government must try to increase the **mobility of labour**. Workers need help to gain new skills through Government-backed training schemes such as **Employment Training**.

5 (Revise Chapter 9)
(a) A trade barrier is any artificial restriction imposed by a country or group of countries to reduce imports of goods from other foreign countries. Examples include tariffs (a tax on imports); subsidies (helping to keep home-produced goods artificially cheap); quotas (an agreed maximum number of imports over a period of time); bureaucracy (minimum standards and much form filling).
(b) One argument used to justify the imposition

of high trade barriers on Japanese goods would be that they represent a very high percentage of British imports and are destroying British manufacturing and therefore jobs. It has been said that every Japanese car driven in the UK represents lost British jobs. Japan has risen to become the world's third largest exporter but Japanese imports represent only a small proportion of UK imports (less than five per cent). The imposition of high trade barriers, even if they worked to reduce Japanese imports, would have only a small effect upon the UK. There is no guarantee that UK consumers would switch to UK-produced goods – they might buy German or French cars!

A second argument used is that of the infant industry. If UK firms were late in developing video tape recorders compared with Japan, then they have yet to expand and gain the economies of scale so as to be able to compete fairly with Japan. This argument was used by the EC to impose quotas upon Japan for the import of VTRs during the early 1980s. It had little effect due to the number of multinational firms. Many UK-produced VTRs have Japanese electronics. Many Rover group cars are part Honda and it is becoming increasingly difficult to identify the country of origin for most goods. Unless foreign-owned firms were to be banned from the UK such barriers seem a waste of time.

In addition to these technical difficulties it must be remembered that the UK is a signatory to the General Agreement on Tariffs and Trade which sets out to reduce all trading barriers. The UK is also a member of the EC in which we agree to maintain a common external tariff. In many respects the UK is not free to impose high trade barriers upon Japan.

Finally, even if such a course were open it is not clear that the UK would win. If Japan were to retaliate it could reduce trade between the two countries and thus effect unemployment. The barriers could increase prices of many goods we enjoy in the UK and therefore inflation. Many goods we enjoy in the UK were developed in Japan and to limit their importation would seriously reduce the choice of UK consumers. For these reasons I do not think that the UK would be better off if it were to impose such barriers upon Japan.

6 (Revise Chapters 1 and 17)

(a) The records of all consumer durables do not begin in 1972 because some were not invented until after this date and many were not readily available until later. For example, the video recorder did not become available to households until 1983.

(b) Of those shown in the diagram the refrigerator is found in most (95 per cent) of homes. (However, one would have thought that all homes had some form of cooker which is not shown).

(c) Six

(d) (i) The standard of living is a measure of the number of goods and services a household can purchase. When used for a country it is a measure of average prosperity within that country.

   (ii) It is usually measured for a household by looking at their final income and for a country by measuring real GDP (gross domestic product) per head.

(e) The evidence indicates that during the period 1972 to 1985 the number of households able to purchase the nine consumer durables displayed here increased. 73 per cent of homes had refrigerators in 1972 as compared with 95 per cent in 1985 and so on. This might suggest a rise in the average standard of living. This is only one indication, however, as to the general standard of living and one would need to know much more before it is possible to state that the standard of living for all people within the country improved. These nine might distort the full picture although that is unlikely since they seem to be standard items.

It would be good to see figures which show the real gross domestic product per head. But this is merely an average and can mask difficulties. The general level of unemployment rose throughout this period and, as a result, many households experienced a fall in their real incomes. Hospital waiting lists grew. It is interesting to speculate whether a colour television increases one's standard of living if one is waiting for an operation to remove cataracts! In conclusion, although this information gives a good general indication of a rising standard of living much more information is required to make a firm statement.

7   (Revise Chapters 5 and 12)

(a) (i) Gross pay is a person's total earnings in a given week or month. It includes all pay – normal rate plus any overtime and bonuses. Net pay is the total amount the employee takes home. That is gross pay less income tax, National Insurance, superannuation (pension) and any other deductions such as for clothing etc.

(ii) Wage rate is the agreed hourly or weekly rate of pay. Earnings as seen above is the total amount earnt by the employee and included overtime and bonus payments.

(b) A bonus is an additional payment made to employees over and above the agreed rate of pay in recognition of achieving a production target, or undertaking additional duties or dirty and dangerous work. Bonus payments are often agreed in advance and are used as an incentive.

(c) 'Piece-rate' means payment by results. That is an employee works for an agreed payment per task satisfactorily completed. Clearly in the case of a bricklayer, he or she could be paid per brick laid and that is easy to calculate. Similarly a carpenter could be paid per window frame made. For a managing director it is almost impossible to calculate his or her specific contribution to output and therefore the appropriate rate of pay. (Although managing directors are often given a bonus of shares in the company if the company reaches pre-set profit levels for example).

(d) Carpenters and bricklayers need to serve a four-year craft apprenticeship. This will include both on-the-job training and off-the-job training at a College of FE. Throughout this time they will earn a low wage. Indeed, for the first two years they may well be on a YTS scheme and be paid a low training allowance from the Government. At the end of this they have a 'skill'. The labourer, although often knowledgeable, has no skill and has had no training. If skilled employees were to be paid the same as unskilled there would be no incentive for young people to train. Because not all people can gain a skill there are fewer skilled than unskilled people which means that employers must pay skilled employees more to attract them.

(e) The Government runs re-training programmes in order to increase the mobility of labour and thus reduce unemployment and skill shortages. In a developed economy, technological progress will make some jobs unnecessary and create new jobs. For example the computer has reduced the need for welders in car factories but increased the need for computer engineers and programmers. To avoid unemployment, people with redundant skills must re-train and to avoid skill shortages they must re-train in shortage skills. This needs government support and planning since the trainees must know which skills to train in and need an income while training. The current major scheme run by the Government is called Employment Training. This is open to anyone who has been unemployed for more than six months and is over 18 and younger than 59. Initially they are seen by an independent training agent who draws up an action plan. They will then undertake up to 12 months training while receiving benefits from the state plus an additional £10 per week. Travel expenses over £5 per week are paid and there is a £50 per week payment to loan parents to pay for childcare. A training bonus is paid on completion of the action plan. The training will be appropriate to the trainee and the area using colleges of FE and government skill-centres. The Government also pays grants to employers who re-train existing employees.

8   (Revise Chapter 2)

(a) (i) An internal economy of scale is any saving in costs available to a firm as it increases in size. Large firms can buy in bulk and therefore reduce the unit cost of raw materials. An external economy of scale is where savings result from the increase in size of the whole industry. Where firms in the same industry are grouped together there are economies of concentration for example where transport facilities which help the industry develop or local specialist skills develop.

(ii) Firms seek economies of scale in order to reduce costs and therefore increase profitability. Where they are in competition with other firms, the larger firms can charge lower prices and increase market share.

(b) (i) With a limited company ownership is divided among the shareholders. With a small private limited company this may be a handful of family or friends. In a larger public limited company ownership may be spread over hundreds of thousands of small shareholders as has occurred in recent government privatisations like British Telecom. The advantage to the shareholder is that of limited liability. In law, a limited company has its own identity thus it is possible to sue the company rather than the owners. This in effect means that shareholders are only liable for the funds they place into the company and cannot lose their own wealth should the company fail.

A limited company will therefore last for ever or until it is officially liquidated since ownership is transferrable.

(ii) Limited companies are able to sell shares in order to raise finance. In the case of a PLC this can mean an offer for sale to the general public. Because a limited company has registered with the Registrar of Companies it is able to borrow funds more easily and often at a lower rate of interest from the financial institutions. For these two reasons limited companies

have considerable advantages in gaining finance over the one-man business and partnership types of business enterprise.

(c) (i) One method of company growth is merger. This is where two or more companies join together to produce one larger company. This will enable a company to gain economies of scale and through rationalisation reduce costs and increase profitability. Where companies are engaged at the same level of activity mergers are known as horizontal integration. A good example would be the merger of British Airways and British Caledonian which led to 2000 job loses and reduced the number of half-empty internal flights.

(ii) Another form of merger is where a producer merges with a supplier of raw materials or retail outlet. This is known as vertical integration. Business engaged in the same industry but at different levels within that industry merge to form one larger company. An example would be farms owned by Tesco. Again, this will produce economies for the company and secure supplies. In both cases it reduces competition and choice for the consumer. This could lead to an abuse of monopoly power so that government moniters such mergers and can refer them to the independent Monopolies and Mergers Commission which, if it finds that a proposed merger is not in the public interest can recommend that the Government prevents the merger from taking place.

19 Course work

The GCSE introduced for nearly all subjects an element of course work to be included in the final assessment of a candidate. In most cases it counts for between 20 and 40 per cent of the final mark, although it can be as high as 100 per cent. Course work can take different forms. In some subjects it might be something made; in others it could be a tape or video. In economics it normally involves a piece or pieces of individual research or 'finding out' about a particular topic, business, issue, group, dispute or question.

For many students course work appears to be unimportant, a waste of valuable time or even a bore. Students who feel this way will often leave course work until the last minute and copy a few pages from a book or newspaper and expect to gain good marks. They do not!

It is true that students taking many subjects in the same year face a great deal of course work and may feel under much pressure. It is important to space course work out throughout the one or two year course to avoid a panic at the last minute. The school or college should help in this and teachers will be sympathetic in genuine cases of 'bunching'. Remember to look at the exact requirement. *Students often write far too much.* Your teacher is interested in quality rather than quantity.

Course work is a *friend* because:

- It reduces the importance of the final exam. Candidates who work hard can have marks 'in the bank' before that dreadful day in June.
- It enables all work to be rewarded – not just what the candidate does in the exam.
- Candidates learn from their mistakes. Where more than one piece of course work is counted it is possible to improve technique and acquire skills throughout the course.
- The candidate sets the question. Even where the board sets the topics there is usually some freedom of choice.
- A candidate can use the skills learned in the course work to discover something about his own locality – often something original.
- It is fun. Setting questionnaires or collecting facts is certainly more fun than sitting in a classroom. It gives the opportunity to find out what lies behind those factory gates or 'Staff Only' signs. One can discover something about the real world – first hand!

So do not moan about it – *enjoy it!*

Approaching course work

It is difficult to set general rules for tackling course work. Pupils and syllabuses differ but there is a simple word to help. Course work *kindles* an interest in a particular area of the syllabus and gives the student the time and ability to study that topic in depth. But we use each of the letters to illustrate how to tackle course work:

K – Know what is required
I – Identify questions to be answered
N – Notify your teacher
D – Data/information collection
L – Layout/present your findings
E – Evaluate/interpret your findings

Know what is required
This must seem obvious. Of course you know what the course work requirements are of your particular economics GCSE syllabus – or do you? You may have been told but check *before you start*.

The following details are important:

- What **choices** do you have? Is it a free choice or a prescribed topic?

- How long ought your work to be?
- How ought it to be presented? Details such as size of paper, title page, and completion date are also important.

These are all fairly obvious but something you ought to ask your teacher which is perhaps more important than these is; which of the assessment objectives is the course work component designed to test? This may sound like educational jargon – which it is – but it is important to fully understand what this means. Suppose you were training to be a chef and as part of the course you had a practical test. This was designed to test not only your technical cooking skills but also your ability to plan an appropriate diet for a particular category of person. The person you are given is a person suffering from diabetes. You expertly prepare a delicious meal but it contains far too much sugar and starch. The technical skills have been demonstrated well but the understanding of different foods and their effect on the body have not. Your final mark would depend upon the weighting given to these two different skills – one demonstrated well, the other badly. Someone wandering around the practical assessment, upon seeing your excellent finished dishes, might suppose you had passed well and would be shocked to find that you had not. They do not know the assessment objectives.

The MEG economics syllabus, at the time of writing, is designed to test the following objectives:

- Collection and presentation of relevant data (15 marks)
- Analysis, interpretation and evaluation of data collected (25 marks)

There are several important points to notice. Collection and presentation are important. To gain anywhere near the full 15 marks you must demonstrate knowledge of how to collect data scientifically and choose the appropriate method of displaying that information. Note also the word **relevant**. Further note that the marks are weighted 5:3 in favour of analysis, interpretation and evaluation. Over half of the marks are awarded for using the information collected; *not* information collected by someone else, from this or any other text book but your own unique set of data . . . 'of data collected'.

Many candidates make the mistake of collecting lots of data. Displaying it in a variety of ways – some appropriate and others not and then write pages copied from text books. It can correctly be argued that correct presentation aids analysis and interpretation. A skillfully drawn graph may well illustrate trends *but* if the candidate does not point out such trends and discuss their likely cause and effects he has not demonstrated evaluation.

Identify questions to be asked

It is important that before starting the course work you draw up a plan of campaign. What do you need to ask? Who do you need to see? What do you need to find out? Where do you need to visit?

Write out a list of facts you need to know. Where the topic or area is large break it down into subsections.

It is important to remain flexible. Events do not always turn out as planned; but if you have a plan it can always be modified.

Notify your teacher

Most teachers will wish to see your plan and check that you are on the correct lines. Most course work will form part of the course and time will be given in lesson time to work on the course work and seek help. Teachers can help you if you are stuck; but you must ask! Of course, they cannot write the course work for you but they can advise and answer your questions. It is better to ask a teacher than waste weeks of work on irrelevant material.

Data collection

There are two main sources of information open to any researcher.

Primary sources – information collected by you:

- Observation (e.g. factory tour)
- Interview (e.g. manager of local firm)
- Questionnaires (e.g. survey of workers)

This is often called field research.

Secondary sources – information collected by others: reference books, statistics such as census returns or local government statistics on housing or employment. (Many of these will be held in your local reference library and librarians are generally pleased to help.) Newspapers, both local and national, are an excellent source of information, and back copies of newspapers can be found in your local reference library. The majority of the statistics quoted in this book can be found in: Social Trends, Britain an Official Handbook, Economic Trends, Financial Statistics, Annual Abstract of Statistics, New Earnings Survey all for 1988, published by HMSO. It is also possible to write to companies, trade unions, pressure groups, local councillors, etc. Keep a copy of your letters and replies and place them in an appendix at the end of your work. This is often called desk research.

Obviously desk research is cheaper, quicker and easier, but you can only use *existing* data. Often the information you require will have to be found using your own field research. Field research is fun. It also involves techniques or skills which many syllabuses wish you to demonstrate. It is possible that some or all course work must be based on your own field research. Check if this is the case.

When making observations try to be as scientific as you can. Take notes and listen to what is being said and watch what is going on.

When conducting interviews it is important to:

- Be polite
- Be prepared
- Be precise
- Be careful (not to embarrass or influence people)
- Be off (be as brief as possible – people are usually very busy).

Always ask permission before conducting observation or interviewing.

Questionnaires are a very popular way of finding out about opinions. They are a series of structured questions for people to answer either in writing or orally. Opinion polls during an election campaign are examples of questionnaires.

There are two important considerations:

- Who to ask
- What to ask

It is unlikely that you can ask everyone you are studying. For example in conducting a shopping survey it would be impossible for a professional organisation (let alone a student) to ask all the customers of a particular shop to fill in a questionnaire. For this reason researchers use a *representative sample*. They ask a small number of the population being studied and take the results to be representative of the whole. But . . . the sample must reflect the make-up of the whole population faithfully or the results are biased.

Example you wish to conduct a survey to find out how school pupils spend their pocket money. Your school has 1200 pupils. You have time to ask only 30 pupils.

One seemingly good way might be to put all the tutor groups into a hat and to select one at random. You pull out 1X, a first year group. During registration you give 30 questionnaires to Form 1X. Would the answers reflect accurately the true spending of pupils in your school?

Clearly not. How an 11/12 year old spends money would be very different from a 17/18 year old. A better way would be to select people to answer the questionnaire upon the basis of their sex and age in proportion to the number in each sex and age group in the total school population. If half the school were female and half male ask fifteen boys and fifteen girls. If 10 per cent of the school were in the sixth form ask three sixth formers and so on. In this way the sample reflects the total population and bias is reduced. This is the way opinion polls are carried out and the results can be very accurate even though the sample size is small (*see* Fig 19.1).

Marplan Poll 9 April 1987		Actual result of General Election 11 June 1987
Conservative	38%	43%
Labour	32%	31%
Liberal/SDP Alliance	27%	23%
Others	3%	3%

Designing a questionnaire is very easy; designing a good questionnaire is extremely difficult. It is useful to conduct a mini (or pilot) survey to test your questions before you have anything printed and before you take off to the High Street clipboard in hand. Some questions just do not work!

The 'rules' are similar to those for interviewing. It is once again important to be polite, brief, etc. for obvious reasons. Try to be simple, straightforward and unambiguous. (A form from my son's new school asked: 'Can he put on his own shoes? □always □sometimes □never.' Of course it depends what type of shoe: he cannot tie laces (he is only four years old), but copes with velcro/elastic shoes. The question would have been less ambiguous had it asked whether he could tie laces.)

Closed questions are preferable to *open*. An example of a closed question is: Which of these types of television do you like to watch? □Comedy □Soaps □Drama □Films □Variety □Documentary □News/Current Affairs. The subject has a simple choice. Analysing the results of such a questionnaire is quite straightforward and quick. We could see what proportion of the sample liked to watch comedy.

You could ask the open question: 'What television do you like to watch?' and leave several lines to be filled in. The subject is not constrained by your choices, but the analysis takes far longer since you will have to classify the results.

Only ask questions the subject can answer. If you were to ask: 'How many hours of television do you watch per week?' the answers would not be very accurate. People simply do not keep a record of such things and would only guess; they genuinely do not know. To find the answer to this you would need to ask people to keep a weekly diary or perhaps ask them to tick which programmes they watched from the previous night's list in the newspaper.

Check with your teacher before conducting any survey.

Layout/presentation

When all your information has been collected it must be presented. You can present information in a number of ways:

- Written
- Table
- Graph
- Diagram
- Picture
- Map
- Video/audio tape

The key to good presentation is effective communication. Use a variety of forms of presentation choosing the appropriate form for the given information so that you pass on your answers in the best way.

Written

Much of your course work will be in written form. Try to break up passages into separate paragraphs with side headings. Follow a logical order. Do not try to present too much detail. It is often a good idea to put nonessential detail in a separate additional chapter at the end of the study – this is called an appendix. Explain things in your own words – do not copy chunks from books or company reports.

It may prove difficult to find out all you wish to know. Include letters, once again in an appendix, to show the direction and scope of your investigation.

Because of the importance of your written presentation, it is worth writing it out roughly so that you can check spelling, order of material, etc. before writing your finished copy. If you have no time to do this, at least check it thoroughly before handing it in.

Tables

UK new car registration (%)	1985	1986
UK produced	42	44
Foreign imports	58	56

Tabulation means putting data into rows and columns. It is a neat way of presenting information and may be much quicker than the written word. It helps analysis. In the very simple table above it is easy to see that in both years more foreign cars were registered in the UK than British built cars. It can also be seen that the percentage of foreign registrations fell by two per cent between 1985 and 1986. Tabulation enables the reader to compare values and detect trends: X is bigger than Y but Y is growing and X is falling.

Remember to make it clear what any figures represent. In the above example it is clear that percentages are given, that 1985 and 1986 are years and that the table refers to car registrations in the UK. Too often a table gives little or no useful information because it lacks clear labelling.

Graphs

Sometimes a graph may be better than a table. A graph is a diagram which shows the relationship berween two variables each measured along a calibrated axis. They come in three main forms: line, bar, pie. It is certain that you have drawn all three at some time during your school career.

A *line graph* is ideal for showing how a variable changes over time. It is, for example, the chart seen at the foot of a patient's bed in hospital showing how their temperature varies hour by hour. This is often called time series data (*see* page 214).

Bar charts are ideal for comparing relative size. This could be across time or for different firms, countries, areas, etc. at the same time (*see* page 215).

A *pie chart* is used where you wish to display the relative importance of the component parts of a whole. The circle (or pie) represents the whole, and slices are 'cut' to represent the relative sizes of constituent pieces. Although perhaps more time consuming, these look very attractive and are good for showing relative size – but not trends since the human eye is not as good in detecting small changes in segments as it is in detecting small changes in the heights of columns. (*See* page 206.) Pie charts can become confusing if too many segments are used.

Remember: label all graphs clearly.

Diagrams

A diagram can save much written explanation and make your work clear. A flowchart which shows the production process is a good example (*see* Fig 19.1).

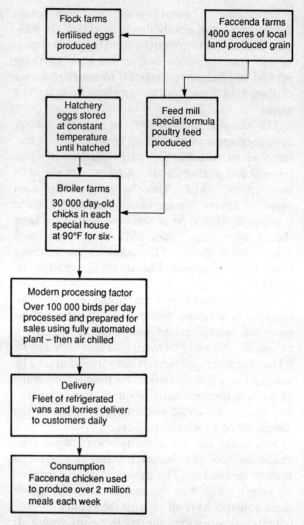

Fig 19.1   *The production process*

When considering the use of a diagram decide whether:

- it would make your work clearer
- it would reduce written explanations
- it would make analysis easier

It would be foolish to use diagrams to pad out a thin piece of work.

Pictures

It is tempting to fill a piece of course work with pretty pictures. Firms will often send you glossy brochures full of them. Cutting out pictures and sticking them in is largely a waste of time. The *right* picture can, however, be very useful. Ask yourself the same questions as with diagrams. If they help the explanation use them. In particular try to take your own: the parking problems in a town centre, pollution of a local river, pickets outside a factory gate, the production line of a local firm, the new robot machine compared with the old manual process, the new factory estate being constructed, different types of advertisement. (Many schools will have cameras and their own developing facilities which it may be possible to use – ask!)

Remember: always ask permission before you take pictures on or inside business premises.

Maps

A map can be very helpful. It might be a plan of a business, a map of the local area or a map of the region. (*See* page 94.)

This figure contains much important information about the Dagenham site and the reasons for its choice by Fords for a major manufacturing plant in Europe in the late 1920s. It once again saves written explanation and clearly makes its point.

Video/audio tape

Many syllabuses are pleased to accept these types of communication. They are expensive and often not appropriate for our purposes. A tape can provide a permanent record of something which is only likely to occur once, such as a technology project where a new design of submarine is tested in the school swimming pool. A video might be useful if the candidate can only demonstrate a skill visually, as perhaps in drama, child care or home economics. In these subjects the board normally appoints outside moderators to visit each school to see what each candidate can do.

It is clear that the use of video and audio tape is limited in Economics since we can normally use the other mediums of communication listed above. A tape is a good idea when interviewing people, if they do not mind, as it will give you a chance to listen to their answers over and over again. It would probably not be necessary to include the tape, however, in your course work. Ask yourself whether it would contribute positively to your work and then ask your teacher for advice.

Evaluate/interpret/analyse

Your work should not be merely a description of a firm, topic, group, etc. When you have collected your information you should select information from your study to illustrate the work which you have done in class. Show that you understand, for example, how firms grow by reference to the growth of the firm you have studied. If the firm has remained small try to state why (Lack of finance? Lack of market? Lack of entrepreneurial skill?). You may wish to show why the firm is located close to your home, selecting those special features which existed to attract the business to your locality.

Choose themes which your study helps to illustrate. Your experiences might make it impossible to comment upon the impact of technology if you were not allowed on the shop floor – but you may be able to ask questions about training and the work of the personnel department. Be flexible and positive. Write about what you did find out, not what you could not. Examiners call this *interpretation*, i.e. you can take the information collected and interpret (explain) it in terms of the work that you have done throughout the course.

Where you have collected data use it. Analyse the results of questionnaires and desk research. Do not be afraid to state the obvious. Look for trends (Which is largest? Which is growing faster? Which was most popular and why?).

Where you have asked questions try to give an answer. This may even be that you were unable to find an answer to the question you set yourself. For example, you might set out to discover the effects of a by-pass upon the retail businesses of a town. Elaborate questionnaires could reveal that most businesses think they will be unaffected. The conclusion is that retail business will be unaffected by the by-pass. A negative result is just as interesting as a positive one.

Presentation is important. Remember your course work may be sent to a moderator to be re-marked. It could then be sent to the chief moderator to be checked and even be sent to the board to help to decide grades. It is not just your teacher who will see the work.

It is important therefore to have the following information on the front cover: your name, the centre name, candidate number, centre number, syllabus name, syllabus number, title of work, item of course work. (Some boards prepare a title sheet for you to supply this information.)

Arrange your work in order and fasten the sheets together but do not put it into a file.

Underline side headings and make sure that all graphs, diagrams, maps, pictures, etc. are correctly labelled.

Any extra information such as letters you sent or received, documents, examples, etc. can be put in appendices at the end of the work and should be clearly labelled.

You should list all sources of help such as books, etc. and acknowledge any help individuals or firms have given.

Do not write in the first person unless instructed to, nor make direct reference to the moderator. If you had problems explain them to the teacher and they will make notes to the moderator where necessary.

Have fun, enjoy yourself and remember the existence of course work makes your eventual grade far less a matter of luck and far more a matter of how hard you work throughout the course.

Course work study guide 1

General aim

To keep a diary following an economic issue, using cuttings and with comments.

Questions

There are several suitable questions you may like to consider if set this topic.

1 An industrial dispute (other than wages). The closure of a plant or firm and the reaction of the workers. Why is the plant to be closed? How will effect employment and the local area? How do the Unions react? etc.

2 A wage dispute. Who was involved in the original negotiations? What was the original claim and offer? What industrial action was threatened/took place? What were the results of ballots on industrial action? Were any outside parties involved ACAS, TUC etc? What was the eventual settlement?

3 Take-over bid. What was the original offer? Was this accepted by the business to be take-over or contested? What benefits were given in favour of the take-over for shareholders, workers and consumers? Was the take-over referred to the Monopolies & Mergers Commission? If yes what were the findings?

4 Privatisation. Which corporation is to be privatised? How will the shares be sold? Are there safeguards to ensure the small investor and employee gain a fair share? Is the corporation to be split to bring about more competition? What benefits are given for the privatisation? What is the offer price and is it at a premium? How was the issue underwritten? Were all the shares sold?

Method

The aim is to follow an event preferably to its conclusion. By watching the television news in the evening you will get a good idea of the issues in the following mornings newspaper. Try to keep cuttings from more than one quality newspaper. (Your local or school library will have them and it is cheaper to take photocopies than to buy several heavy-weight newspapers each day.) Write to the parties concerned. Addresses can be found again at your library. The TUC handbook will have the addresses of Union head offices. Your careers teacher probably has directories with the addresses of many large companies.

Presentation

Present your work as a diary. You will not make an entry for each day but only when there has been an important development. (Look back at my 1988 Ford dispute.) Record the events in chronological order with comments. (yours not those of the newspaper).

Conclusions

Your conclusions ought to reflect upon what has happened. Who benefited, who lost? Could the event have been handled differently? What is likely to occur in the future?

Course work study guide 2

General aim

Local shopping basket survey

Questions

Three main questions should be considered:
1 Where is it cheaper to shop in the local area?
2 Why are some shops cheaper than others?
3 Why do more expensive shops survive?

Method

Select three widely different types of shop from which to sample prices but make sure they sell the same products. The easiest is groceries. Take a small single branch independent shop, an independent retailers who is part of a voluntary chain (Mace, Londis, VG etc) and a national supermarket chain. Select 10 well known branded items which are regular items in most household's expenditure such as bread, baked beans, etc. Visit the chosen shops and draw sketch maps of locations, note parking (free?), bus stops etc. Record the prices of the chosen branded goods at each shop. (If there is an own-label alternative record that price too). Try to interview the branch manager/owner and discuss turnover, pricing policy, supplier etc. Record answers. Or perhaps conduct a sample survey amongst shoppers why do they use the store? How often? etc. Perhaps conduct a count of shoppers entering each shop over a given period (use same time for each shop).

Presentation

Clearly a map of each location will help and the prices can be appropriately displayed using bar charts. Do not forget the ten item total for each retailer. Calculate the percentage difference. How much cheaper is it to buy non-branded goods?

Conclusions

Are large multiple supermarket chains cheapest? Even when all factors are taken into account? Who uses each type of shop and for what? Will the small corner shop survive? Use the evidence you have collected to reflect upon these questions.

Course work study guide 3

General aim

To determine where it is 'best' to save in a local community.

Questions

This will depend upon the person who is being advised. Are they tax payers? Might they require a mortgage in the future? But before this can be taken into account you need to conduct a survey and find out:
1 In how many different institutions is it possible to save? (Do not forget the Post Office which offers many different ways or life assurance endowment schemes. It might be fun to compare these with keeping it under the bed!)
2 Find for each the following information:
Rate of interest (on the same day)
When the interest is paid
Is the standard rate of income tax paid?
Is there a minimum deposit
Can cash be withdrawn on demand without penalties?

Method

There is no subsititute for leg work – visit each institution. Most will have current rates displayed and will provide leaflets describing the various schemes. It might be a good idea to design a questionnaire and to conduct a survey. Find out where they save, why they save and why they save where they do. You may find that people of your own age are unaware of the tax advantage of saving with a Post Office Investment account.

Presentation

This question gives scope for a large table, like a 'Which' report. You could even design your own symbols.

Conclusions

Why do different saving schemes offer different terms?

Take different groups of people and indicate the advantages to them of different saving schemes. Compare your conclusions with your survey. What motivates the direction of saving, interest rates, tax advantage, convenience, future loans, ignorance?

This is a wide topic – if the length of the course work is limited you may look at a few of the aspects detailed above in detail.

Course work study guide 4

General aim

To conduct a study of a town, village or the area around the school classifying business functions and types and explaining their presence and importance to the community.

Questions

For each business the following information could be collected:

- Legal type of business (private company, part-nership etc)
- Level of production (primary, secondary etc)
- Size: number of employees; turnover/output
- Number of plants
- Percentage of employees who live locally
- Percentage of output exported
- Number of years at present location
- Main reason for choice of site (communication, market, raw materials etc)
- Future growth plans

Method

In a large industrial area it might be possible to share the data collection whithin the class (if this is allowed within the GCSE Board's rules). It would be a good idea to design a card on which to record the information. It might be necessary to make an appointment and give a rough idea of the information required. Most firms are most helpful and are happy to help, but they do not want to give the same information to 30 pupils at different times.

Presentation

Many different methods possible and the most appropriate will depend upon the type of area chosen. A map with a key and different symbols and colours will display the information. The analysis of the information collected – which is the most important part – lends itself to 'pie' charts. These could show percentage of different types of business, percentage in different sectors etc. This will cover the classification of types and functions.

Conclusions

Two important conclusions are required. Why are the business types in your area? (or if there are not many and/or are leaving, why is this?). You ought to be able to tell from the answers to your questions.

How important are local businesses to your local community? Employment is, of course, a major factor but don't forget consumption. Services and food production (local baker) will be locally consumed.

(This course work title does not lend itself to small rural communities where we discover local farms, employing very few and a village shop!)

Course work study guide 5

General aim

To conduct a survey of local house prices and explain the factors which influence demand, supply and price.

Questions

The results of your survey ought to show how house prices vary according to type and location.

- Are certain locations better than others and therefore in greater demand?
- What makes one location better than another? (school catchment area, close to park, quiet – lack of traffic noise, close to public transport)

- Which types of property are most sought after? (age, style, size, number of rooms)
- Do 'improvements' such as double glazing, a new bathroom/kitchen etc increase the price by the cost of the improvement?

Method

Clearly one way to determine the answers to these questions is to ask an estate agent. This would be a good idea and perhaps your teacher will arrange a talk.

The title asks for a 'survey', however. Here you need to compare house prices (at roughly the same time since they can move very rapidly). Use the local newspapers and estate agents, who if asked nicely, might give you the detail sheets they prepare on property. Try to compare either similar houses in different locations or different houses in the same location.

Presentation

This type of survey lends itself to a map with key and different price ranges.

Conclusions

Try to use the evidence you have collected to arrive at the conclusion. Distinguish between the supply of new housing and second-hand housing coming on to the market. Why do people move? Demand is a difficult thing to assess but the estate agent knows how many enquiries he gets and how quickly property sells in different areas.

Use the analysis you have learnt to predict price differences and then see whether these are backed up by your findings.

Course work study guide 6

General aim

To consider how the Authority finances and spends its budget and to comment on its priorities.

Sample different groups within your neighbourhood and evaluate the effects of the budget on individuals.

Questions

Several questions to answer:

1 What services are provided by your local authority and how much is spent on each?
2 Has the pattern of spending changed over the last few years?
3 What proportion of the local authorities budget is financed by:
  (a) The Community Charge
  (b) Central Government Grants
  (c) Borrowing
  (d) Charges
4 How does the pattern of local authority spending affect different groups within the community:
  (a) Single employed
  (b) Married couple (no children)
  (c) Family
  (d) Council tenant
  (e) Unemployed

Method

There are several sources of information. The local authority will send a leaflet outlining much of the information required for the first part, towards the end of the financial year (31 March), when it has calculated the community charge for the following year. In addition, a trip to the local library will help. The Council itself will help but normally only to a letter from your teacher for your whole class and not individual student enquiries.

For the second and perhaps most important part you will need to conduct a survey. It would be a good idea to try to find out what people pay (full community charge or reduced amount), and which of the Council services they 'think' they benefit from. Rather than giving a list it might be interesting to ask them for a list.

Presentation

Plenty of scope for pie and/or bar charts. It might also be possible to present the results of your survey in tabular form. Although the Council normally gives a map of the area, I do not think this helps here.

Conclusions

You ought to be able to come to conclusions about the Council's spending priorities, how it has changed and how it benefits different groups within the community. It should also be possible to determine how many people actually know which services provided by the local authority they benefit from.

Course work study guide 7

General aim

To undertake a survey of second-hand cars. What factors do advertisers consider important to stress? What factors do you consider determine the prices of second-hand cars?

Questions

The title of this piece of course work contains the two questions you must ask:
1   Do different sorts of advertisers give different information? Does the amateur, private advertiser give different information to the professional car salesman?
2   Clearly the demand and supply for a particular car determines the price; but how can you produce evidence to illustrate this?

Method

The first question can easily be answered by looking at a local newspaper or specialist car magazine. Select a popular car and then look at all the advertisements for such a car and record what is mentioned. Keep separate dealers and private advertisers.

To look at the factors which determine the price it is important to only look at the same product. You would not compare the price of a vintage champagne with that of a bottle of Spanish plonk so do not compare a Porsche with a Mini. Compare the same make and model. By taking different years, you will be able to illustrate depreciation but the same year will show how mileage, condition and optional extras, even colour, affect price. Do not forget that the price asked is not always the price paid. It might be a good idea to arrange to interview a second-hand car dealer.

Presentation

Clearly you will soon have a great deal of information. To analyse it you must use graphs – the best for this are column and pie for the first question and line graphs for price variation over time.

Conclusions

You will easily reach some conclusion about what advertisers think it important to stress and how this varies with different types of seller. The second question is more difficult. Having traced depreciation, try to explain in terms of supply and demand the different rates of depreciation between those cars which hold their value and those which do not. Perhaps look at so called 'classic cars' which can cost more second-hand than they did new. And the good old Skoda – why does it depreciate so quickly?
(Remember – I would like to drive a big red Porsche, just like you, but you will not get marks for a piece of economics course work if all you write is how nice they are and how you intend to own one!)

Course work study guide 8

General aim

To follow the price of a chosen commodity over a period of time and record and account for price changes.

Questions

Your questions sound deceptively easy:
1   How have prices changed over the time period?
2   Why have prices changed over the time period?

Method

First you must select your commodity. You could choose one of those commodities dealt in on the London commodities markets. Things like coffee, tea, oil, gold, sugar, wheat etc are traded in London and prices change from day to day. These prices are reported in quality newspapers and can be seen on 'Teletext'. Most good papers have a commodities report. (I used one in the exercise on Tea). But why choose something so remote from you and your school? Perhaps, like me, you live near a livestock market (Banbury) or fish market. Take the price of year old barley beef or cod. If you have friends or relations who work at such a market get them to take you along. Local newspapers will have prices and reports. Talk to the farmers/fishermen, they have a wealth of knowledge. You must live near a street market. There they will sell fresh fruit and vegetables. Follow the price of tomatoes. Watch what happens if one stall holder has a lower price than another.

Presentation

Prices changes over time are easy to display using line graphs. You can easily write by the dates along the horizontal axis special events. Try to keep it in chronological order.

Conclusions

Try to explain price changes in terms of demand and supply and draw curves which explain the figures you have recorded.

Index